.N *April 16.. 1746*.

MBERLAND, *drawn up in three Lines; the Front consisting of Six Battallions of Foot, the Second of Five, the Third was*

n upon the left of the Dukes Front Line, where their Rashness met with its deserved chastisement from the Fire and

er Hawley & Bland, are describ'd as passing through a breach that had been made for them in it, to attack the rear of

of the Rebels met our Dragoons in their Center, on which began the total rout of these disturbers of the Publick Repose

Battles
In Britain

and their political background

Volume 2

1642–1746

Battles
In Britain

and their political background

Volume 2

1642–1746

William Seymour

Drawings, Maps and Battle Plans by W. F. N. Watson

HIPPOCRENE
BOOKS, INC.

By the same author
ORDEAL BY AMBITION
BATTLES IN BRITAIN, Volume I

To Jenny
Whose map-reading passeth all understanding.

Illustration on page 2: A musketeer, from a seventeenth-century exercise manual for musketeers

Acknowledgements:
Cooper Bridgeman Library, 146; Editions R. Laffont, 59; Mary Evans Picture Library, 18, 38 (top), 40, 47, 51, 57, 80, 85 (btm right), 100–1, 121, 140, 144 (top right), 161 (top right), 184 (top right); Mansell Collection, endpapers, 2, 11, 12, 13, 38 (btm), 60, 72 (top), 85 (top left and right, and btm left), 91, 111, 114 (top right), 117, 124–5, 128, 142 (top), 143, 158, 163, 175, 178, 183 (top left, and btm left and right), 184 (top left), 189 (btm), 202; National Portrait Gallery, 72 (btm), 114 (top left), 142 (btm), 144 (top left), 161 (top left), 183 (top right); Radio Times Hulton Picture Library, 56, 139

William Seymour photographed the illustrations (copyright ©) Sidgwick and Jackson Ltd) on pp. 45 (btm), 62–3, 76–7, 94–5, 119 (btm), 133 (btm), 135 (btm), 152–3, 170–1, 193 (btm), 219 (btm)

W. F. N. Watson drew the maps, battle plans and drawings (copyright © Sidgwick and Jackson Ltd) on pp. 23, 25, 33, 45 (top), 61, 75, 93, 104, 105, 106, 107, 119 (top), 126, 133 (top), 135 (top), 137, 146 (top), 151, 169, 193 (top), 199, 207, 211, 213, 219 (top)

HIPPOCRENE BOOKS, INC.
171, Madison Avenue   New York, N.Y. 10016

ISBN 0-88254-379-2

Library of Congress Catalogue
Card Number 75-34555

Printed in Belgium

Contents

Preface

In the introduction to the first volume of this work, which covered battles from Stamford Bridge (1066) to Pinkie Cleuch (1547), I stressed the point that our knowledge of the battles is far from precise: eyewitness, or contemporary, accounts are often at variance with each other, because they were not committed to paper until some time after the event. It is unwise to be dogmatic about battles that were fought hundreds of years ago. The historian's task, therefore, is to sift through the facts and where they are open to more than one interpretation, or the exact site of any battle cannot be certainly determined, to present them to the reader in a straightforward and easily understandable manner, so that he can have the enjoyment of walking the site and deciding for himself just how it happened, and in some cases where.

An excellent example of this that occurs in the present volume is the Battle of Cheriton (March 1644). Although in this case the sequence of events and many details of the fighting have been accurately chronicled, the actual positions of the contending armies have never been satisfactorily determined. I have accordingly treated the chapter on this battle somewhat differently, and devoted extra space in which to present the case for my own and other writers' ideas: for on the position of the battle line depends the site of the battle. The reader can then form his own opinion as to which position is correct.

In both volumes of the work I have eschewed the temptation to pursue the might-have-beens of history – to forecast the possible outcome of any battle had the losing side been the victors. There was not space for this fascinating, but usually fruitless, undertaking. However, a more practical exercise for those who have studied both volumes is to examine the reasons why the percentage of men killed to the total numbers engaged in battles during the hundred years between 1450 and 1547 was more than double that of the hundred years between 1642 and 1745, when increased knowledge had produced more destructive weapons. The difference cannot be entirely accounted for by the massive slaughter at Towton, for the percentage figure was nearly as great at Sedgemoor, nor were the victors noticeably more merciful in their treatment of the defeated foe during the Civil War and at Culloden: but possibly

TABLE OF BATTLES BY COUNTIES

pursuits were better controlled and less barbarously conducted in the last hundred years of British battles.

In the two chapters on the Jacobite rebellions I am aware that in occasionally describing the supporters of the Old and Young Pretenders as 'rebels' I may incur the wrath of many Scots. Nevertheless, they were in rebellion against the legitimate government and this description, as an occasional variation from the constant use of the word 'Jacobite', seems permissible. Similarly the words 'English' and 'Scottish' are sometimes used to describe the rival armies. Technically this is wrong, and is only done for convenience and simplicity. The government forces included a number of Scots loyal to the crown, and latterly in the 'Forty-five campaign some Hessians. Prince Charles Edward's army contained Irish and French contingents and even some English Jacobites. Both armies claimed to be royalist, but in these chapters that designation is applied only to King George's troops.

To many of the people who so kindly helped me in the writing and preparation of the first volume I owe a further debt of gratitude for their continued assistance in this part of the work. I hope that they will forgive me if I do not mention them again individually; but there are others, not called upon earlier, but who were good enough to give me their time, encouragement and specialist knowledge in the preparation of this volume. Mr Charles Chenevix Trench, the Reverend J. W. S. Mansell and Colonel Angus Cameron have read through parts of the manuscript and given me the benefit of their advice, and Colonel Cameron also drove me across half Inverness to visit battlefields. Mr Bernard Bruce of Cauldhame was equally helpful in my endeavours to reconstruct the rather complicated Battle of Sheriffmuir. Mr Sharpe France, county archivist, Lancashire Record Office, supplied me with the plan of Preston, reproduced on page 189, and once again I am indebted to the director of Ordnance Survey for permission to base the battle maps on the Ordnance Survey sheets. To all of them I offer my grateful thanks.

William Seymour
Falconer's House
Crichel
Wimborne
Dorset

CHAPTER 1

The First Civil War

The Protagonists:
Their Arms, Armies and Armaments

The First Civil War lasted from 1642 to 1646, and fighting took place throughout much of England and Scotland, while in Ireland the savage rebellion that broke out in October 1641 had considerable influence on the war. It is not possible in a single short chapter to recount the progress of the Civil War, in which there were more than fifty battles, sieges and skirmishes of note, but its origins, and the composition of the two armies that took part in it, have been traced in outline. In subsequent chapters five of the principal battles in the First, and one in the Third, Civil War will be dealt with in detail. See pp. 32–6 for brief descriptions in chronological order of the more important battles and sieges of the First Civil War.

The origins of the Civil War stretch back to the end of the Tudor era. It was not the Stuarts' fault that they inherited an economy moving rapidly towards inflation, and an unfinished Reformation – though Charles I, through his extravagance and obstinacy, certainly exacerbated the situation. The eventual crisis that precipitated the outbreak of hostilities was a political one: in essence Charles's complete refusal to yield to his opponents in Parliament. But basically it was a quarrel whose ingredients of recalcitrance, religion and economics opened wide gulfs and chasms as the unhappy reign unfolded. From 1629 for eleven years Charles ruled without a parliament, and during that time many of his subjects became increasingly discontented with government through a council of courtiers who were often inept, sometimes corrupt, and nearly always factious; a council presided over from time to time by a monarch who had a high sense of God-given duty, which he strove to perform conscientiously, if often misguidedly, and who saw himself as the absolute arbiter over people and events in a society where 'a subject and a sovereign are clean different things'.

It is wrong to think that at the beginning of the seventeenth century religious discontent was confined to Puritan strongholds in East Anglia and certain other parts of the country. Calvinist theology dominated the Church of England (even Whitgift, who

9

persecuted Puritan parsons for their failure to perform certain rituals, held Calvinist views), and although the doctrine of the Dutch theologian Arminius, with its leaning towards certain aspects of Roman Catholic ritual, was beginning to gain ground, in most country churches there was neither surplice nor church music, while the altar occupied a central position. Charles himself was a sincere Protestant, but he favoured a more elaborate ritual than most of his subjects. His appointment of William Laud, a convinced Arminian, to succeed George Abbot as Archbishop of Canterbury opened the way to a doctrinal split in the country.

Laud, and other high church prelates, found Charles anxious to believe that a return to the more elaborate ritual would meet with general satisfaction, and that dissent and criticism could be expected only from a small minority. Nothing could have been further from the truth, least of all in Scotland. Here, in 1638, the National Covenant was drafted as a protest against Laud's imposition of the new Prayer Book and the appointment of bishops and churchmen to civil posts, and the two Bishops' Wars were entirely religious in origin.

In England, although the bishops came in for much obloquy as the enforcers of Laudian measures and the religious problem generally was perhaps the most important underlying current of discontent, this was not the immediate cause of the Civil War. There were other equally grave problems, and among them the more earthy economics played their part. The value of money had been steadily falling since the days of Elizabeth, and Charles quite simply had not the means to finance his foolish and quite useless military adventures in France, the upkeep of an expensive court and an extravagant, although informed, taste in art and architecture. His determination to rule without Parliament presented fiscal problems that, inevitably, were eventually insoluble. Nevertheless, his enforcement of tonnage and poundage, a manipulation of the customs duties and an agreement with Spain to transport bullion in English ships for the payment of Spanish troops, enabled him to exist for a while without recourse to Parliament. The Spanish agreement was most unpopular with merchants and Protestants, for it favoured a nation openly hostile to countries with which the former did trade and for which the latter had religious sympathies. But it was the reintroduction of ship money that caused the greatest furore.

This tax had been imposed under Elizabeth as a levy on the coastal counties and sea ports for the benefit of the navy. As such it was a sound tax and not greatly resented. But when Charles

Above: John Pym, champion of the
rights of Parliament against
Charles I. Right: The Earl of
Warwick, one of the foremost
objectors to ship money. Below:
The House of Commons in 1648

Cancellarij Sedes vz

Left: Charles I in the House of Lords, from a contemporary print.
Above left: Charles I, after Lely. Above right: Archbishop Laud, his
controversial Archbishop of Canterbury. Below: Execution of Strafford
at the Tower on 12 May 1641

A. Doctor Vther Lord Pri
   te of Ireland;
B the Sherifes of London
C the Earle of Strafford
D. his kindred and Friend

attempted to extend it to inland counties he had gone too far. Many of his subjects came out in open defiance against this imposition. Prominent among the objectors were the Earl of Warwick and Lord Saye and Sele, but the man who was to gain immortality through his contumely was an influential Buckinghamshire landowner called John Hampden. Hampden was one of many who refused to pay this tax, and the crown prosecuted him in 1637 to show reason why he should not pay twenty shillings levied on his lands. The case rumbled on for many weeks, first before the four barons of the Exchequer and then before the judges of the King's Bench and Common Pleas. In the end Hampden won his particular case on a technicality, but by a slender majority the judges upheld the legality of ship money. It was a hollow victory for the King and gained him nothing, for by 1640 resistance to the tax was almost nationwide.

His subjects' refusal to pay ship money was not in itself sufficiently damaging for Charles to have to terminate his personal rule. It needed the First Bishops' War* and the clear, cogent and closely reasoned arguments of his greatest servant, Thomas Wentworth, Earl of Strafford (whom he was so soon to sacrifice), before at last, in April 1640, a parliament was summoned. Wentworth, with considerable experience of successfully managing the Irish parliament, felt confident that he could manipulate the less turbulent members who would assemble at Westminster. But he was wrong. He found men in the Commons who were too strong for him, and who had come there determined to plunge Parliament into constitutional assertiveness. This was not at all what Charles wanted, and three weeks after it first met he dissolved the Short Parliament. No money was forthcoming to pay the reluctant levies now being raised to bring the dissident Scots to heel. The result of the Second Bishops' War was a foregone conclusion: Charles's largely untrained, ill disciplined and indifferently led force was no match for 20,000 Covenanters under tried military commanders such as Alexander Leslie and William Baillie. At Newburn (near

---

* In 1637 Charles I attempted to impose the new Prayer Book upon Scotland; this was bitterly opposed and led to the forming of the Covenanting party in Scotland. Matters went from bad to worse, and the Assembly, sitting without the bishops in defiance of Charles's command, ordered the abolition of episcopacy. There followed in 1639 and 1640 what became known as the Bishops' Wars. General Leslie had command of the Covenanting army and Montrose acted as his second-in-command. In the second battle at Newburn in August 1640 the Scots gained a very easy victory over the English, and the King had no alternative but to offer terms.

Newcastle) on 20 August 1640 the English were routed, and the Scots thereupon occupied the five northern counties of England, demanding payment of £850 a day until the occupation could be terminated by treaty.

It was very obvious, indeed it was a stipulation of the Treaty of Ripon, that another parliament must be called to raise money for the indemnity and to arrange terms for the withdrawal of the Scots. Accordingly, on 3 November 1640 what became known as the Long Parliament assembled. Civil war was far from anyone's thoughts when this parliament first met; nevertheless the atmosphere was tense, filled with the presage of storm. This time there could be no quick dissolution, for the Commons held the purse strings. There were at that time about 300 Members, mostly country squires and merchants, and they knew their position to be a strong one; nor could Charles expect overwhelming support in the Lords, for many who sat there were uneasy at his apparent disregard for what they considered their indefeasible privileges. Moreover, throughout both Houses there was a broad streak of Puritanism, dedicated men for whom no toil was too hard in pursuance of their high ideals.

Until his death at the end of 1643 the leader of the Lower House was John Pym. When the Long Parliament assembled he was fifty-seven years old, a widower and a man who lived entirely for his work. He stood out above all his colleagues, remarkable alike for his intellect, eloquence, cool judgement, administrative ability and leadership. He was supported by able men such as Lords Brooke, Mandeville, Saye, and Warwick; and in the Commons by Hampden, William Strode, Denzil Holles, Arthur Hesilrige and Harry Vane. But his was the guiding hand, he the chief architect of reform and revolt. Pym was no warmonger – he stood rather for peace, tolerance, justice and a freedom of the spirit – but the cataclysm of events and the stubbornness of Charles edged him towards the brink and beyond.

This is not the place to detail the actions of the Long Parliament, whose initial proceedings though drastic and mostly abhorrent to Charles gave promise of a settlement. It is only necessary to catalogue briefly some of the principal events that in spite of this early promise inevitably widened the gulf between king and people and eventually led, inexorably, to civil war.

Almost Parliament's first act was to set up a committee to deal with what they considered the misdemeanours of the Earl of Strafford. On 11 November Strafford was impeached, and he was brought to trial in March 1641. Unable to topple him through impeachment Parliament resorted to a bill of attainder and the

King found it necessary, in the interests of peace and the safety of his queen, to bow to the inevitable. At noon on 12 May this loyal and able statesman was beheaded. Strafford was but the first of the King's councillors and intimate circle to feel Parliament's displeasure; others had to flee the country to escape impeachment, and Archbishop Laud, who disdained flight, was eventually beheaded after a long imprisonment.

In January 1641 Parliament passed the Triennial Act, and later followed this up with a bill to ensure that it could not be dissolved without its own consent. Ship money had been declared an illegal tax in the previous December, and steps were taken to close the door on all non-parliamentary taxation. In July the prerogative courts were abolished, and by the time Parliament rose for a short recess the King, albeit reluctantly, had given his assent to most of the important measures that Pym had included in his programme. Only the religious question remained outstanding. On this the House was deeply divided and Pym was not anxious to precipitate action for the present.

It seemed to many that by resolute and dexterous management the most dangerous reefs had been avoided, and that the ship of state might now sail on into calmer waters. But in fact Charles had granted nothing that he did not intend to repudiate as soon as he could regain the initiative. And Pym – unlike most of his colleagues – knew this very well. Some signs of returning popularity gave Charles encouragement, and he still held two trumps; he retained the right to appoint his councillors, and he controlled the armed forces of the state. With a confidence that was characteristic, but scarcely justified, he proceeded to Scotland, where he hoped to gain a party among the Scottish nobles. While he was there an event occurred, the results of which were eventually to bring the country to civil war.

In October 1641 the Irish Roman Catholics revolted against the English and Scottish settlers. They greatly feared that the upsurge of Puritanism in England would bring still further repression and confiscation of land upon them. From north to south the flame of revolt quickly spread; the slaughter was appalling and mischievous rumours were afoot. It was given out (falsely) and widely believed that Charles was in sympathy with his Roman Catholic subjects and had given them licence for what they did. An army had to be raised immediately to quell the rebellion, but Pym's belief that the King could not be trusted with such an army prompted him to challenge one of the last of Charles's remaining prerogatives. On 8 November Parliament agreed to request the King that he should

16

appoint only those councillors and ministers approved by them. A fortnight later the Grand Remonstrance, the most damaging indictment that foe and faction could devise, passed the Commons by the narrowest of margins. Soon afterwards an earlier suggestion, made by a backbencher called Oliver Cromwell, to wrest control of the armed forces from the King, was taken up and embodied in the Militia Bill.

Parliament was no longer unanimous in its thinking; none of these measures was passed without a struggle. Gradually the two parties – Royalist and Parliamentarian, or pejoratively, Cavalier (cavaliero) and Roundhead – took shape. Nevertheless, war was still not inevitable, although in January Charles did his best to make it so. Accompanied by some 300 troopers he came to Westminster to arrest five Members of the Commons who were the ringleaders in a move to impeach the Queen. Warned of trouble the Members had escaped by river, leaving Charles looking remarkably foolish and his opponents greatly strengthened. On 10 January he and his queen slipped furtively out of London. When he next entered the capital it was as a prisoner on trial for his life.

From London to Hampton Court, from there to Windsor and then to York. For the country a period of agonizing suspense; for the Royalist faction a period of advice and counter-advice. The Queen and certain hotheads of the court were constantly advising the King to sever the last hopeful strands of peace; the moderates, who comprised Charles's few remaining friends in Parliament – men like Hyde and Lord Falkland – urged him to negotiate while it was still possible. The King seemed to accept their advice; he made many concessions in matters of church and state, and he even went some way towards a compromise over the question of the armed forces. But Pym was not fooled; he knew very well that these were delaying tactics. The King was taking steps to secure important ports; he was looking to the north for support, and to Ireland for an army. Meanwhile the Queen was to go overseas taking the crown jewels with which to buy foreign aid.

In March 1642 the Commons passed the Militia Bill as an ordinance; it was a step which virtually signified that sovereignty had passed to them. The country was sliding, with gathering momentum, towards civil war. In June Pym passed through a greatly reduced and now pliant Parliament nineteen propositions, which made religious as well as secular demands on the King. Charles had always stood uncompromisingly for the absolute rule of kings, defying any interference or advance of democracy; had he accepted

Costume of noblemen in
early seventeenth century

the nineteen propositions he would have become little better than
the puppet of Parliament. The choice before him was to surrender
or to fight. Charles chose to fight.

On 22 August 1642 King Charles unfurled his standard at Nottingham. The country moved into civil war with the utmost repugnance;
for much of its course both sides were looking for opportunities
to patch up the quarrel, although Charles and the extreme
Royalists were never prepared to give an inch of what they
regarded as hallowed ground. Almost to the very end the Parliamentarians persisted in the myth that they were not fighting the
King; it was the same story as 200 years earlier in the Wars of the
Roses: one reason, so they said, that they took up arms was to
free the King from his 'evil councillors'.

The population in England and Wales at this time was about
four and a half million, with perhaps another million in Scotland
and Ireland. This was not a class war, for the ruling class was
split down the middle on the issue, but it is possible to see certain
sections of the population adhering to one or other party. The
Stuarts had created the majority of the 125 peerages then in
existence, so it is not surprising to find more than twice the number
of peers in the Royalist camp as in the Parliamentarian. The

merchants, on the other hand, tended to side with the Parliamentarians. The landed gentry, who formed the largest part of the ruling class, were about evenly divided, and to some extent they influenced the lower classes, for they could raise their tenantry in support of the side they favoured. Labourers, craftsmen and artisans, not owning loose allegiance to any overlord, seemed mostly to favour Parliament. It can be seen, therefore, that both sides had an almost equal pool from which to draw volunteers; but what little military talent there was available at the outbreak of hostilities was mainly Royalist, for in their ranks were the most soldiers of fortune with experience of war on the continent.

If the parties were more or less equal in the availability of manpower, Parliament held the advantage geographically, in that their support came mostly from the rich eastern and south-eastern counties and they held London. Royalist strongholds were in Wales, most of the north – other than certain parts of the West Riding and Lancashire – the western Midlands, and the south-west. Parliament was operating on interior lines, and the longer the conflict went on the greater advantage would accrue to them.

In 1642 there was no standing army as such. The defence of the kingdom rested in the first instance with the navy, and in the event of invasion there were fortress garrisons and the county militia, known as the trained bands. The navy, which was soon to be put in charge of the capable Earl of Warwick, was small but efficient; the conditions of service had been so bad under the King that when hostilities broke out most of the officers and men sided with Parliament. This was a great loss for Charles, for it meant that the important Parliamentarian ports could be supplied by the fleet. It made it extremely difficult for Charles to obtain foreign aid even if such could be arranged, and the very fact that the navy was hostile to the Royalist cause made foreign countries wary of proffering the much desired help.

The militia, or trained bands, were mostly infantrymen – musketeers and pikemen. They came directly under the lieutenant of the county and were officered by local gentry. The name 'trained bands' indicated that the men were available for training rather than that they had been trained, and with the notable exception of those from London and Cornwall they were almost entirely untrained. The London men were easily the best organized and equipped; they almost alone could be persuaded to fight outside their own county boundaries, and their well drilled and trained regiments, comprising some 8,000 men, were a formidable ready-made force for Parliament. In addition the Honourable Artillery

19

Company sent out a number of competent officers to the Parliamentarians (and a few to the Royalists) trained in their New Artillery Garden.

It was important for both sides, particularly the Royalists who were deprived of the Tower's large arsenal, to take possession of the major ports and garrison towns in order to obtain their ordnance. Charles's attempt to gain Hull in July had been thwarted by the navy, and when hostilities broke out Colonel Goring, Governor of Portsmouth, found himself blockaded by the fleet and attacked by land. He surrendered the port and escaped to Holland to join the Queen. Dover Castle was seized from the Royalists and both Plymouth and Bristol declared for Parliament. The latter was taken by the Royalists in July 1643 and proved an invaluable source of supply for the successful Royalist army in the south-west. In spite of these serious losses Charles secured many of the county trained bands' magazines, and early victories brought him a rich haul in warlike stores. Up and down the country the King's commission of array was read in the principal towns with varying results – sometimes being greeted with enthusiasm, sometimes in silence and at other times resulting in hostile clashes. Wherever Charles found the trained bands unwilling to march with him he disarmed them and used their magazines for equipping his volunteers.

The build-up of the armies in the first instance was from volunteers, and both sides had a ready supply. But the majority of those enlisting were without military experience, and very undisciplined; nor could they be officered by men of experience. In August the King received a welcome addition to his handful of men with battle experience when his nephews the Princes Rupert and Maurice joined him from Holland with some men, arms and ammunition, having overcome a number of adventures at sea. The King also had a possible reservoir of trained men from Ireland, and some battle-hardened officers from the English regiments in Dutch service managed to reach him. But getting troops to England with the navy hostile was a continuing problem, and in the first years, while both armies were gaining experience, it was a very amateurish war.

For at least two months prior to the outbreak of hostilities the Royalists had been actively recruiting, and Members of Parliament had left Westminster in good time to stir up support for their cause, but by 22 August Charles was still without an army, having scarcely more than 800 horse and 300 foot. However, at the beginning of September volunteers began to come in from Yorkshire and other counties. A small amount of artillery was also acquired. On 13 September the King left Nottingham and made for Shrewsbury, where some 6,000 infantrymen and 1,500 dragoons were said to be assembling, with whom he intended to secure Chester in order to safeguard communications with Ireland.

Money was an even greater problem for Charles than it was for Parliament, but, apart from the invaluable financial assistance rendered by the Prince of Orange, there were those at home most generously disposed. Many of the landed gentry either came themselves or sent their sons with a horse and arms, and usually money to support them; some of the wealthier magnates, such as the Marquis of Worcester, were even more generous and subscribed huge sums to the cause, or raised and maintained quite large bodies of armed men. These scions of patrician England both led and filled the ranks of Charles's cavalry. Their greatest asset was derived from the hunting field, which had given them 'an eye for a country' and the courage to cross it at speed. It had also given them better horses and a higher standard of horsemanship than their enemy. Oliver Cromwell, probably the most proficient of Parliament's soldiers, soon saw the need to improve the standard of his own troopers to fit them to 'encounter gentlemen who have courage, honour and resolution in them'.

Both parties thought that a single battle would decide all. The

Cuirassier ('Lobster'), wearing close helmet and three-quarter armour of laminated plates. Dragoon in burgonet and breast-and-back over buffcoat, snaphance musket, powder flask and bullet pouch slung at right side. Each man carries two pistols in saddle holsters

King foresaw a return to London at the head of a victorious army and the chance to start afresh with a new parliament of a more friendly shade. The Parliamentarians, equally sure of victory in the field, would bring the King back to his capital to sit in state carefully and tightly trammelled. By the middle of October Charles felt himself ready to put his cause to the hazard and march on London. As he rode across England his army gathered strength. At Bridgnorth there was a warm welcome and more recruits, and at Wolverhampton further levies from Wales joined his standard. By now he had mustered 13,000 men: fair material, but unfortunately insufficiently armed.

Meanwhile, Parliament had raised and equipped an army formidable in numbers if not in professional skill, which was marching towards the King under the command of the Earl of Essex. The London trained bands formed an important nucleus, but by and large Parliament raised its men in the same way as the King – volunteers from those areas under its influence – and its cavalry leaders were men of much the same stamp as the Royalists, many of them being armigerous (men entitled to bear heraldic arms). John Hampden armed his tenantry and turned them out in dark green, while Oliver Cromwell recruited a troop of horse* comprised of Huntingdonshire volunteers. Lords Brooke, Bedford, Mandeville (later Manchester), Stamford, Robartes, and Saye and Sele, Sir Arthur Hesilrige (with his fully mailed troop of 'Lobsters'), Denzil Holles and many such others all raised men and commanded one of the nineteen regiments of foot, or seventy-five troops of horse, which with five troops of dragoons made up the bulk of Essex's army. By 10 September Essex had brought this army as far as Northampton. A steady stream of raw recruits kept trickling in, so that soon he had under command some 20,000 men. But even before the first major engagement at Edgehill (see p. 32 or chapter 2 for full details) this number had somehow dwindled to no more than 13,000–14,000.

Both armies experienced great difficulty in keeping up their numbers. Pay was usually in arrears and men, who with a few notable exceptions were only interested in the money and the loot, were inclined to drift away when neither was forthcoming and the fighting had receded from their own neighbourhood. There was also a certain amount of wastage in unnecessary garrisoning of towns, castles and even houses. Nor was there any sensible system

* In Essex's army the cavalry was at first raised in single troops of about sixty to eighty men, but the strength of the infantry regiment was the same as that in the Royalist army—1,200 men.

Pikeman and infantry officer. The officer carries a half-pike. Both armies had basically similar arms and accoutrements

of recruiting losses; the King relied mainly on commissioning officers to form new regiments and in consequence there were many regiments hopelessly under strength. In spite of this problem, and apart from the need, by both sides, to have resort to impressment by 1643, there was little change in the composition, equipment and strength of the armies until in 1644 Parliament gained the support of an 18,000-strong Scottish army.

Parliament made more positive attempts to strengthen morale and discipline in the early stages of the war than did the Royalists. They tried to overcome the difficulty of getting men to serve outside their counties by forming associations of counties, such as the Western Association which comprised troops from Bristol, Gloucester and neighbouring areas. But this military grouping by districts was only really successful in the Eastern Association, and that because Cromwell provided the necessary drive and energy. The lack of discipline and the harm this did was apparent to most commanders, but only Cromwell seems to have taken real measures to combat it in the period before the New Model was formed. In raising his regiment he tried to select men who 'made some conscience of what they did', and his insistence on the observation of Christian principles was accompanied by strict, not to say severe, discipline. Such steps as these went some way to offset the undoubted advantage of better officers possessed by the Royalist army, at any rate during the first part of the war.

It is only possible to give the bare outline of the arms and equipment in use at this time; to the student of war fuller details are available in books by such eminent authors as J. W. Fortescue, C. H. Firth, H. C. B. Rogers, A. H. Burne and Peter Young (see bibliography for this chapter). The Royalist cavalry from the beginning of the war (and the Parliamentarian soon afterwards) was organized in regiments of six or more troops, the troop being commanded by a captain with a lieutenant and cornet under him. There were occasional slight variations in the cavalryman's arms: basically he carried a pair of pistols and a sword, but in Essex's original army there were some cavalrymen carrying carbines, and Cromwell's first troop was described as consisting of arquebusiers. Again at the beginning of the war there were a few regiments of cuirassiers, but these soon disappeared (with the exception of Hesilrige's 'Lobsters'), because apart from their being cumbersome there were too few horses suitable for mounting them. The more usual defensive armour was a light headpiece known as a pot, and back and breast plates worn over a buff leather coat.

Gustavus Adolphus was responsible for recent changes in

Musketeer with 48-inch barrelled matchlock and rest, and sleeveless
buffcoat and bandolier with wooden bottles containing charges of
powder. Cavalry trooper in lobster-tailed pot, with breast-and-back over
apron-skirted buffcoat. Vambrace or bridle gauntlet on bridle arm

cavalry tactics, but formations and use of cavalry in England in 1642 mostly followed the old continental pattern, for those officers with experience had fought mainly in the Dutch and German armies. Cavalry was drawn up six ranks deep (usually on the wings) and advancing at a trot would discharge their pistols by ranks until the opposition had been sufficiently battered to allow them to close in with the sword. But Prince Rupert, who had served under Gustavus Adolphus, soon changed these tactics in the Royalist army, and advancing only three ranks deep at a fast trot, or even gallop, thrust in with the sword and only then used the pistol. Cromwell, too, quickly adopted these more mobile tactics. Such were the cavalry tactics in theory, but a cavalryman is a more difficult article to train than an infantryman, and in practice matters were often very different.

Dragoons were mounted infantry and rode an inferior type of horse. They were armed with sword and carbine and in battle were usually used in support of cavalry, but on account of their mobility they were sometimes sent forward to hold key points such as bridges. Loosely organized according to the tactical situation, they almost always fought on foot, one in every ten men remaining in the rear with the horses.

The infantry regiment of 1,200 men was organized into ten companies, but certainly in the Royalist army this was very much a paper strength and formation. Before the end of 1642 many of Charles's regiments had only one or two companies, although Parliament's practice was to amalgamate weak regiments to maintain the full strength where possible. Each company had a captain, subaltern and ensign with usually three sergeants, of whom two were in charge of the musketeers and one the pikemen – there being at the beginning of the war two musketeers to every pikeman.

The pikemen, who were still considered the élite of the infantry even though the increase in musketeers was giving this arm more effective bite, carried a pike that was in theory eighteen feet long, but invariably shortened by the men to about sixteen feet. The pikemen also carried a cutting sword; it was not of much value and General Monck was of the opinion that a rapier-type weapon would have been better. Pike drill was fairly complicated, but when properly executed was most effective. There were many instances in the Civil War when the fortune of the day was decided 'at the push-of-pike'. The pikemen usually formed the centre of the line, and would fall in six deep with the musketeers on their flanks. They were severely handicapped by their defensive armour:

an iron helmet and back and breast plates – known as a corslet – were most unpleasant in the warm weather and at all times restricted mobility.

Musketeers were armed with the matchlock (with the exception of the small artillery guard, who usually carried an early flintlock), which was a cumbersome, inaccurate weapon that fired a heavy bullet of about an ounce for a distance of up to 400 yards, although there was no hope of accuracy above 100 yards and not much at that range. They usually marched carrying twelve cartridges apiece, and the rate of fire was so slow, owing to the reloading problem, that even fighting six ranks deep the leading rank, who after discharging their muskets retired to the rear, only just had time to reload before coming to the front again to continue the 'rolling fire'. The burning match, a two-foot piece of impregnated cord that the musketeer had to carry, made his role a hazardous one, for it was not unknown for a spark to explode all the charges in a man's bandolier. The matchlock was very prone to misfire, most unreliable in wet weather and could completely eliminate surprise in any night attack. The musketeer also carried a sword, but preferred to use his musket butt for close quarter fighting. He was more mobile than the pikeman, but much more vulnerable to cavalry.

The Earl of Essex seems to have placed much reliance on the role of artillery, not only for siege purposes but also in the field. Having the benefit of the London and Hull arsenals he was able to start the war with a well provisioned ordnance and artillery train, whereas it took the King some time to gain parity. Nevertheless, although the principal armies on both sides had many cannon, their chief value was in siege warfare, and in most of the set-piece battles one does not find them playing a very prominent or decisive part. The rate of fire, even with light cannon, was very slow, and sometimes as many as eight horses were needed to drag the guns over the bad roads, while teams of oxen were required to haul the heavy siege pieces – the exception to such slothful progress being the light guns of the Royalist army mounted on carriages with their gunners riding; these were the forerunners of horse artillery and another innovation borrowed from Gustavus Adolphus.

The culverin, a five-inch calibre gun firing a fifteen-pound shot, although not the heaviest type of siege gun was the one principally used: the demi-culverin (nine-pounder) was a dual purpose cannon, used occasionally as a siege gun, but also in the field as heavy artillery. The field guns were generally drakes, a collective name

27

for the lighter calibre sakers, minions, falcons, falconets and robinets. Range was seldom a problem, for armies were usually drawn up for battle well within the range of even the lightest cannon, and for siege purposes the gunners liked to open fire just outside musket range. A gun crew normally consisted of three men, and, although the heavy artillery was organized in batteries and came directly under the officer commanding the artillery train, pairs of the lighter field pieces were allotted to regiments and took up positions in the front line.

It is a fallacy to imagine that until the New Model Army was dressed in red coats, differing only in the colour of their facings according to regiment, the two armies were without uniforms or uniformity. It is true that officers and sergeants might be permitted to wear what they chose, but an attempt was usually made to clothe the private soldiers in some form of standard dress. Nevertheless, colonels of regiments dressed their men as they thought fit, and in consequence there was often a kaleidoscope of colours – red, purple, green, grey and blue. In due course a few regiments could be distinguished by the colour of their coats. Hampden's men in green have already been mentioned, the Earl of Newcastle dressed his in white, Prince Rupert favoured blue, Colonel Montagu preferred red faced with white, and Lord Manchester green faced with red; but surely the sartorial prize must have gone to Lord Brooke, who had his men in purple.

However, although one colour (such as red in the regiments of the Eastern Association) might predominate, there was no easy means of telling friend from foe and often the two sides wore distinguishing scarves of orange and red, or even simpler emblems. Sir Thomas Fairfax, having had his cavalry worsted at Marston Moor, rode to safety through the enemy lines merely by removing the white handkerchief, which was the Parliamentarian token for that day, from his hat (see p. 98). The term 'Roundhead' probably originated from the cropped heads of the apprentices who championed the Parliamentarian cause before hostilities began, when the name was first used. It seems that at the beginning of the war some Parliamentarian officers lived up to their soubriquet by wearing their hair short, but soon shoulder-length hair styles were the fashion in both armies.

The New Model Army warrants a special mention, for although it should not be allowed to eclipse the fine record of many of the other armies that took part in the struggle it was the precursor of our regular army and the first successful attempt to weld together an efficient fighting machine. When it first took the field in May

1645 it was only one of many Parliamentarian armies and smaller formations – at this time, with the Scots, Parliament had about 70,000 troops on its pay roll. The First Civil War was now drawing to its close and one has, therefore, to look further ahead to see the New Model as an instrument of ultimate victory.

The need for a properly organized, disciplined and permanent force was first brought to the attention of Parliament by General Waller in June 1644, but the composition of the New Model underwent some paper changes and a good deal of delay at the hands of the Committee of Both Kingdoms. It was eventually decided that its total of 22,000 other ranks was to be derived from eleven regiments of horse, each of 600 men, twelve infantry regiments of 1,200 men each and 1,000 dragoons. Unfortunately the list of artillery for the New Model, which was reported to the House of Commons on 19 April 1645, was not printed in the Journals, but the army was provided with a formidable train of artillery and we know that the field guns were principally demi-culverins and sakers. The cavalry were well mounted on medium-weight horses of fifteen hands or just over, and were all volunteers. The infantry, however, were a scratch lot to start with. It was found impossible to make up their numbers even with pressed men and Royalist prisoners of war, and when they first took the field they were 4,000 short of establishment, although within a month or two their numbers had been made good, but with untrained recruits.

The question as to who was to command this new élite force caused some argument between the two Houses. The Lords were inclined to favour Essex or Manchester, but the Commons pressed the case strongly for Sir Thomas Fairfax, against whom there could be no complaint on military or other grounds. He was a professional soldier who had distinguished himself in the field, and he had taken no part in politics and so did not come under the ban imposed by the Self-denying Ordinance. This ordinance disallowed a member of either House to execute any office or command, military or civil.

There was at the time of the ordinance some dissatisfaction with the military leadership, and in December 1644 Oliver Cromwell and one or two others conceived this measure as a means of removing the incompetent Manchester, and even Essex, from their commands. The Lords at first threw the ordinance out, but the Commons won the day with their nominee and Sir Thomas Fairfax was appointed commander-in-chief on 21 January, with Philip Skippon as major-general of the foot and chief of staff. The post of lieutenant-general of the horse was not immediately filled; Cromwell was the obvious choice, but there were difficulties on account of the Self-Denying Ordinance, which the Lords eventually passed in April. However, Parliament could always make exceptions to its own decrees and Cromwell's continuing success in the field, and his own conviction that the Almighty would be seriously displeased if he resigned his command, seemed reasons enough to give him a series of extensions from the ensnaring coils of the ordinance, although his official position in the New Model was not confirmed until 10 June.

The problem of leadership was not confined to the New Model. Throughout the First Civil War there was on both sides a constant obfuscation of command. This was due largely to jealousy and petty squabbling, while the Parliamentarian generals were also confounded by committees. We have said that in its early stages this was an amateurish war; nevertheless in due course it produced commanding generals of some repute. Men like Montrose, Hopton and Newcastle for the King, and Lord Essex, Thomas Fairfax and William Waller for Parliament at times handled their armies with rare distinction, nor were there lacking men of competence, skill and daring among those who held lower rank: Oliver Cromwell, Philip Skippon, Marmaduke Langdale, Prince Maurice, Lords Astley, Digby and Byron, Sir Bevil Grenvile and William Balfour, to name but a few. Some of these men (and others like them), pre-eminent for their leadership and high capacities, were never touched by envy's brush, but unfortunately there were those who often became slaves to self-interest and faction, which at best manifested itself in a preference for local over national patriotism and at worst in insensate jealousy and damaging intrigue.

Many of the King's troubles in this respect emanated from his nephew Prince Rupert, who stands in a class by himself. Young, impulsive, brave and very sure of himself, he was inclined to treat with contempt Charles's older advisers and commanders. He quickly antagonized the first two Royalist commanders-in-chief (Lord Lindsey, killed at Edgehill, and the septuagenarian Lord Forth) by insisting on complete independence as general of the horse; he had little use for Lord Wilmot, and Lord Digby – among others – was jealous of his closeness to the King. A brilliant cavalry leader and a master of siege-craft, it was perhaps a mistake to make him commander-in-chief, for although completely tireless in the performance of exacting duties he lacked many of the qualities necessary for a successful commander of an army. Moreover, he had replaced the popular Forth, who although not outstanding had made no overt blunders and, unlike Rupert, had few enemies at court. The mercurial George Goring replaced Wilmot as general of the horse in August 1644. An ambitious, unscrupulous and somewhat dissolute man, he shared Rupert's audacity, powers of endurance and quick insight, but beyond that the two men had nothing in common and were the worst of friends. The King's generals must have tried his patience very sorely; yet he seldom made reproaches or uttered lamentations.

The divisions within the Parliamentarian army in some ways went deeper than those that Charles had to contend with, for they involved affairs of conscience. There were the inevitable petty quarrels and personal slights: Lord Essex and Sir William Waller disliked each other intensely, and Lord Manchester and Oliver Cromwell gravely mistrusted each other. There were also accusations of incompetence and cowardice, resulting on one occasion in Lord Saye's son Nat Fiennes being sentenced to death. But more disruptive than these was the dissension on the fate of the King, and more particularly on religion. The strong Anglican and Presbyterian element throughout Parliament and its army found its dogmas vitiated by the Independents, as the various sectaries of the old Separatists were now collectively called. These people, chief among whom was Cromwell, held differing political as well as religious views which deeply disturbed their more orthodox colleagues and put an almost unbearable strain on the Scottish alliance.

The Parliamentarian commanders were also a prey to the objurgations of controlling committees. Both sides set up county committees for the purpose of maintaining their armies in a particular county, but the higher command in the Royalist army was not fettered by frequent armchair operational advice from a collection of civilians. That the conduct of Parliament's war should have been in the hands of a committee is understandable, but commanders in the field can never give of their best when they know that they are constantly in danger of interference from a remote controlling authority. The Committee of Safety was succeeded by the Council of War, which in turn gave way to the Committee of Both Kingdoms when Scotland entered the war. To these committees Parliament delegated operational responsibility, until on 9 June 1645 Fairfax was informed that they were 'leaving it wholly to you who are upon the spot to do what by the advice of your council of war you shall judge most conducive to the public interest'. Thus, with future operations properly confined within the narrow ambit of personal command, Fairfax could prepare the way for a decisive punch and death grip.

31

Principal Battles and Engagements of the
First Civil War
in Chronological Order

1642: 23 September
Powick Bridge. The first engagement of the Civil War was a cavalry skirmish south of Worcester in the meadows surrounding Powick Bridge. Prince Rupert, while covering Sir John Byron's intended withdrawal from Worcester, defeated an advanced cavalry force of Lord Essex's main army under Nathaniel Fiennes.

1642: 23 October
Edgehill. The first major battle of the Civil War. The two armies were fairly evenly matched numerically with around 14,500 men apiece. The Earl of Essex commanded the Parliamentarian army, but although the King was present at the battle, and took an active part, he had delegated command of the Royalist army to the Earl of Lindsey, who was superseded by the Earl of Forth just before the battle began. The two armies were drawn up for battle shortly after midday, the Roundheads some two miles south of Kineton and the Royalists just north of Radway. Prince Rupert commanding the Royalist cavalry on the right wing and Lord Wilmot that on the left were entirely successful in their first charge, but the fight in the centre was most stubbornly contested. The Royalist centre was gradually pressed back almost to its start line, and after three hours' hard fighting both armies had had enough. Victory in the field went to neither side, but the King had forced Essex to withdraw, leaving the road to London open. For full details of this battle see chapter 16.

1642: 12 and 13 November
Brentford and Turnham Green. On the morning of 12 November Prince Rupert attacked Denzil Holles's regiment under cover of a morning mist, and after a sharp engagement drove it back into Brentford. The battle in Brentford against Holles's regiment and that commanded by Lord Brooke was short and sharp and resulted in the Royalists gaining possession of the town. But on the following day King Charles found his way to London barred at Turnham Green by a large Parliamentarian army, which included the City trained bands. Charles felt unable to take on this large force with an army greatly weakened by cold and hunger. He withdrew to Reading and the threat to London was removed.

1642: 6 December
Tadcaster. Lord Newcastle, having won a victory at Pierce Bridge on 1 December, and now in command of all the Royalist forces in the north, attacked and defeated Lord Fairfax at Tadcaster. The victory was important, for it drove a wedge into the Parliamentarian defence of Yorkshire. This victory, however, was somewhat offset when Sir Thomas Fairfax (Lord Fairfax's son) captured Bradford, Leeds and Wakefield from Sir William Savile in January 1643, which successes forced Newcastle to fall back upon York.

1643: 19 January
Bradock Down. Sir Ralph Hopton and Sir Bevil Grenvile fell back with the Royalist army across the Tamar into Cornwall before Parliamentarian troops commanded by the Earl of Stamford. Once in Cornwall the Royalists were heavily reinforced by the Cornish trained bands and at Bradock Down, near Liskeard, Hopton and Grenvile utterly defeated Stamford and took more than 1,000 prisoners together with a number of guns and some ammunition.

1643: 2 and 4 March
Lichfield. The battle here, in which the Royalists lost the city, was a comparatively minor one, but in it Lord Brooke was killed while in command of the Parliamentarian forces. His death was a considerable blow to Parliament – there had even been talk of his succeeding Essex as commander-in-chief.

1643: 19 March
Hopton Heath. This successful Royalist skirmish, some two miles from Stafford, was part of the King's plan to regain Lichfield. It is chiefly notable because in the hour of victory the Royalist commander, the Earl of Northampton, was killed. As a sequel to this fight the King sent Prince Rupert to the Midlands where he took and sacked Birmingham on 3 April, and after a stiff resistance he gained Lichfield Close and Cathedral on 21 April.

1643: 16 May
Stratton. Following James Chudleigh's minor success against Sir Ralph Hopton at Sourton Down in Devon on 25 April, Lord Stamford decided to carry the war into Cornwall, for he had more than

double the amount of men under Hopton's command. He took up a nearly impregnable position near Stratton in the extreme north-west of Cornwall. Hopton advanced from Launceston to meet him, and the assault was entrusted to Sir Bevil Grenvile, who was familiar with every inch of the countryside. The battle was fiercely contested before the Cornishmen, sweeping up the hill in a four-pronged attack, put the enemy to flight, killing 300 men and capturing a further 1,500 including Chudleigh.

1643: 18 June
Chalgrove Field. Rupert, acting upon information from the turncoat Colonel Hurry, marched from Oxford on 17 June in an attempt to intercept a valuable treasure convoy and to deter Essex from his intended blockade of Oxford. He narrowly missed the convoy, but surprised some sleeping enemy troops in the village of Chinnor. While falling back on Oxford he was overtaken by the Roundheads commanded by Sir Philip Stapleton and John Hampden. Rupert, with considerable superiority of numbers, and having cleverly forced his enemy to fight at a disadvantage, routed them with his cavalry. John Hampden received a wound in the shoulder from which he died six days later.

1643: 30 June
Adwalton Moor. Lord Fairfax and his son Sir Thomas, realizing that they could not withstand a long siege in Bradford, marched out to give battle to Lord Newcastle's army, which although numerous comprised for the most part untrained peasants armed only with scythes. However, Newcastle did have 4,000 properly armed soldiers and this was sufficient to defeat the Roundheads decisively. The Fairfaxes retreated to Hull, and with Bradford captured other towns quickly fell, and soon the whole of the West Riding was in Royalist hands.

1643: 5 July
Lansdown. Lord Stamford's defeat at Stratton enabled Hopton to leave Cornwall and join forces with Prince Maurice and Lord Hertford. After an inconclusive affair against General Waller's army at Chewton Mendip on 12 June, both armies manoeuvred for position around Bath. Eventually

Marston
Moor ⚔
⚔Tadcaster
Hull ●
⚔Adwalton
Moor

Winceby ⚔
RowtonHeath ⚔ ⚔Nantwich ⚔Newark

⚔Hopton Heath
⚔Lichfield

⚔Naseby

Powick Bridge ⚔ ⚔Edgehill
⚔Cropredy Bridge

● Oxford
⚔Chalgrove Field

● Bristol ⚔Aldbourne Chase ⚔
⚔Newbury Brentford
Lansdown ⚔ ⚔Roundway ● Basing House
Down

⚔Langport ⚔Cheriton
⚔Torrington ● Sherborne
⚔Stratton Castle
● Exeter

withiel ⚔ ⚔Bradock
Down

WFNW

Waller gained the commanding Lansdown Hill, and on 5 July Hopton's Cornishmen, again led by Sir Bevil Grenvile, forced their way against stiff opposition, which included well sited artillery, to close in hand-to-hand battle. The position was gained at heavy cost. The cavalry losses were extremely heavy, and worse still Sir Bevil Grenvile fell in the hour of victory.

1643: 13 July
Roundway Down. Waller had been defeated at Lansdown, but not destroyed. The Royalists were tired and short of supplies, particularly powder. They were further disheartened when, on the day after the battle, their general was seriously injured by the explosion of almost their last ammunition wagon. The army conveyed the wounded Hopton first to Chippenham then to Devizes, where Waller laid siege to the town. The Royalist position was hopeless, and surrender would have been inevitable had not Prince Rupert brought cavalry relief from Oxford under Lord Wilmot. Waller withdrew his cavalry from the outskirts of Devizes to meet this threat on the chalk hill a mile above the town called Roundway Down. Here his cavalry, including Hesilrige's formidable 'Lobsters', was utterly defeated and scattered. The abandoned infantry soon surrendered. It was a total disaster for the Roundheads, who lost more than 1,500 men and all their cannon, ammunition and baggage.

1643: 23–6 July
Siege of Bristol. After the defeat at Roundway Down Waller withdrew towards London leaving the way clear for Rupert to join forces with the western army, and together, on 23 July, they laid siege to the important city of Bristol. On 26 July an assault from the Somerset side by Cornish troops was repulsed with heavy loss, but Rupert managed to slip in a posse of troops on the Gloucestershire side. Before the situation became completely desperate the governor, Nathaniel Fiennes, surrendered. He was later sentenced to death for incompetence (but not cowardice), which sentence was remitted. The capture of this city was an important prize for the Royalists.

1643: 28 August–4 September
Surrender of West Country towns. Sir John Digby's minor victory at Torrington against local levies won the towns of Barnstaple and Bideford for the Royalists at the end of August, and on Warwick's failure to relieve Exeter from the sea the city surrendered to Prince Maurice on 4 September.

1643: 18 September
Aldbourne Chase. On 26 August Lord Essex at the head of some 15,000 men marched from Hounslow to relieve Gloucester. Having attained his objective he so confused the King, who commanded the Royalist army, by skilful manoeuvring that he had reached Cricklade before the Royalists started in pursuit. Prince

Rupert at the head of a flying column came up with Essex's army – dangerously extended – at Aldbourne Chase, which lies between Chiseldon and Aldbourne. The action that followed was inconclusive, but it had the effect of slowing down the Roundhead army and allowing the Royalists to get to Newbury ahead of them. For fuller details see chapter 17.

1643: 20 September
First Battle of Newbury. Advancing from Wantage on 19 September Essex found Newbury already in the hands of the Royalist army. The way back to London was effectively barred, and to get there Essex would have to give battle. The First Battle of Newbury was fought to the west of the town round the area of Wash Common, Enborne Heath and Skinner's Green, the fighting being heaviest at Round Hill, Wash Farm and Enborne Heath, although the opposing lines extended almost to the river Kennet. It was a confused battle in which artillery played its most important part in all the Civil War battles. The cavalry fight on the southern flank was a fierce affair in which the Royalists came off best, but their infantry fought poorly. As at Edgehill there was no clear-cut victory, but the Royalists, finding themselves short of powder, left the field during the night. For full details see chapter 17.

1643: 11 October
Winceby. This was a small cavalry engagement between a Royalist force commanded by Sir John Henderson, Governor of Newark, and Oliver Cromwell (whose horse was shot under him during the scuffle), helped by Sir Thomas Fairfax, put the Royalists to flight. Many were killed in the flight, and others drowned in the waters of the fens.

1643: 11 and 12 October
Siege of Hull. On the same day as Cromwell's victory at Winceby the garrison of Hull, which was under the command of Lord Fairfax, made a sortie against Lord Newcastle's besieging force and drove them from many of their strongpoints, capturing some cannon. On the next day Newcastle raised the siege, and on 20 October Lincoln surrendered to Lord Manchester.

1644: 25 January
Nantwich. Lord Byron in Cheshire had been reinforced by Royalist contingents arriving from Ireland and with these he hoped to clear the county for the King. He laid siege to Nantwich, the only important town in Cheshire still held by Parliament, but on 25 January Sir William Brereton, whose troops had recently been joined by those under Sir Thomas Fairfax, attacked Byron's besieging army, which had been divided on either side of the river Weaver. Byron was forced to fight against superior numbers on ground very disadvantageous to cavalry. Defeat was made certain when troops from the Nantwich garrison sallied forth and took him in the rear. Byron and most of the cavalry

escaped, but more than 1,000 prisoners were taken, including Colonel George Monck. Many of these prisoners enrolled themselves under Parliament.

1644: 22 March
Relief of Newark. The Royalist commander at Newark was Sir Richard Byron (Lord Byron's brother). The town was of extreme importance to the Royalists as a link between their forces in the north and south. Sir John Meldrum together with Lord Willoughby had laid siege to the town and the King ordered Prince Rupert to march to its relief. Rupert outmanoeuvred Meldrum and on 22 March he surrendered, being forced to leave his siege artillery and a large quantity of muskets and pikes to the victors. It was a very important Royalist success.

1644: 29 March
Cheriton. This was the first decisive major victory that the Parliamentarian army achieved, and it had important consequences. It was fought between General Waller, commanding a Roundhead army of some 10,000 men, and Lords Forth and Hopton with a numerically inferior force of not above 6,000 troops. Cheriton is east of Winchester and close to Alresford, which town the Royalists managed to gain before the battle. Waller's army encamped for the night of 28 March in the field below Hinton Ampner and the battle was fought to the north of their encampment and immediately to the west of Cheriton Wood, which played an important part in the early stages. There is some dispute as to the exact positions held by the two armies, and the details of this together with an account of the battle will be found in chapter 18.

1644: 29 June
Cropredy Bridge. In this inconclusive engagement north of Banbury, Charles, commanding an army of at least 9,000, which included 4,000 cavalry, was attacked by an army inferior in numbers commanded by General Waller, who had the assistance of Major-General Browne. The armies had been marching parallel to each other on either side of the river Cherwell, until Charles, thinking to intercept a force coming to the aid of Waller, pushed forward with his leading troops, creating a dangerous gap between the forward and rear elements of his army. Waller, seizing his opportunity, forced a crossing of the river at Cropredy Bridge, putting 1,500 horse, 1,000 foot and eleven guns onto the east bank, and marched north with the bulk of this force to attack the King's forward element. Lord Cleveland hurrying up with cavalry from the rear had little difficulty in defeating the small force left by Waller to guard the bridge. Waller then found himself trapped between the two halves of the King's army and only with difficulty did he regain the bridge and cross to safety. Casualties were not heavy on either side, but Waller lost all of his eleven guns and a number of standards.

44: 2 July
arston Moor. By the beginning of
ne the Marquis of Newcastle's
my was tightly beleaguered in
ork. Prince Rupert had the King's
rmission to march to its relief, an
eration which he executed with
nsiderable skill. He then decided,
though his instructions were not
ecific on this point, to give battle
the combined Parliamentarian and
ottish army that had been
sieging the city. Accordingly, on the
orning of 2 July he moved his army
the west of York and occupied
ound to the north of the Long
arston–Tockwith road, where later
the day he was joined by Lord
ewcastle's troops. The allied army
ployed for battle on the high
ound south of the road. No action
ok place during the day, but the
lied commanders decided to attack
the evening. The battle, which was
ught partly in a thunderstorm and
rtly under a harvest moon, resulted
a Royalist defeat, and the north
as lost to the King. Full details in
apter 19.

44: 1 September
ppermuir. This brief fight was
ontrose's first success for Charles
Scotland. In command of about
00 men, most of them poorly armed
d with no cavalry, he defeated a
rce of 7,000 under Lord Elcho three
les west of Perth.

44: 2 September
stwithiel. Lord Essex, commander-
-chief of the Parliamentarian army,
vanced into Cornwall on 26 July
the head of about 10,000 men. The
ng, with some 16,000 troops, came
er him and was at Liskeard by 2
igust. Essex had taken up a
fensive position a little way north
Lostwithiel with his headquarters
that town, and he sent 1,000 foot
wn to Fowey to hold the port.
uring August the King was joined
Sir Richard Grenvile with 1,800
ot and 600 horse and on the 26th
sent Lord Goring (who had joined
m shortly after Marston Moor) on a
de flanking movement to seize St
aisey and the port of Par. Essex,
alizing he could not now expect
inforcements either by land or sea,
ped to avoid battle against a
merically superior force and
anaged to evacuate Sir William
alfour and 2,000 cavalry along the
guarded Lostwithiel–Liskeard road.
e foot fell back towards Fowey,
d being pressed took up a position
a line from Tywardreath to Castle
ore where they were attacked in
eir centre and on their left flank by
e troops from St Blaisey. The
uation quickly became hopeless,
d Essex abandoned the army and
ok boat for Plymouth leaving
neral Skippon to surrender. More
an 6,000 men laid down their arms
on generous terms, and the
oyalists took forty guns and a large
antity of small arms.

44: 13 September
berdeen. Although Montrose had a
tter equipped army than the one
at fought at Tippermuir, his cavalry
ly numbered forty-four horse and
was inferior by about 1,000 men to

the Covenanters under Lord
Burleigh, who were drawn up to meet
his advance in a strong position on a
hillside south-west of the city.
Burleigh attacked the flanks of the
Royalist army with his cavalry, but
on both wings they were beaten back
in disarray. The Covenanters' centre
was then charged by Montrose's Irish
brigade, whose determined advance
proved too much for Burleigh's men.
Montrose had now seriously disabled
two of the three Covenanter armies.

1644: 27 October
Second Battle of Newbury. In the
course of his march back from
Cornwall to Oxford, Charles found
the way barred by a large
Parliamentary army in the
neighbourhood of Newbury. He took
up a position north of the town
covering the strongpoints Speen,
Donnington and Shaw House. In the
absence of Essex, Manchester
commanded the Roundhead army and
had about 19,000 men as against
12,000 Royalists. The Roundhead plan
was a daring one involving a wide
flanking march of some fifteen miles
by Waller with 12,000 men round the
front of the Royalists to come in on
their left flank at Speen; Manchester
was to hold the enemy in play in
front of Shaw House. The flank
march carried out on 26–7 October
was entirely successful and Waller
gained some measure of surprise.
Fighting on the Royalists' left flank
(under Prince Maurice) was severe
and Speen was lost, but Waller failed
to break through, and Manchester's
attack, which did not go in until
4 p.m. on the 26th, also made little
progress. In the gathering darkness
the battle ended indecisively. Charles
considered his position untenable,
and early the next day withdrew to
Oxford.

1645: 2 February
Inverlochy. Montrose, returning from
the harrying of Clan Campbell, was
nearly trapped in the Great Glen
between Lord Seaforth's army of
5,000 in his front and 3,000 embittered
Argylls under Duncan Campbell in
his rear. Being unable to fight his
way out with only 1,500 men,
Montrose decided to double back by a
circuitous route and surprise the
Campbells at Inverlochy. In bitter
weather and without much food or
any warmth Montrose marched his
men along the steep, treacherous
ledges beneath the mountain peaks.
And at dawn, from the shadow of
Ben Nevis, his men fell upon the
astounded Campbells encamped
around Inverlochy Castle. Argyll at
once took to flight, but Duncan
Campbell put up what resistance he
could. However, the furious charge
of Montrose's and Alasdair
Macdonald's men proved too much
for the Campbells and the fight was
soon over. Duncan Campbell fought
bravely and was killed together with
some 1,500 of the clan. Montrose lost
only a handful of men but among
them a valued friend in Sir Thomas
Ogilvy.

1645: 9 May
Auldearn. Colonel Hurry,
commanding the Covenanting army,

attempted to lure Montrose into
country that was known to be
unfriendly to him, and there give
battle in circumstances favourable to
himself. He accordingly fell back in
front of Montrose from Elgin almost
to Nairn, and then suddenly turned
upon his pursuer hoping to gain
surprise. Surprise was not achieved,
although Montrose had little time in
which to take up a suitable defensive
position. He occupied the high
ground just north of the village of
Auldearn with a small force of some
500 men under Alasdair Macdonald,
and kept the main body of his troops
on the reverse slope of the ridge
running to the south of the village.
Hurry made the mistake that
Montrose hoped he would of
attacking Macdonald with his entire
force, which left his right flank open
to attack from the Royalists' main
line of battle. Macdonald's men were
nearly worsted in a very fierce battle
for the hill, but the Gordons, who
formed the main part of Montrose's
troops on the reverse slope, smashed
the Covenanters' flank and allowed
Macdonald to rally his Irishmen and
complete the defeat of the
Covenanters. For a fuller account of
this battle see chapter 7.

1645: 14 June
Naseby. This was the last major
battle of the First Civil War. The
defeat of the Royalist army under the
King and Prince Rupert by the New
Model Army under Sir Thomas
Fairfax virtually destroyed the King's
military machine. The battle was
fought over the undulating ground
immediately north of Naseby. Fairfax
with more than 13,000 men, including
6,500 cavalry under Oliver Cromwell
and Henry Ireton, was opposed by
only some 7,500 Royalists. Prince
Rupert on the Royalist right wing
met with initial success, but the
King's cavalry on the left was
defeated by Cromwell. In the centre
the Royalist infantry fought with
great determination and courage,
but after three hours' hard slogging
were eventually overpowered by
weight of numbers and captured
almost to a man. The battle is
discussed in chapter 20.

1645: 2 July
Alford. It was now the turn of
Montrose to draw the Covenanters
away from a strong position into an
area where he thought he had better
prospects of offering battle
successfully. He drew the
Covenanting General Baillie
southwards from Strathbogie, and
prepared to meet him on high ground
south of the river Don at a point
about a mile to the west of the
present town of Alford. Both armies
were almost equal in infantry, but
Baillie had superiority in cavalry.
He was, however, at a disadvantage
in having to ford the river before
bringing his men to the attack, and
Lord Gordon, on Montrose's right,
gave him little chance to regroup
after crossing the Don. In a fierce
fight with troops under Lord
Balcarres, Gordon succeeded in
driving Baillie's cavalry off the field,
and then turned on the Covenanting
centre. At the same time Lord

Aboyne and Colonel O'Kean advanced against the enemy. Montrose gained the victory, but in the pursuit Lord Gordon, his great friend and able lieutenant, was killed. For a fuller account of this battle see chapter 7.

1645: 10 July
Langport. After the Roundhead victory at Naseby, Leicester surrendered and Parliament urged Fairfax to march to the relief of Taunton. This town had long been a tiresome thorn in the King's western side: the garrison under its intrepid commander Robert Blake had resisted three sieges. On 4 July Lord Goring raised the siege for the last time and fell back towards Bridgwater, taking up a strong position in difficult, waterlogged ground near Langport. Goring was outnumbered, and a feint towards Taunton, intended to confuse Fairfax's army, was only partly successful. Fairfax attacked Goring's main position with 1,500 musketeers, backed up by elements of two cavalry regiments and a strong infantry reserve. At first Goring's men fought desperately in the marshy fields bordering the rivers Yeo and Parret, but they were broken and routed. Cromwell's troops, which had not been engaged, joined in the pursuit. About 2,000 prisoners were taken, and others, less fortunate, fell prey to the clubmen. Goring's army, virtually the King's last hope, was destroyed.

1645: 15 August
Kilsyth. Not long after Montrose's victory at Alford he received news of King Charles's defeat at Naseby and he clearly saw the need to cross the border and go to the King's aid. By the middle of August Montrose had under his command his largest army since he first commenced operations, but Baillie was still capable of putting into the field a greater force, and he was not prepared to let Montrose slip away. The two armies met in some meadows a mile north-east of Kilsyth. At that time these meadows formed a basin of what is now a reservoir, and Baillie occupied a commanding position on the high ground which gave him a considerable advantage. However, the Covenanting Committee, which usually accompanied the army in the field, ordered Baillie to carry out a dangerous flank march in full view of the enemy so as to prevent any possibility of Montrose's army escaping from what they confidently considered was a well set trap. The result was disastrous, because before long Baillie was to find his army cut in two. There was, however, a fierce fight on Montrose's left flank, which had become threatened by the

advance portion of Baillie's army. The situation here was brought under control by the veteran Lord Airlie and the Ogilvys, while Alasdair Macdonald, as impetuous as ever, had brought a seemingly unwise attack on Baillie's hilltop position to a successful conclusion. Baillie's defeat was absolute and his infantry almost annihilated. Montrose was, for the time being, master of Scotland. For a fuller account see chapter 7.

1645: 15 August
Capture of Sherborne Castle. Once the castle walls had been breached by a mine, the Royalist garrison under Sir Lewis Dyves was unable to hold out. The siege is notable for the action of the Dorset clubmen. These local peasants came out in strength to meet Cromwell on Hambledon Hill, and, although principally interested in the defence of their properties, they were, in Dorset, in league with the Royalists during the siege of Sherborne.

1645: 23 August and 11 September
Capture of Bristol. With Sherborne Castle taken the way was open for Fairfax to reduce the most important stronghold still left to the Royalists, Bristol. Prince Rupert commanded between 1,500 and 2,000 men in this city but the defences were weak in places and there was a plague epidemic raging. Summoned to surrender on 4 September Prince Rupert prevaricated for some days until on the 10th Fairfax lost patience and mounted an attack. The garrison around Prior's Hill Fort resisted strongly, but was ultimately overborne and slaughtered. Unable to stem Fairfax's cavalry, who had gained entrance where the walls were virtually down, Rupert, on being again offered terms, surrendered the city on 11 September.

1645: 13 September
Philiphaugh. Montrose, the recent victor of Kilsyth and many other battles, now found himself with a pathetically small army of 500 Irish infantry and perhaps 1,000 mounted gentlemen – there were no other ranks among his cavalry. David Leslie, on receiving information of the weak state of the Royalist army, carried out a remarkably swift march to take Montrose's men by surprise as they were camped just below Selkirk. Attacking through the morning mist with some 4,000 horse the result was never in doubt. Montrose and most of the cavalry made good their escape, but only about fifty Irishmen received quarter.

1645: 24 September
Rowton Heath. A cavalry battle fought in difficult cavalry country

two miles south-east of Chester between Sir Marmaduke Langdale (Royalist) and Major-General Sydenham Poyntz. Poyntz was force to attack and was at first worsted, but obtaining infantry support from Colonel Michael Jones, who was besieging Chester, he eventually chased the Northern Horse off the battlefield. This defeat, together wit an unsuccessful sally under Lord Lichfield (who was killed) by the Chester garrison, virtually sealed th fate of the city. Charles marched ou of it the next day with 2,400 horse; Lord Byron surrendered the city on 3 February 1646.

1645: 14 October
The sack of Basing House. Basing House, the home of the Catholic Marquis of Winchester, stood athwart the London–Winchester roa and occupied a position of great strategic importance. It had been held for the Royalists throughout th Civil War, and on 11 October it refused Cromwell's summons to surrender. The heavy guns soon mac irreparable breeches in the walls and at 6 a.m. on the morning of the 14th the defenders were totally unable to repel the storming parties. The destruction of life and property that followed was exacerbated by sectarian intolerance. The house wa looted and completely destroyed. More than 100 people were killed.

1646: 16 February
Torrington. Lord Hopton, with a force of 5,000, most of which were cavalry, did what he could to hold t Devon town. When patrol action flared up unintentionally after dark, Fairfax decided to mount a full-scale attack. After a brief struggle some o Hopton's cavalry, fighting in narrow streets unsupported by infantry, broke, and he would have been unab to hold the town even if his entire stock of powder – stored in the church – had not blown up. The engagement is chiefly notable as being virtually the last in the First Civil War in which there was organized fighting.

1646
End of war. The loss of Torrington left the way open to the west: Launceston and Bodmin were quickl occupied: Exeter surrendered on 13 April and Barnstaple and Dunster Castle a week later. Lord Astley's 3,000 men, confronted at Stow-on-the Wold (21 March) by Roundheads under Brereton and John Birch, showed no wish to fight. Charles gave himself up to the Scots at the beginning of May. Newark surrendered on 6 May, and when Oxford hauled down the flag on 24 June the First Civil War had ended.

CHAPTER 2

Edgehill

23 October 1642

Virtually the entire battlefield is now Ministry of Defence land and being a high security area no admission is possible for the general public, although those with a special purpose or interest can apply for a pass from the headquarters of the C.A.D Kineton. However, an excellent panoramic view of the field of battle can be obtained from Edgehill itself – especially if the visitor has binoculars.

Edgehill is about seven miles north-west of Banbury off the A422, and is the long ridge that connects that road with the Kineton– Knowle End road (B4086). Just opposite the Castle Inn is a car park; a public footpath leads through the wood to fields immediately above Radway Grange, and from here there is an uninterrupted view to Kineton and beyond. The main fight took place south of Thistle Farm, over what was then much less wooded country. Thistle Farm is now used by the army and Battle Farm has disappeared. There are two monuments; one on the Kineton road, which is sometimes said to mark the left of the Parliamentarian line before the battle, but is almost certainly too far to the north-west for this; and the other by the copse known as Graveground Coppice, where many of the dead were buried – but that one is in M.O.D. territory. Local tradition has it that the King had his standard at the tower on Edgehill before the Royalist army began their descent of the hill, in a field at the junction of the Westcote Farm–Kineton–Radway track at the beginning of the fight, and probably near Battleton Holt when it was captured. Prince Rupert's charge took place immediately to the left of the Kineton road and parallel to it.

After King Charles had raised his standard at Nottingham (see p. 18) and determined to regain his former authority through what he hoped would be one decisive trial of strength, neither side was in a hurry to put the issue to the test. The King's army was at first too weak to undertake successfully any military enterprise, and Essex did not march out of London until almost three weeks after Charles had laid down the gage.

Clearly Essex's main task was to ensure that he put his army between London and the King. This he failed to do, and he is often blamed for being slow, indecisive and a poor strategist. Some of

Left: Robert Devereux, Earl of Essex, first commander of the Parliamentarian army
Below: Charles I on the eve of the Battle of Edgehill

these labels stick, although he was lamentably served by his intelligence, not having definite news of the King's advance on London until six days after Charles had left Shrewsbury on 12 October. Furthermore, after Essex left London he dissipated his force quite considerably, leaving garrisons at important places such as Worcester, Hereford and Banbury. It is easy with hindsight to see that had he concentrated his army in the Warwick area he would have outnumbered the Royalists and possibly won a decisive victory, and that by holding on to Worcester for too long he allowed Charles to slip by him. But so long as the Royalists were recruiting on the Welsh marches Essex probably considered it important to keep the south and west Midlands protected.

Whatever his reasons for holding too far to the west, Essex, on reaching Kineton on the night of 22 October, with an incomplete army and artillery train, found that the King had stolen a march on him. Charles spent the night of 21 October at Southam and marched to Edgcote the next day. He had, therefore, a clear run to London. However, during the night of the 22nd information concerning the whereabouts of the Roundhead army came in from Prince Rupert's patrols, and the King decided to take his nephew's advice and postpone the intended attack on Banbury in favour of giving Essex battle. Accordingly the army was ordered to occupy Edgehill.

Owing to their wide overnight dispersion it was gone midday before the Royalist assembly was complete. We are told that it was a bright, cold morning, and as the King's men looked down from their commanding height there stretched before them a flat but beautiful landscape, a scene of pastoral peace with tiny farmsteads, lush meadows and hedges aflame with scarlet hips. But if the King's men had leisure to enjoy this enchanting view, his generals were more concerned with the advance of the Parliamentarian army more than a mile below them.

Throughout all the preliminaries to this battle Essex's staff work, and particularly his intelligence, seems to have been consistently bad. He had a spy in the King's camp and yet it was not until he was on his way to worship in Kineton church (probably about 8 a.m.) that he learned of the Royalist army's change of plan, and that they were assembling only three miles away. The Roundheads' billets, like those of the Royalists, were very widely dispersed, and no arrangements had been made for the army to concentrate early on that Sunday morning. Essex did not, therefore, have his army deployed for battle some two miles south of Kineton until almost the same time as the Royalist assembly was

Truppen aus dem Anfange des siebzehnten Jahrhunderts: 3. Schütze im Marsch. (Ebd.)

Truppen aus dem Anfange des siebzehnten Jahrhunderts: 2. Schütze Pulver ins Rohr schüttend. (Ebd.)

Arquebusier marching and holding his arquebus (left) and loading his arquebus (right)

complete on Edgehill. Both armies now remained motionless, both poised for battle but neither anxious to strike the first blow. Essex was clearly not prepared to attack uphill, so if Charles wished to engage he would have to come down to the plain. The Royalist army began the steep descent about 1 p.m.

Although Essex fought at Edgehill with an incomplete army, he was certainly not inferior in numbers, and it seems that the two armies were fairly well matched numerically with around 14,500 men each. Royalist morale was high, for exactly a month before Prince Rupert had gained the better of an untidy skirmish at Powick Bridge, just south of Worcester. Both parties had been taken unawares, but Rupert's speed of action and élan won the fight. The Cavaliers had the satisfaction of seeing 1,000 Roundhead horse and dragoons put to ignominious flight.

However, this boost for morale was somewhat offset by dissensions among the higher command that came to a head while the army was preparing to deploy for battle. Charles was, of course, the titular head of the army, but he had delegated command to the Earl of Lindsey, and Prince Rupert had been given the independent command of the cavalry – a fact that had annoyed Lindsey. While the army was at Shrewsbury it had been joined by a much abler soldier than Lindsey who, like Rupert, had fought under Gustavus Adolphus: this was the Scottish veteran Patrick Ruthven,

40

Earl of Forth. He now supported Rupert in advising the King to deploy for battle after the Swedish fashion, rather than the Dutch, which was what Lindsey favoured. The Swedish brigade formation, with two forward wings, a withdrawn centre and an advance element of musketeers, was much more flexible than the Dutch, but needed experienced men if it was to work effectively. In the circumstances Lindsey was probably right to advocate the simpler Dutch formation (and in fact the result was a sort of compromise), but the King overruled him, whereupon he resigned his command and put himself at the head of his own regiment. Lord Forth succeeded him as commander-in-chief.

Prince Rupert retained his independent cavalry command and was himself on the right of the Royalist line, having under his immediate command a squadron of the Lifeguard and four regiments of uneven strength – perhaps a total of 1,700 men. The cavalry on the left was under Lord Wilmot, who had five regiments comprising 755 men in the first line and 300 in the second.* The Royalist foot, consisting of five brigades, was drawn up with three brigades forward and two in the second line. The strength of the brigades was uneven and their armament even more so. The brigade commanders were Charles Gerard, Richard Feilding, Henry Wentworth, John Belasyse, and Sir Nicholas Byron. Most of the brigades had three regiments – Feilding's had five – and the total foot was probably no more than 11,000. The infantry was not up to strength in musketeers, and there were a good many men fighting only with the most elementary weapons. There were some 1,000 dragoons operating in advance of the cavalry, and the army had fourteen light cannon and six heavy pieces. The siting of the artillery must be speculation, for there is little reliable contemporary evidence. Probably most, if not all, of the light pieces were allotted to the brigades and placed between the forward regiments, while the heavy demi-cannon and culverins were sited well in the rear and certainly at one time were firing from the lower slopes of Edgehill, having been brought down the steepest part with the utmost difficulty. As the battle proceeded they were probably hauled up the road towards Battleton Holt.

---

* These and some other figures for the two armies engaged at Edgehill are taken from Brigadier Peter Young's *Edgehill 1642*. He admits that his calculations are only approximate, in the absence of official strength returns, but after studying the various suggestions put forward by historians past and present it seems to the writer that Brigadier Young's figures—the result of deep research—are probably as near correct as we shall get.

The Royalist army was deployed for battle just north of Radway with the right wing on – or possibly a little beyond – the Kineton–Knowle End road and its left in the vicinity of Brixfield Farm. Certain familiar features of the battlefield were not present in 1642. Edgehill had hardly any trees on it: Radway church stood a little to the south of the present one; The Oaks and the two spinneys, Graveground Coppice and Battleton Holt, were not there. But the country, particularly in front of the Royalist left, was enclosed by a network of hedges – which was probably the reason for Lord Wilmot's being allotted the larger body of dragoons.

It cannot be said with certainty exactly where Lord Essex deployed his men for battle; in most contemporary accounts the landmarks are hazy and features exaggerated. Sir James Ramsey, another veteran with Swedish experience, was in command of the left wing, and he has left a fairly detailed account of his tactical dispositions. There is also a report written directly after the battle and signed by four brigade commanders, which tells us that the left wing had to be considerably extended, because the wind was much to the Royalists' advantage. From neither can it be determined exactly where the left wing rested, but probably on the Kineton–Knowle End road near Radway Ground, with the line running through the southern end of Graveground Coppice to a little way beyond The Oaks.

Lord Essex, who favoured the Dutch formation and tactics, had three brigades each of around 4,000 men; that commanded by Charles Essex was on Ramsey's right and slightly in the rear, and it had four regiments in line; Sir John Meldrum's brigade was on Charles Essex's right with three regiments in line and one in the rear; and the third brigade, commanded by Thomas Ballard, was behind Essex's in support of the left wing, and some of his musketeers were interspersed between Ramsey's horse, and also placed *en potence* on the extreme left. There is some difficulty over the position of the remaining horse. Lord Feilding had his regiment on the right of Meldrum's brigade and perhaps all the 700 Parliamentarian dragoons were on the extreme right. It is probable that Balfour's and Stapleton's regiments were placed in the rear of Meldrum's brigade to strengthen that part of the line which was weakest in infantry. In all there were forty-two troops of horse totalling about 2,200 men, around 12,000 infantrymen, 700 dragoons and an artillery train of which we have few details, but in numbers of guns it exceeded the King's.

The fight at Edgehill falls into four fairly well defined phases. A brief preliminary, and virtually harmless, cannonade; the Royalist cavalry advance, which was successful on both flanks; the main battle in which two Roundhead cavalry regiments mauled the Royalist infantry so badly as to prevent what looked like being a decisive victory; and a state of utter exhaustion with the Royalists back more or less on their starting line and the Roundheads unable to do more than leave them there.

Possibly to tempt Charles down the hill – and if so it succeeded admirably – we know from a statement by Edmund Ludlow that Essex opened the fight by ordering his gunners to fire into the enemy, and they laid their aim at what appeared to be the King's entourage. The ball fell short and the place is known to this day as Bullet Hill. But a slightly more intensive, although equally ineffective, artillery duel took place when both armies were deployed for battle. Its immediate result was to make Prince Rupert, always eager to be at the throat of his adversary, decide it was time to charge Sir James Ramsey's force, which was awaiting him up the Kineton road.

Rupert, for all his impulsiveness, found time to ride round his troops instructing their commanders to keep close order and to use their swords only, until such time as they had penetrated the enemy lines. What he failed to do – and it is difficult to blame Lord Forth for this, for Rupert had an independent command – was to provide for a proper cavalry reserve other than the small band of fifty Pensioners. This omission was to cost the Royalists dear. We have a picture of a well controlled, steady advance at a pace no faster than a trot. The dragoons, under Colonel James Usher, had already done good work in chasing the enemy musketeers from hedge and ditch; nevertheless, this splendid array of cavalry, riding almost knee to knee, was assailed by cannon fire and the rattle of intense musketry – most of which did little harm.

On nearing the enemy the pace would have been increased; and for Ramsey's men, most of whom had had no previous experience of warfare, to the terrifying spectacle of this concentrated charge was to be added the consternation of treachery. It seems that Rupert may have known that a gentleman, with the singularly inappropriate name of Sir Faithfull Fortescue, was planning to lead his troop over to the Royalists at the moment of attack. This he did, but in their haste to perform this act of treachery some of the men failed to remove their orange scarves, and about eighteen of the troop were killed by their new allies. Their desertion, coupled with the lines of Rupert's horse bearing down upon them in irresistible strength, was too much for Ramsey's men who, with few exceptions, turned away from the flailing swords and firing pistols and made all speed for Kineton, hotly pursued by the victorious Cavaliers. Nor was Prince Rupert able to check more than a very small portion of them; this was finally achieved by John Hampden's force, whom they met on the Warwick road north of Kineton. Thus almost the entire right wing of the Royalist army vanished from the battle.

It was much the same story on the left flank, but here the opposition was less numerous and through the efforts of one or two determined officers not all of the men went plundering in Kineton. Lord Wilmot's advance was almost simultaneous to that of Prince Rupert, but he had more difficult country to cross. The dragoons to his front, under Sir Arthur Aston, had done as good if not better work than that done by Usher's men on the right, and Wilmot had only Lord Feilding's cavalry and Sir William Fairfax's infantry regiments to deal with. It is possible that had these two regiments made any show at all, the two cavalry regiments under Balfour and Stapleton would have come to their assistance; but Wilmot's men went through Feilding's regiment as a cutter through corn, and Fairfax's soldiers did not stay to argue the toss. However, Sir Charles Lucas, Lord Grandison and one or two others managed to rally some of the triumphant Cavaliers before they had gone too far, and brought them back to take a further part in the battle. In both these charges – particularly Rupert's – the Roundheads almost certainly suffered considerable casualties, for although plunder may have been the victors' principal aim we can be sure that there were those among them unmoved by the process of death and mutilation.

Sergeant-Major-General Sir Jacob Astley, possibly the most experienced soldier of them all, had command of the Royalist foot. His well known prayer, 'O Lord, Thou knowest how busy I must be this day. If I forget Thee, do not Thou forget me', followed by his exhortation, 'March on, boys', set the infantry in motion about the same time as the two cavalry brigades began their charge. The advance proceeded at a steady pace, for regiments six deep in the ranks cannot be hurried and still keep station. The attack was to be launched with all five brigades in line, and as they marched Gerard's and Byron's brigades moved forward into the gaps between the three originally deployed in the front line. It must have seemed to the Roundhead infantry watching this long wall of red, blue and buff, their steel glinting in the October sun, that nothing could stop the onslaught. Already their left wing was in disarray, for when Ramsey's men broke the horse had stampeded through Denzil Holles's regiment, and bravely as Holles struggled

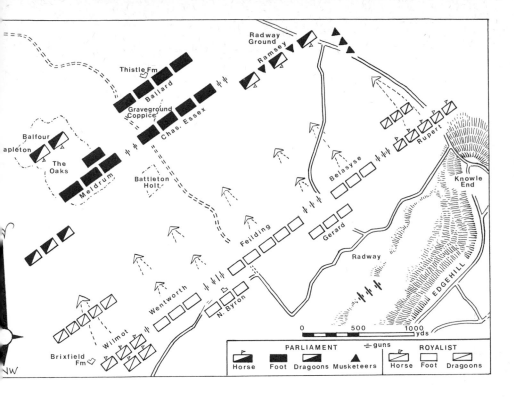

Above: Battle of Edgehill: the armies deployed at the start
Below: Battle of Edgehill

to maintain some semblance of control, only with difficulty did he prevail upon three companies to stand. Worse still, Charles Essex's brigade had left the field without firing a shot; Rupert's whirlwind to their left and the sight of the Royalist columns to their front had quite overcome their courage. What was there to prevent the utter destruction of Parliament's army? The answer lay in two not very large cavalry regiments.

Amid the smoke and carnage of an ever-shifting infantry battle it is not easy for the participants to know exactly what is happening on their immediate front, let alone along the rest of the line. In consequence we get a number of somewhat confusing personal accounts from which to piece together what probably happened on that October day almost 350 years ago. We can be fairly sure that Stapleton's and Balfour's regiments (Stapleton on the right) had formed up behind Sir John Meldrum's brigade, and that there must have been a good many gaps in the Parliamentarian line, for out of twelve regiments and forty-two troops of cavalry there were now only seven regiments and fifteen troops left on the field. It seems, therefore, that the cavalry had no need to ride round the flank to attack, but that they could easily have passed through the infantry to meet the advancing Royalists in a frontal charge.

This they almost certainly did, even though some accounts say that the whole Royalist line had come to push-of-pike before any cavalry engagement, because Wentworth's brigade, which was on the left of the Royalist line, was not attacked by the cavalry and could scarcely have been bypassed. Stapleton rode at Sir Nicholas Byron's brigade and after stubborn fighting was repulsed, or at any rate held, by the courage of the pikemen; but Balfour had complete success against Richard Feilding's brigade, and scattering two regiments he carved his way to the battery of heavy guns and cut their traces. On his way back he was fired upon by his own artillery. Fortunately the guns were manned by Stapleton's cavalrymen, as the gunners had fled, so the damage was slight. At this stage of the battle the King, seeing the discomfiture of his centre, sent the young princes (the future Charles II and Duke of York) back to Edgehill and himself rode forward to encourage his infantry, exposing himself for a time to considerable danger.

At the time of Balfour's return to the fighting line, Byron's brigade – now with one flank in the air – had been mauled but was still defiant; on his left Wentworth's regiments were virtually unscathed, but at the right of the Royalist line the brigades under Belasyse and Gerard were being hard pressed by Ballard. Lord Essex, who had been fighting in the forefront of the battle, pike

Prince Rupert's charge at Edgehill, after which almost the entire
Royalist right wing vanished from the battle

in hand, now ordered Lord Robartes's and Sir William Constable's regiments of foot to join Balfour and Stapleton in a combined attack upon Byron. The fighting here was some of the fiercest of the whole battle, for in Byron's brigade were the Lifeguard and Lindsey's regiment, the pride of the Royalist infantry. But fighting at push-of-pike to their front, and taken in the flank and rear by the cavalry, the brigade gradually gave ground. Sir Edmund Verney, who carried the Banner Royal, was killed and the standard snatched from his dying grasp (it was recovered that evening by the courage of Captain – later Sir John – Smith), while Lord Lindsey was mortally wounded and his son, Lord Willoughby d'Eresby, who went to his assistance, was captured.

It is difficult to know how Wentworth's brigade was employed at this time, for its three regiments would seem to have had only one opposed to it. Out of Meldrum's brigade two regiments were fighting with the cavalry against Byron, and Sir William Fairfax's men had fled the field some time previously, so presumably only Sir John's own regiment was opposing Wentworth. It was as well, for this brigade retiring in good order enabled the guns (which Balfour had been unable to spike) to open up with case shot, and with the help of the returning cavalry this stabilized the Royalist line during its withdrawal. While all this was going on Colonel Lucas led the 200 troopers whom he had managed to hold back from the pursuit on the left against Essex's rear. This could have been serious for the Roundheads had Lucas's men not got side-tracked into capturing the colours of those formations that had already decided to make for Kineton. Nevertheless they were able to add to the confusion that was now becoming general over the entire field.

The battle had started about 3 p.m. and only darkness was to put an end to it. In the failing light the cavalry began to return – and there were those who felt sure that had the horse been able to deliver a further charge at this crucial stage the Royalists would have won a decisive victory. It is impossible to say; but clearly neither men nor horses were in a fit state to charge, even had darkness not intervened. We cannot blame Rupert for failing to halt his troops once committed, for it is an almost impossible task; but had Sir John Byron's men on the right and Lord Digby's on the left been kept in reserve the story of the Civil War might have been quite different and many battles left unfought. As it was, all that the cavalry was capable of doing was to shore up the infantry line as, fighting every yard of the way and somehow still in possession of their guns, whose traces Balfour had cut, the

Royalists fell back pivoting on their right flank to a line parallel to, and almost on, the present link road running from Radway to the Kineton road.

Both armies had had enough; it was for most of the men their first taste of battle, and after three hours of hard slogging they were utterly exhausted. The night was cold, food and fuel were short, and the armies sought what comfort they could. The morning of 24 October found the Royalists back on Edgehill, and the Roundheads, who had retired in the night towards Kineton, now reformed below the hill. Lord Essex had received considerable reinforcements: John Hampden had arrived with two infantry regiments, and a cavalry regiment and some guns had also joined him. The King had received no reinforcements, but his cavalry – unlike Essex's – was virtually intact. Neither side seemed anxious to resume the contest, and Charles sent Clarenceaux King at Arms to offer pardon to all those rebels who would lay down their arms. The herald received short shrift, and as he was blindfolded for most of the time that he was in the enemy lines he had little of use to report to the King on his return. Later that day Charles ordered his men back to their billets around Edgcote, and Essex took his men to Kineton and then on to Warwick.

Many attempts have been made to assess the casualties in this battle, but the true figure will never be known. As is so often the case, both sides put out unrealistic claims of enemy losses, while playing down their own. Although accurate strength returns are not available there is plenty of evidence to show that many regiments were sadly depleted as a result of the battle, but a good proportion of these may have been runaways who never returned to the colours. The Royalist cavalry suffered only a handful of casualties, and no doubt the Parliamentarian horse that fled were swift enough to avoid much bloodshed, but the large numbers of infantrymen who broke on their left wing may not have been so fortunate. Undoubtedly the heaviest battle casualties took place in the fighting around Byron's and Feilding's brigades, and here the Royalists probably came off worst. They certainly lost more men of note, but not necessarily of senior rank. To hazard a figure could be misleading, but if forced to do so from the unreliable evidence available one must stop at 2,000 killed altogether and perhaps as many again severely wounded. Lord Bernard Stuart's letter of 28 October 1642 says of the Royalists, 'What is killed and run away I think is about 2,500 and that is the most'. This figure, which excludes the wounded, is probably too high, and anyway deserters would account for the greater part of it. The Roundheads must have lost more men through desertion and may have suffered heavier casualties than the Royalists.

It is often said that the first major engagement of the Civil War was a drawn battle. As far as the actual fighting on the afternoon of 23 October went this assessment is fairly true, but the victory went to the King. Essex, in spite of the considerable reinforcements he had received, evidently considered his army too badly mauled to achieve the object for which Edgehill was fought, and in going off to Warwick he left the road to London open. Moreover, his withdrawal seems to have been a somewhat disorderly affair, for on the morning of the 25th Prince Rupert fell upon the rearguard and captured or destroyed a considerable amount of ammunition and other valuable stores. It was, too, the Royalists and not the Roundheads who gained the most important trophies from the field – seven cannon, two of them much needed twelve-pounders. How and when this happened is not entirely clear. Sir Edward Sydenham, writing to Ralph Verney, says, 'My Lord of Essex is retired in great disorder to Warwick, for the next morning he suffered his cannon to be taken away within muskett shott of his armie, and never offired to hinder them'. It is possible that Rupert grabbed them along with his other prizes that Tuesday morning.

To say that the King had won the battle is no hyperbole. Urged by many to remove himself far from the battlefield, he not only disregarded this pusillanimous advice but insisted on his army holding the field the next day. Essex refused the challenge and marched away. Had Charles shown the same resolution in the days that followed he could have won the campaign and probably the war. There were two possible ways in which he might have saved his country the agony of a prolonged civil war: by annihilating Essex's army at Edgehill, or by holding it at bay and getting to London first. His nephew's haste contributed to the failure of the first, and his own tardiness to the second of these possibilities.

Banbury was taken on 27 October and the King entered Oxford two days later, where he stayed for a few days before arriving at Reading on 4 November. His caution may have been due in part to not knowing exactly where Essex's army was, but he must have known that he had the advantage of distance, which could be – and in fact was – soon lost. Prince Rupert's idea of a flying column of some 3,000 men to reach London hard on the news of Edgehill might conceivably have succeeded, but the Londoners were busy putting their defences in order and there were 8,000 of the London trained bands in arms. Meanwhile Parliament put out peace feelers, which the King probably never intended to take seriously, although he received the commissioners while postponing any decision on one pretext or another. Windsor Castle had defied Prince Rupert's summons to surrender on 7 November, and Essex, now safely back in London, had been ordered to take the field again – but not to precipitate any action.

Charles was at Colnbrook on 11 November and still outwardly considering the possibility of a settlement, when with typical double thinking he decided he would obtain better terms from a frightened Parliament, and ordered Rupert to attack Essex's troops in Brentford. Advancing under cover of a dawn mist on 12 November, the Prince eventually overwhelmed the two regiments in the town (Holles's and Lord Brooke's), killing or capturing almost the entire force. The Cavaliers then proceeded to sack the town. It was a victory that availed them nothing, for Parliament and the Londoners were now thoroughly roused and troops poured out of London. At Turnham Green the King found the way to his capital blocked by 24,000 men. He fell back before this formidable host, leaving Brentford to be retaken, and entered Kingston.

A bold stroke south of the river might yet have gained the victory; but Charles, perhaps sensing that he had missed his opportunity, withdrew to Reading, which town he re-entered on 19 November. The Edgehill campaign was over, and the King, as a free man, would never again come so close to London.

Prince Rupert at the siege of Bristol. The city surrendered on 26 July 1643

CHAPTER 3

The First
Battle of Newbury

20 September 1643

The battle was fought a little over a mile to the south-west of the town. Leaving Newbury on the Andover road (A343), the visitor should fork right at The Gun public house (three-quarters of a mile out of Newbury, opposite the Falkland memorial) and go down Essex Road. The site of the battle is not an easy one to pick out, for except for the roads, which do in fact surround the battlefield, it cannot be viewed from any public access. The south part of the battlefield, which saw much of the heaviest fighting, is now almost completely covered by a recently built housing estate. The rest of the ground is still fairly open – in fact at the northern end more open than at the time of the battle – but it is all in private ownership.

The fighting took place in three principal areas. Wash Common and Enborne Heath, which are now built over to a great extent, but still have some traces of heath; the centre in the area of Skinner's Green and what is now called Round Hill; and the flat northern part stretching from Skinner's Green almost to the river Kennet. These latter portions of the field can be seen very well from a track running across Wash Farm, but permission to walk along it must be sought from the farmer. Wash Farm is on the corner of Essex Road and the road leading off it towards Round Hill, exactly on the division of two one-inch Ordnance Survey maps (sheets 158 and 168) – which does not make the visitor's task any easier!

For the first nine months of 1643 the Royalists had on balance much the better of the conflict. This was particularly so in the south-west, where by September it seemed that only the destruction of Essex's army was needed for total victory. In this task the King failed, and never again was he to hold such an overall advantage.

The opportunity occurred when Essex marched to the relief of Gloucester. The annihilation of General Waller's army at Roundway Down (see p. 34) made it possible for Prince Rupert to assault and capture Bristol on 25 July (see p. 34). Weymouth, Portland and Dorchester surrendered to Prince Maurice and Lord Carnarvon in August (although they failed against Lyme and Poole) and at the beginning of September Exeter also surrendered to Prince Maurice. This left Gloucester remarkably isolated: it was in fact the only garrison still held by Parliament between the Bristol Channel and Manchester.

Charles has often been criticized for ordering the Oxford army to march against Gloucester, rather than combining with the army in the south-west in a bid for London. But given the situation prevailing at the time, especially in the north, where Newcastle's (Royalist) army was meeting with many difficulties, the decision to clean up Gloucester – thereby gaining control of the Severn valley and opening up the road to South Wales – was probably a wise one. The refusal of Colonel Massey, Governor of Gloucester, to surrender the city when Charles summoned it on 10 August, and his very determined resistance thereafter, came as something of a surprise to the Royalists, and brought fresh hope to a dispirited Parliament. The losses at the assault on Bristol had been very heavy, and the King was in no mood to repeat them, so he had occupied the heights above the city, and although lacking proper siege material had felt confident that he could reduce the small garrison of 1,500 men before any relief could reach them.

Meanwhile, the threat to this important outpost was causing grave anxiety to the Parliamentarian leaders in London. It was originally decided by Parliament that Sir William Waller would command the army designated to relieve Gloucester, but Lord Essex, as commander-in-chief of the Parliamentarian forces, decided to take personal command. On 24 August he reviewed a large assembly of troops on Hounslow Heath – business in London was virtually at a standstill to enable the London trained bands and auxiliaries to muster at full strength – and on 26 August he set out on what must have seemed a fairly desperate venture. At Brackley Heath the army was reinforced by a strong artillery and horse contingent, bringing Essex's total force up to about 15,000 men, of which 4,000 were cavalry. As he marched through Bicester to Chipping Norton and Stow-on-the-Wold, Prince Rupert and Lord Wilmot hung about his flanks, but caused him little trouble, and by 5 September Essex was in sight of Gloucester.

Frantic attempts to induce Massey, whose powder was down to three barrels, to beat the chamade failed. Charles, not wanting to fight Essex with an unsubdued garrison at his back, raised the siege and made off to Sudeley Castle. Essex, his first task accomplished, entered Gloucester in something of a triumph on 8 September. He now had to get his army back to London. His recent march, much of it through enemy-held country, had been a remarkable feat, and he was about to display further skill in some complicated manoeuvring which completely baffled the Royalists, whose primary purpose was to bring him to battle on the most favourable terms.

Leaving much of his heavy ordnance and powder in Gloucester, Essex set out for Tewkesbury on 10 September, and the next day Charles, so as not to lose touch, moved ten miles north to Evesham. Throughout this campaign Essex displayed strategical skill and a sense of calm and power that was well above his average, and now through a series of feints he had the Royalist intelligence thinking that he meant to strike north for Worcester, or even enter Warwickshire, whereas he had all along determined to regain London by the road running south of Oxford. On the night of 15 September he led his army out of Tewkesbury, and before the King had realized what he was up to he had surprised some 200 Royalist soldiers in their beds in Cirencester, had captured a badly needed supply train and was on his way to Cricklade.

When Charles discovered that he had been given the slip he set off in pursuit, and sent Rupert in advance with rather more than 3,000 troops to intercept the enemy. The Prince, displaying his usual energy, was at Faringdon by the time Essex was leaving Swindon, and striking south he caught up with the Roundhead army between Chiseldon and Aldbourne. Although Essex was marching across Aldbourne Chase with his army dangerously strung out, the opportunity to defeat the various sections in detail with a comparatively small cavalry force was probably never there, although Sir John Byron states that it was missed. Colonel Hurry, at the head of 1,000 men, had been detached to attack the column in the rear, while Rupert fell upon the flank. Hurry's attack caused considerable confusion among the five regiments of horse that comprised Essex's rearguard, but Sir Philip Stapleton in command of the van had time to draw back onto the main body, and Prince Rupert's charges were repulsed. Nevertheless, the action had the important effect of forcing Essex to put the river Kennet between him and the Royalist army and preventing his getting further than Hungerford on the night of 18 September.

The Royalists camped that night at Wantage, so Essex still had the shorter distance to go to Newbury, where his half-starved army would have obtained welcome rations from that Roundhead stronghold. But the resolution he had displayed hitherto seemed now to desert him, or else he sadly misjudged the dynamism of the King's nephew. The next day he continued somewhat leisurely

54

on his way, and the advance party sent to arrange billets in Newbury was rudely handled by Prince Rupert's cavalry, who had
ridden into the town a few hours ahead of the main Royalist army.
Essex, who was apprised of this unpleasant situation as he trudged
the miry road out of Kintbury, had no alternative but to halt his
army for the night in the rain-soaked fields lying between the
rivers Kennet and Enborne.

The King now clearly held the advantage. He had placed his
army between the Roundheads and London; he had acquired the
food supplies destined for his enemy; and although he was short
of powder this was expected to arrive from Oxford at any time.
He therefore led his men out of Newbury to the west on the evening
of the 19th, so as to be ready to meet Essex on the morrow. His
main camp was on the flat ground north and east of Skinner's
Green, but cavalry patrols were sent to occupy the ridge east of
Wash Farm. There is some reason to believe that Prince Rupert
advised against attacking until such time as the ammunition
supply had been assured.* Apart from the fact that such advice
would have been quite out of character, it does not make much
military sense. The King's objective was to beat the Roundheads
before they could regain London, and conditions could scarcely
have been more unfavourable for Essex – indeed, as we shall see,
he himself had little alternative but to fight. Behind the King
Waller commanded an army 4,000 strong and Charles was not to
know how little inclined Waller was to help Essex. It seems,
therefore, that the council of war's decision that evening to seize
the vantage points in readiness to attack the next day, and defeat
Essex before Waller could come to his relief, was a wise one.
Unfortunately, it was imperfectly executed.

And what were Essex's thoughts? Having undertaken this
hazardous enterprise in preference to a subordinate he disliked,
he could not afford to fail. There is a Royalist letter extant† in
which the writer says that the Royalists expected the enemy to
withdraw during the night, and no doubt Essex would have liked
to go on his way unmolested. But to attempt to slip past to the
south of the Royalist army would have been fraught with danger.

* Eliot Warburton, *Prince Rupert's Diary*, Vol. II, p. 292. In the Wiltshire
  Country Record Office there are three manuscripts, from which
  Warburton has drawn his work. They form a near-contemporary
  series of notes intended to form the basis of a biography of Rupert.
  Their precise origin is not known, but Colonel Thomas Benett,
  Rupert's secretary, may have been their author. They are certainly
  not a diary written by Prince Rupert.
† *Thomason Tracts*, E.69.

The ground was low-lying and difficult to move over, and his flank and rear would have been constantly exposed to attack. No, the road to London lay straight ahead through the enemy; and furthermore it lay along the ridge and plateau that jutted out as a broad finger between the two river valleys. Essex had been dilatory out of Hungerford; the lesson had been learned and he determined to have the high ground before first light on the morning of 20 September.

The First Battle of Newbury was a most confused affair, and as so much of the battlefield is now built over the visitor is bound to find it difficult to follow even the most lucid account. There are numerous documents and letters written by participants of both sides, but they are disconnected and usually view the fight from a narrow personal angle. Moreover, their site descriptions are often dangerously vague. From these we can build up some sort of picture, but it is impossible to be certain as to exactly how the battle was fought. We cannot even be sure of the numbers engaged, although it is known that the Cavaliers were considerably superior in horse, but the overall figure may have been much the same as at Edgehill and the armies almost equal at around 14,000. Essex may have had 10,000 foot to 4,000 horse and the King only 8,000 foot but 6,000 horse. Both armies appear to have had about the same number of guns (twenty), and at least six of them were heavy cannon.

The King took personal command at this battle with Lord Forth acting as chief of staff. Prince Rupert, Lords Carnarvon and Wilmot, Sir John Byron and Charles Gerard commanded cavalry brigades, while Sir Jacob Astley was again in command of the infantry and had under him, as brigade commanders, Sir Nicholas Byron, Sir William Vavasour, Sir Gilbert Gerard and John Belasyse. The Roundhead infantry consisted of four brigades each of three regiments and the London trained bands, who were not brigaded and at first formed the reserve. The cavalry was divided into two wings; Sir Philip Stapleton commanded on the right and John Middleton on the left. For some reason, possibly because he did not think his brigade commanders up to the task, Essex took command of the army's right wing (a foolish involvement for the commander-in-chief), while Sergeant-Major-General Skippon commanded the left wing and reserves. The Roundhead guns were under Sir John Merrick, who used them with considerable skill.

On the evening of the 19th the two armies were encamped almost opposite each other on the low ground south of the Kintbury road, along which the Roundheads had marched. Essex had left his baggage wagons in the area of Hamstead Park, and in the early hours of the morning he deployed his men for battle. Before he did so he issued – presumably through his brigade commanders – what would later be called an order of the day; he warned the men that the struggle would be a stern one and that the enemy held

Left: Cavaliers and Roundheads, from 'A dialogue or parley between Prince Rupert's poodle and Tobie's dog Peper', 1642

Right: Military costume, c. 1645

all the advantages of terrain. The troops needed no reminder of their present desperate plight and they were soon to show, as others after them would do, that when times are difficult Englishmen become determined, and when they are desperate they become indomitable.

The important ground lay to the south of the two army encampments. The Royalists had already sent a cavalry patrol as far as Wash Common and had brought up some guns, but through a carelessness that was to prove extremely costly they failed to take any steps to occupy the feature of tactical importance that became known as Round Hill. The southern part of what was to become the battlefield (Wash Common and Enborne Heath) was fairly open and good cavalry country, but to the west of this plateau the ground was much more broken, and narrow, steep-banked lanes ran down from the spurs intersecting the flat ground, which was covered by enclosures and the occasional copse. Essex extended his line to where Bigg's Cottage still stands,* just south of Boame's Farm, and before first light pushed his right onto Enborne Heath. General Skippon had orders to occupy Round Hill before dawn, and the guns, which had difficulty in traversing the very broken country, were brought up to the Crockham Heath area near where the London trained bands were at first positioned.

These manoeuvres by the Roundheads to seize the high ground were carried out unopposed, and when dawn broke the Royalist commanders were distressed to find that their position was overlooked by the enemy, who far from disappearing in the night had now imposed themselves upon ground from which it was vital to dislodge them. At the same time the Roundheads realized that they had paid too much attention to the right flank, and that the Royalists had a big concentration of troops opposite their baggage train. Skippon at once deployed men to cover this valley. A part of Lord Robartes's brigade and the Red Auxiliary regiment occupied the Skinner's Green area, and a contingent under Major Fortescue reached to and beyond the Kintbury–Newbury road.

The fortunes of the day would be decided on the Round Hill spur and the edge of the plateau between that hill and Wash Farm and immediately to the west of the farm. The Roundheads needed the high ground if their artillery was to be of value and, as we have seen, they had by first light a precarious footing on part of it. The task of dislodging them fell chiefly to Sir John Byron's cavalry

* It is possible that Essex spent a part of the night 19–20 September in this cottage, in spite of its position on the extreme right of his line, which makes it an unlikely place for his headquarters.

brigade and his uncle Sir Nicholas's infantry brigade. Sir John has left a graphic account of this part of the battle, in which he starts by deploring the negligence that made the assault on Round Hill necessary. In the pearly softness of a September dawn he received his orders to support the foot with his own and Sir Thomas Aston's regiments of horse. The fight began at about 7 a.m. and the leading infantry (Colonel Lisle's regiment) were soon in trouble assaulting over difficult country a hill held by determined men supported by two light cannon. Sir Nicholas threw more regiments into the attack, but they too got bogged down and called for cavalry support.

The infantry had attacked the hill from the east. Sir John assures us that this was not cavalry country, and he rode forward to reconnoitre before committing his regiments. Even now one would think twice about assaulting this hill with cavalry, but then the fields surrounding it were smaller and more thickly fenced. In obtaining a lodgement on Round Hill Sir John and his men displayed great courage and skill. He seems to have attacked from the low ground to the north-east of the hill close to Skinner's Green. Here he found the enemy infantry screened by a high hedge with a gap only wide enough for one horse to pass through at a time. While he was giving orders for it to be widened his horse was shot in the throat and he had to seek a fresh one; during his absence Lord Falkland, Charles's Secretary of State, 'more gal-

Siege warfare, from a seventeenth-century treatise on military regulations

Try your match.	*Guard your pan.*	*Present.*
Give Fire.	*Come up to your Musket.*	*Return your match*
Take up your rest.	*Blow of your loose Powder and cast about your Musket.*	*Trail your rest & open your*

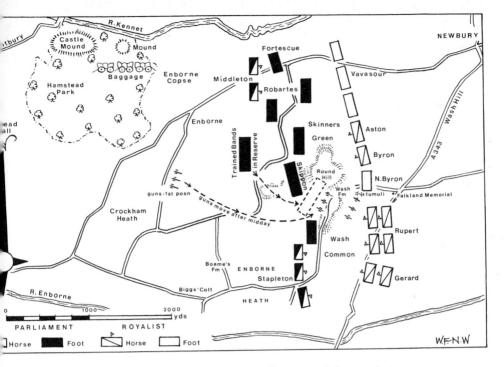

Left: Plate from a seventeenth-century exercise manual for musketeers,
showing various different positions
Above: First Battle of Newbury
Overleaf: First Battle of Newbury

lantly than advisedly' spurred his horse through the gap and was
killed instantly. As soon as the hedge had been flattened Byron's
men galloped through and into a hail of musket balls and case shot
from the two drakes. The punishment they received was too severe
to be withstood, and amid a tangle of flailing hooves and rearing
horses the order to withdraw was carried out.

Throughout this battle it is impossible to be certain of the timing,
because most narratives disregard such details. We know that
action along the whole line began at about 7 a.m. and that sporadic
firing was still going on as late as 10 p.m., although as might be
expected the main fighting stopped at nightfall; we also know
from a contemporary account that 'the fight was at its hottest at
4 p.m.'. It must have been well into the morning therefore before
this cavalry attack took place, and some time must have elapsed
while Byron rallied his men for another charge, during which the
Roundheads removed their cannon to the rear. This second attack

61

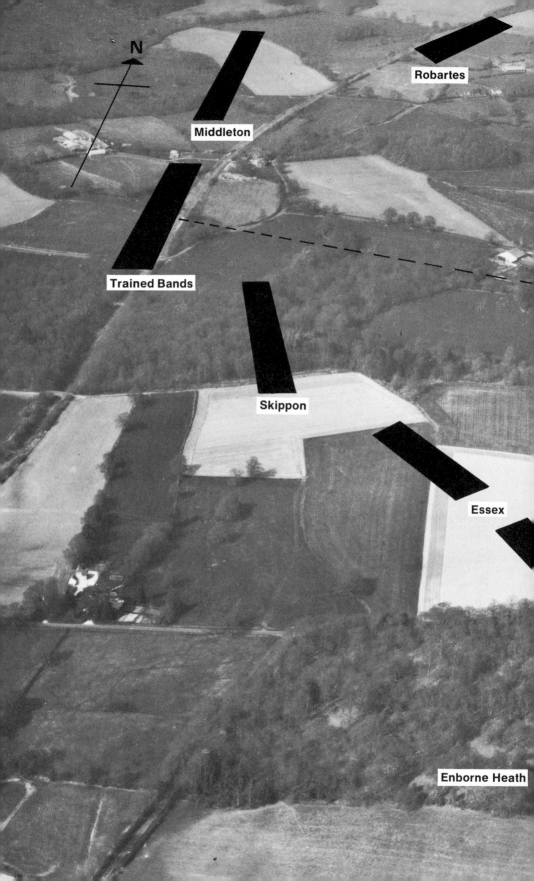

N

Robartes

Middleton

Trained Bands

Skippon

Essex

Enborne Heath

scue

Vavasour

Round Hill

Byron

Tumuli

Wash Hill

N. Byron

Rupert

Gerard

Stapleton

carried out by Sir John's and Sir Thomas Aston's regiments drove the Parliamentarians back from the summit of the hill until they had their backs to another high hedge. Here the fight became more stubborn, and once again the cavalry were unable to make headway against the flying shot and bristling pikes. Another pause in the battle while Skippon altered his position to hold Skinner's Green Lane, and then a third cavalry charge completely routed the enemy, who were only saved from total disaster by the thickness of the hedges, the steepness of the banks and the fact that Skippon had also brought up the four London regiments he still had in reserve. The cavalry suffered heavy casualties in these assaults, but they did a magnificent job.

It was probably about midday when Sir John Byron finally withdrew his brigade from the Round Hill area, leaving what he had captured to be held by the infantry. And now the main battle switched to the Wash ridge and the high ground to the south and east. Fighting had been heavy on this plateau for many hours and was to continue, in one form or another, with the utmost ferocity for the rest of the day. Some say the King had meant to stay on the defensive here, but it was good cavalry ground and Prince Rupert, who revelled in the intensity of risk, was never one to stay inactive: he led three full-blooded charges mainly against Sir Philip Stapleton's cavalry wing. Charge and counter-charge, cut and thrust, with the fortune of war going first to one side then to the other. Stapleton's men beat Rupert's first charge right back onto their main body. A second charge fared little better, for the Roundheads had been able to deploy more troops; but in the third charge Stapleton found himself outnumbered and assailed from front and flank and his men were gradually pressed back to the edge of the heath, although those Cavaliers who followed into the lanes were mercilessly dealt with. The Royalists had lost three standards and the Roundheads two, the ground was a mass of bodies, but Stapleton's cavalry had been driven off to play no further part in the battle. It was now the turn of the Roundhead infantry, who by their courage, cohesion and pertinacity were to gain the chief honours of the day.

Lord Essex's first biographer (Robert Codrington, writing in 1646) tells us that the Lord-General was everywhere encouraging his men, and that when Rupert's horse had broken through Stapleton's regiments he rallied them and 'with undaunted courage stormed with them up the hill'. This no doubt was most admirable, but hardly the duty of a commander-in-chief, and clearly it was Skippon who master-minded much of the battle. Having retained a footing on a sizable slice of the Round Hill–Wash Farm ridge, he brought up his cannon to engage the Royalist artillery, which had been doing considerable damage firing from the vicinity of the tumuli on Wash Common. He advanced the London trained bands to hold the mouth of Skinner's Green Lane, and in response to an appeal from Essex he sent his commander the Red Auxiliaries, having already sent the Blue to strengthen Fortescue, who was being pressed on the left flank.

Once Skippon had stabilized the Roundhead centre and got the heavy cannon into the firing line, matters improved considerably. The Royalist guns, which had been giving the Red Regiment of the London trained bands a considerable hammering, were now switched to engage in what was probably the fiercest and most sustained artillery duel of the whole war. The Blue Regiment had been placed on the right of the Red and it too had had to withstand some pounding, and this regiment also bore the brunt of a further charge from Prince Rupert's cavalry. Through it all, we are told, the Londoners 'stood undaunted like a grove of pines in a day of winde and tempest, they only moved their heads or Armes, but kept their footing sure, unless by an improvement of honour they advanced forward to pursue their advantage on their Enemies'. Had the Royalist infantry behaved with the same spirit, the King would most likely have won the battle, but with the exception of Nicholas Byron's brigade they appear to have been, if not cowardly, certainly spineless.

The fighting continued, often sharp and bitter, to around seven at night – and sporadically thereafter. The men must have been desperately weary, for at some time all had been committed, and most of them time and again. It was a very confused fight and there were incidents whose place and timing are not easily pinpointed. The Roundhead paper *Mercurius Civicus* in its account of the battle states that the Royalists 'wheeled about a great body of Horse, and a little below the hill fell upon the rear of our army, which occasioned us to withdraw a part of our army from off the hill to assist those which were engaged'. Some of these cavalrymen, or others shortly afterwards, had stuck green branchlets in their hats, which was the Parliamentarian emblem for that day, but the ruse was quickly detected. The hill in question must have been Round Hill, but the timing in the day's events of this particular mêlée is uncertain.

Little has been said about the fighting on the northern part of the field. It was never so vital as in the centre, or on the southern plateau, where both sides were endeavouring to turn the other's flank; but it was at times hotly contested and we have seen that Fortescue had to be reinforced, for little stood between him and the baggage wagons at Hamstead Park. On this flank too there was a curious incident mentioned in Lord Digby's account of the battle, but never fully explained. During the afternoon a party of Round-head troops (presumably either from Middleton's cavalry or Fortescue's infantry) attempted to seize a ford over the Kennet in the Guyer's Field area, but were driven back by Sir William Vavasour's men. It is difficult to understand what they hoped to attain – unless they had had enough and were making for home.

As darkness enveloped the bloodstained field the fighting dwindled to desultory fire and the occasional skirmish among stragglers. Both sides were weary beyond measure. The Round-heads had on balance fought the better of the two, but the King's army still lay intact between them and Newbury – it might be said between them and starvation. Essex's men settled down for a few hours' rest, ready to break through, or die in the attempt, on the morrow. But in Charles's camp there were the usual arguments and dissension. Lord Henry Percy, who commanded the artillery, reported that they had used eighty barrels of powder (sixty more than had been used at Edgehill) and had less than half a day's supply left – the expected barrels from Oxford having still not arrived. In spite of this Prince Rupert (who, it will be remembered, is reported as not having wanted to engage in the first instance) and Sir John Byron were for holding their ground. At the council of war they were overruled and the King, who with Lord Forth must take ultimate responsibility for the decision, ordered a withdrawal into Newbury for what remained of that night, and then on to Oxford.

Of the two principal antagonists Essex was the most deserving of the victor's crown. When on the next day – slightly puzzled – he fired at where the enemy should be, he found them gone. He had achieved his object: the road to London lay open before him. Charles is usually blamed for making a disastrous decision. But who can be certain that he was not right? He had suffered heavy casualties, especially among his leaders; a tough, desperate army was prepared to fling itself at him, and his guns were incapable of firing for more than a few hours. The greatest loss he suffered in this battle was perhaps in the death of one man – Lord Falkland. This nobleman appears to have sought death deliberately, because his spirit was broken by the sad state into which his country had lapsed. Had he lived his wise counsel and his overriding desire for a peaceful settlement might have influenced the King. Lord Digby, who replaced him as Secretary of State, was an altogether smaller man.

Besides Lord Falkland, Lord Carnarvon had been killed returning from one of the cavalry charges on the plateau, and Lord Sunderland had also fallen, together with many much valued senior officers. The Parliamentarians lost far fewer men of note – only six colonels compared with eleven Royalists. Any attempt to assess the total killed could be misleading. There are accounts of the numbers of dead seen on the field the next day, but in each instance some sixty cartloads had already been taken off for burial. From the little contemporary information available one might get an overall figure of 3,500 at the most, and possibly the Royalists were just the heaviest losers.

Essex, still uncertain as to his enemy's whereabouts, was careful to keep south of the Kennet in the early stages of his march to London. He took the route through Greenham Common, Brimpton and Aldermaston. In a narrow lane between Aldermaston and Padworth the column was attacked by a party of Royalist cavalry and musketeers. Before he left Newbury Prince Rupert is alleged to have said that 'although the Roundheads were marching unto Reading they would make calves of many of them before they came unto the Veale [Theale]'. And it seems almost certain that he commanded this raiding party, although Lords Northampton and Wilmot and Colonel Hurry are sometimes mentioned in this capacity. Essex's rear was brought up by Sir Philip Stapleton's cavalry, then came a forlorn hope of 600 musketeers and after them the London trained bands. Stapleton's men, who had received considerable punishment the day before, panicked and stampeded through the infantry; for a short while the situation looked ugly for the Roundheads, but once again they were saved by their infantry, who lined the hedges and poured such effective volleys into the Royalist force that they were beaten off with the loss of more than 100 men.

Essex continued his march through 'the Veale' into Reading, and on 28 September he and his weary, but triumphant, men entered London to bask resplendent in the City's gratitude. Essex had achieved all that he had set out to do, and for this campaign (despite his occasional lapses into the role of regimental commander) he richly deserved his colleagues' encomium. He had halted the Royalist tide of success, he had put London still further from the King's reach and, at least for the time being, he had shown himself to be the linchpin of the Parliamentarian chariot of war.

CHAPTER 4

Cheriton

29 March 1644

Until quite recently there was little or no dispute as to the site of this battle; but in 1973 a full-length account of the campaign was written in which the author disagreed with the generally accepted position of the battlefield.* The present writer, having spent many hours walking round the whole area, and having closely studied the contemporary letters and papers, is not convinced that the evidence contained in them justifies this new siting. That is not to say that the more usual siting is absolutely correct, and indeed this account is a slight variation.

In any event the whole area is easily viewed from public footpaths and tracks. It is generally assumed that the battle took place to the east of Cheriton (Cheriton is two and a half miles south of New Alresford) between that village and Cheriton Wood, perhaps a little to the south of the crossed swords on the Ordnance Survey one-inch map, sheet 168. The small by-road running east from Cheriton goes through the battlefield, and by walking along the lane running north and south of the road (which passes immediately to the west of Cheriton Wood), and the footpath which connects that lane with another running parallel to it nearer Cheriton, the visitor gets an excellent view of the ground. The battlefield has not greatly changed in the last 300 years, except that the slopes of the two ridges, which encompass the site in the form of a horseshoe, were much more enclosed in 1644.

John Adair thinks the Royalists occupied the southernmost ridge of the horseshoe (running south-west from Cheriton Wood) and that the Roundheads were positioned in the area of Hinton Ampner, the battle taking place in the low ground just north of the A272 Winchester–Bramdean road. This site can be viewed from the same tracks.

The Battle of Cheriton had important consequences, but as a fight it quickly developed into an untidy, muddled mêlée. It is not easily pieced together from the confused contemporary accounts, and most descriptions suffer from an over-simplification, or go to the other extreme of plunging the reader into an impenetrable tangle

---

* John Adair, *Cheriton 1644.* See also his biography of Sir William Waller.

of detail. Perhaps the most fascinating task for the student of military history is to decide from the slender evidence available not how it was fought, for that in outline is moderately simple, but where it was fought. For that reason this chapter has been treated somewhat differently from others. The usual run-up to the battle is followed by only a brief account of the actual fight, and then space is devoted to trying to solve the riddle of the battlefield.

During the six autumn and winter months that separated the Battles of Newbury and Cheriton both sides achieved successes and suffered setbacks in approximately equal proportion. Prince Maurice made little progress in the south-west; Sir John (now Lord) Byron was sent north to form a new army in Cheshire, with which he caused Sir William Brereton some trouble before being decisively beaten when attempting to take Nantwich in January 1644 (see p. 34); two months later Prince Rupert won a resounding victory against Sir John Meldrum's force that was besieging Newark (see p. 34); in the south Arundel Castle changed hands twice; and on 13 December General Waller won a fiercely contested fight for Alton.

By the end of 1643 it had become obvious that the contestants were fairly evenly matched and that neither side could expect a swift or easy victory. Charles could brood over wasted opportunities, and the Roundheads had yet to win a victory of strategical importance. But in January 1644 there came the first great turning point of the war. On the 19th of that month a Scottish army numbering some 20,000 well trained troops crossed the Tweed to range itself on the side of Parliament. With the ending of the Irish war the previous autumn the King had obtained some of the Duke of Ormonde's English regiments, but neither in quality nor quantity could these match the Scottish invaders. It was not difficult to see how the fortunes of Parliament could now improve through the succeeding months.

However, no one could accuse the Royalists of losing the initiative through idleness. As soon as the army was back at Oxford after the Battle of Newbury the council of war set about making new plans that would once more point the way to London. While the Oxford army was to be principally employed in containing Essex north of the Thames, a new western army was to be raised and placed under the command of Lord Hopton* with a directive

---

* The day after defeating Waller at the Battle of Lansdown (see pp. 32–4) in July 1643 Sir Ralph Hopton (as he was then) received serious wounds when a powder barrel blew up close to him. He was probably not completely fit again when assuming command of this army.

to clear Dorset, Hampshire and Wiltshire of the enemy. His adversary was Sir William Waller, who was in command of the Southeastern Association. Here then were two great generals once again in opposition, who in happier times had fought on the continent as comrades in arms.

In this campaign Lord Hopton, no longer in command of his valiant Cornishmen, for whom his raw Hampshire levies and contingents out of Ireland were poor substitutes, proved no match for Waller. It is true that he was usually outnumbered and he was further handicapped by a lack of confidence at Oxford. He was anxious to make a start in Dorset and Wiltshire, where he could quickly have cleaned up the remaining Parliamentarian garrisons, but the King ordered him to support Sir William Ogle at Winchester, and then he was lured further east. Arundel Castle surrendered to him early in December 1643, but this strong fortress was poorly provisioned and its garrison contained an element of treachery, so that after only a fortnight's siege Waller retook it on 6 January. Three weeks earlier the Cavalier losses in the fight at Alton had been unpleasantly severe, so it was a decidedly chastened Hopton who fell back on Winchester thankful that the chilling voice of winter and the snow-covered ground kept Waller at a respectable distance.

Early in March Charles sent Hopton some sorely needed reinforcements – cavalry, infantry and four guns. His army now totalled about 6,000 men, of which 2,500 were cavalry, but with them came the Earl of Forth, which could be taken as a further mark of the King's lack of confidence in Hopton, for Forth being senior was to take command. Forth's position in the Royalist army was that of commander-in-chief under the King, who had actually assumed command at Newbury, relegating Forth to chief of staff. He was a man of immense experience and courage, but he was old, deaf and more fond of the bottle than it was of him, with the result that he suffered considerably from gout. He was obviously aware of his inadequacy as a commander in the field, for only with difficulty could Hopton prevail upon him to act in that capacity, and even then much of the campaign and battle was conducted by Hopton.

The Parliamentarian plan made that February was that Waller should open the spring campaign by taking Basing House, which dominated the London–Winchester road, and then advance on Winchester. When Charles had reinforced Hopton with 800 cavalry, Lord Essex had sent Waller 2,000 under Sir William Balfour, his best cavalry commander; Waller was therefore immeasurably stronger in this vital arm. The garrison of the strategically important Basing House was under command of the owner's brother Lord Charles Paulet, and there was reason to believe that he was prepared to betray his trust. However, before the opportunity presented itself he was himself betrayed. Sir Richard Grenvile,* a soldier of considerable experience, had offered his sword to Parliament on being captured soon after his arrival from Ireland, and had been made a Lieutenant-general. This wild and unreliable turncoat was totally unsuited to the mournful rigours of a Puritan host, and he soon made his way to Oxford with a great deal of valuable information, including the plans for Waller. Paulet was arrested, and Waller decided to bypass Basing House and march straight for the Royalist army at Winchester.

The approach marches of both armies to the battle area are not easily understood from contemporary accounts. For example, Lord Hopton and Colonel Slingsby give different dates for leaving Winchester, and Waller's London brigade under Major-General Browne seem to have done an extraordinary manoeuvre if the place called 'Trafford' is really Twyford as is generally assumed. The certain facts are that Waller advanced from Midhurst to camp in the area West Meon, Westbury, Warnford, where he skirmished with what was probably a Royalist reconnaissance force, for Hopton's main army does not appear to have come so far east. On the 28th Waller sent Balfour to secure the important town of Alresford,† but Hopton, correctly divining his intention, beat him to it by the narrowest of margins. When he saw that the attempt had failed Waller halted his army in and around Hinton Ampner, a small village three miles south of Alresford.

The Royalist army bivouacked the night of the 27th on Tichborne Down. The next day there was some skirmishing in the area that was to become the battlefield. Waller had hoped to occupy the ridge immediately above his encampment, which was the southern part of a prominent horseshoe-shaped ridge whose toe encompasses Cheriton Wood and whose heels point westwards towards Cheriton village, but in this he was unsuccessful: Hopton, who had advanced his main army to occupy the northern ridge, had by the evening of the 28th established an outpost under Colonel Lisle on the southern ridge. It is probable that Waller's attempt to take the ridge was not seriously pressed, because a decision to fight had not

* The story of 'Skellum' Grenvile is delightfully told in Daphne du Maurier's book, *The King's General in the West*.
† At that time the London–Winchester road ran through Old Alresford and Bighton.

71

Ralph, Lord Hop
appointed
commander of th
new Royalist
western army

Sir William Waller,
commander of the
Parliamentarian army at
the Battle of Cheriton

been definitely agreed upon. The Committee of Both Kingdoms had expressly ordered Waller not to engage the enemy 'except upon advantage', and there were those in authority advocating withdrawal. This was craven counsel, because for once, with an army of 10,000 men, of which 3,500 were horse, and an artillery train of sixteen cannon, they were very much stronger than their adversaries.

However, Sir William Waller was not the sort of man to pay much heed to committee decisions, and it seems that during the night he overruled the plan to withdraw – although he may have had some difficulty, for Lisle reported hearing the rumbling movement of wagons in the early hours. Certainly when dawn broke through a thick mist on the morning of the 29th the Roundhead army was preparing for battle. Under cover of the mist Waller sent 1,000 musketeers under Colonel Walter Leighton to occupy Cheriton Wood. Waller was renowned for his expert tactical eye; he was quick to perceive the important features of any battlefield, and on the previous evening he had decided that Cheriton Wood held the key to the ground over which the battle would be fought, for the possessor of the wood had a covered approach along either of the two ridges, and could therefore mount an attack without being forced into a frontal approach up the thickly enclosed slopes.

The sun was already beginning to disperse the mist before Hopton discovered what was afoot. He had ridden from the higher northern slope of the horseshoe across the valley and up to Colonel Lisle's outpost, when firing on his left told him that the enemy, far from retreating, were now in the wood. Lisle's position had become untenable and he was withdrawn; a few minutes later it was occupied by the main body of Roundheads. Hopton had as good a tactical eye as Waller, and fully realized the importance of Cheriton Wood. It is possible that he may have been deterred from occupying it earlier by Lisle's report that the enemy were withdrawing, but he wasted no time in trying to regain the initiative.

Lord Forth, whose gout was troubling him, had spent the night in Alresford, but as soon as he got Hopton's report he hastened to the battlefield. The contemporary account, as published in the *Bellum Civile,* indicates that Forth ordered Hopton to bring the Royalist army forward – possibly to the reverse slope of a lower and shorter ridge west from Cheriton Wood almost exactly halfway between the two arms of the horseshoe – 'and, seeing the posture the enemy was in, [he] commanded the Lord Hopton to draw the whole army and cannon up to him to that ground ... And placing the foote and horse that the Earl of Brainford [Forth] brought with him on the right whing, himselfe with his owne foote and horse drew to the left, which was over against the woody ground that the enemy had newly possest.' It is not generally accepted that this intermediate ridge was the one occupied by the Royalists during the battle, but there are indications that it could have been. Certainly it seems from the above account that the army advanced from the north ridge, and although Hopton in his account of the battle does not specifically mention that Waller occupied the south ridge on Lisle's withdrawal, it would seem to have offered him the best possible position. The centre ridge was 'over against the woody ground' and is high enough to give protection to troops on the reverse slope.*

As soon as the army had come up Hopton ordered Colonel Appleyard with 1,000 musketeers to clear the wood. But as these troops breasted the ridge they came under intensive musket fire – perhaps from the enemy position on the ridge, but certainly from those in the wood – and Hopton decided to reinforce their attack by a flanking movement with one 'division' of commanded musketeers under Lieutenant-Colonel Edward Hopton. This double assault was quickly successful, for these particular Londoners (the White and Yellow Regiments) were undisciplined and inclined to be mutinous, and they were driven headlong from the wood. Hopton was now anxious to mount a strong attack on the enemy's vulnerable right flank, which could have been done under cover of the wood, but the more cautious Forth preferred to stand on the defensive and allow the enemy to attack him, if they did not in fact lose heart after their recent reverse and withdraw. It is impossible to guess what the outcome of a flank attack by Hopton on a somewhat shaken enemy would have been, but probably it offered the best chance of success for any army outnumbered by almost two to one.

Hopton is said to have accepted this decision of Forth's with good grace, but on riding back to consult with his chief he was alarmed to find that the right of the line was already engaged. It must have been about 11 a.m. when the young gallant Sir Henry Bard, probably disregarding orders and certainly acting 'with more youthfull courage then souldierlike discretion', launched his regiment down the slope and into the arena entirely unsupported. Sir Arthur Heselrige's 'Lobsters' quickly cut off his retreat and

* The same report states that Hopton took advantage of the ground 'and drew all his horse and foote in order on the side of the hill that was from the enemy'.

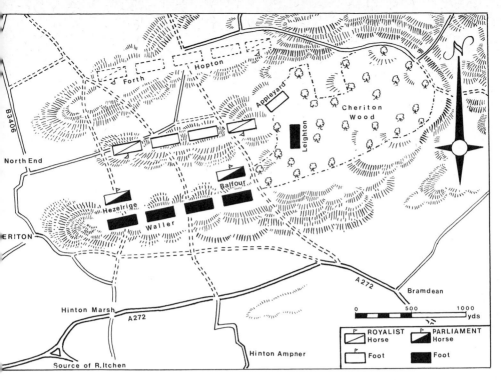

Above and overleaf: Battle of Cheriton

within a short space of time his whole regiment was either taken or killed – Bard himself lost an arm and was captured.

After this fateful beginning the whole affair from the Royalist side seems to have got out of hand. The spectacle was tragic as regiment after regiment rode down the narrow bridleways into the battle-scarred arena merely to be chopped before they could deploy. Royalist accounts of the battle endeavour to show that all was not confusion and that Lord Forth operated to some form of plan, but in truth there was little direction from on high. By early afternoon the infantry had joined the cavalry and the tangled mass of fighting men swirled around in a shapeless pattern.

There were many individual acts of heroism, and the bearing of the proud Cavaliers as they rode into battle was magnificent, but cruel losses were suffered among the senior officers. Lord John Stuart, lieutenant-general of the Horse, and Sir John Smith, sergeant-major-general of Hopton's army, were both killed in the last forlorn effort, when Lord Forth ordered Sir Edward Stowell's brigade to charge. By that time all the cavalry save Sir Humphrey Bennet's regiment were committed, and the Royalist right flank had virtually collapsed. Even so there were musketeers still lining the hedges and keeping the Roundhead cavalry, often led in person

75

Alresford

Royalists' original line

Hopton

Waller

Hinton Ampner

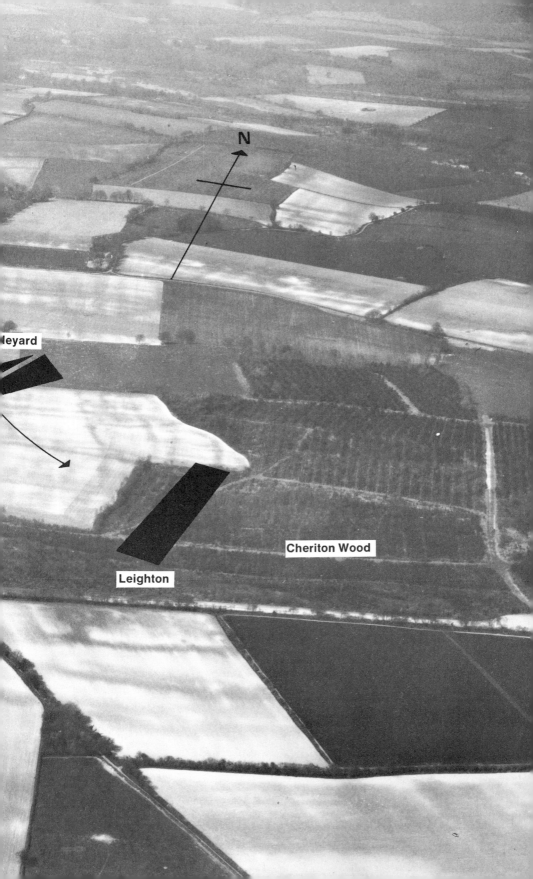

N

Meyard

Leighton

Cheriton Wood

by Sir William Waller, at some sort of distance. According to Colonel Slingsby it was the initiative of an officer on the Roundhead left wing that finally decided the issue, when he led his regiment in a sweeping hook against the fast crumbling Royalist right. But probably by about 4 p.m. the weight of numbers was telling and the whole line had become enveloped in a Roundhead pincer movement.

Lord Hopton conducted a masterly withdrawal in the face of this overwhelming disaster. The action fought by Stowell's brigade had given him valuable time, and the Queen's Regiment, which contained some Frenchmen, including its commander Captain Raoul Fleury, staged a most important and courageous delaying action, in which Fleury lost a foot. According to the Royalist paper *Mercurius Aulicus,* Colonel Richard Neville's regiment also covered the retreat, which was certainly not the uncontrolled rout described by the Roundhead Elias Archer. This cavalry screen enabled Forth and Hopton to get the bulk of the army with its guns back to Tichborne Down. Here the Cavaliers appeared to be contemplating a further stand, but when the Roundheads brought their cannon into action a few rounds sufficed and the retreat continued – although not before Hopton had withdrawn to safety all but two of his cannon.

On Hopton's advice the main army made for Basing House. Alresford was fired by the retreating soldiers, but only about five houses were burned, and if we are to believe Captain Harley many of the incendiaries (who seem to have been mostly Irish) were slain before they could get clear of the town. The Royalist army reached Basing House that night, and were soon back at Oxford. Winchester city – but not the castle – surrendered to Waller on 30 March, and before long he was in control of all Hampshire.

Even more so than in most Civil War battles it is difficult to assess the casualties at Cheriton. Harley put the Roundheads' loss at about sixty and the Royalists' at 300. There are other estimates (almost certainly exaggerated) of between 900 and 1,400 respectively. It seems to be agreed that no more than 800 Royalist horse out of some 2,500 rallied on Tichborne Down – but, of course, many had made off in other directions. We know that the Royalists lost two generals and five colonels killed, and Lord Forth (whose conduct throughout the retreat was most courageous), General Stowell and many other officers were wounded, so their total losses during a long afternoon of hand-to-hand grapple were almost certainly in excess of 300.

The Parliamentarian victory at Cheriton had most important

consequences. To begin with it was the first decisive major victory they had won: there had been minor successes and Essex had successfully barred the King from London, but here was defeat, naked and brutal, for a Royalist army that had sought battle. Morale rose and sank in the respective forces accordingly – and not only in the Roundhead army did morale rise, for the result of the battle gave a boost to the war party in Parliament. The King was at least temporarily forced onto the defensive, and could no longer expect to gain control of the south-east. The Royalists had been humbled, but were some way from being broken. Nevertheless, Lord Clarendon and Sir Edward Walker were justified in their appreciation of the results of Cheriton when the former said that the battle had 'altered the whole scheme of the King's counsels', and the latter that it 'marked a watershed in the war'.

Any attempt to retrace our ancestors' fights, to release the springs of historical imagination, requires that we should stand on the site and walk the ground on which the battle was fought. Our guide to the right place usually comes from the various maps, contemporary accounts, burial grounds, relics and, sometimes, local tradition. In the case of the Battle of Cheriton there is no contemporary map or plan extant, and in trying to locate the exact site of the battle it is first necessary to assume that the wood, which is the key to the whole question, is Cheriton Wood – in spite of the fact that this large, rather straggly wood is described by Captain Harley as 'a little wood on the top of that hill with a fense about it'. There are then certain facts from contemporary accounts that seem to be fairly well established, for they figure in most of them. They are:

1 During the skirmishing on the day previous to the battle Waller hoped to gain a foothold on the southern ridge of the horseshoe, but was unable to do so, and the day ended with Colonel Lisle on that ridge.
2 The Roundhead army encamped on the night of 28 March in Lamborough Fields just north of Hinton Ampner. Waller himself stayed with Lady Stukeley at Hinton Ampner House.
3 The Roundheads debated the advisability of withdrawing, but eventually decided to give battle.
4 In the early hours of the morning Waller sent Colonel Leighton up to Cheriton Wood, about 800 yards to his right front.
5 At about 7.30 a.m., when the mist had cleared, Hopton discovered the Londoners in Cheriton Wood. He immediately sent word to Forth, who rode out from Alresford.

6 When Forth arrived, which could not have been much before 8.45 a.m., he ordered Hopton to draw the whole army forward. They took up a position on a reverse slope, 'within muskett shott' of the enemy, which must mean within 400 yards.
7 The Londoners were evicted from Cheriton Wood and withdrew in disorder onto the main body.
8 Hopton asked permission to turn their flank, 'finding that he had from thence [i.e. Cheriton Wood] a faire way to fall upon

Basing House, which fell to Parliament on 14 October 1645. The house was looted and over 100 people killed in the sack that followed

the flancke of their whole army'. 'Faire' here meaning 'easy'. Permission was refused and the battle began with the impetuous action of Sir Henry Bard.

9 Harley states that when the enemy [i.e. the Royalists] had the wood the Roundheads, 'not to be outdared by their horse . . . drewe downe all our horse into a heathe, which stood betwixt the two hills where they did fight, but under favour of the enemy's ordinanse, the hills being one from another not a whole culvering shott'. He was presumably referring to a demi-culverin, which firing 'at utmost random' had a maximum range of 2,000 paces, but was not effective much above 400 paces.

10 Again in Harley's account there is mention of a village on the Roundhead left, which the Royalists obtained during the fight and set alight.

This is virtually all we have to go on, for what few battle relics have been found do not help us to determine the site, and the only known burial ground in the vicinity is not a Civil War one. It must be remembered that many contemporary accounts were written some time after the battle, when memories may have become confused; they are often contradictory and almost always biased. The student of the battle, viewing the ground from every angle, has carefully to consider these few facts and, working on what the late Colonel Burne called 'inherent military probability', decide for himself the location of the battlefield.

The fourth fact in the above list seems to be important. Why did Waller send a force of 1,000 musketeers into Cheriton Wood, 800 yards to his front? If he had intended to occupy the Hinton Ampner range there would seem to have been little point in sending a small force 800 yards or more ahead of the main line to be defeated in detail. Surely the reason for occupying this strategic position was to prevent the enemy from doing so, and Leighton's task was to advance ahead of the main army and threaten Lisle's troops. In this he succeeded, for Lisle must have been withdrawn before Forth appeared upon the scene.

The sixth fact gives the range from the top of the reverse slope. If Hopton had advanced as far as the south ridge of the horseshoe the enemy would have been firing from Cheriton Wood into his left flank at almost point-blank range; the reverse slope must have been to the north of this main ridge. The intermediary ridge favoured by the present writer is 650 yards from the south ridge and about 250 from what is now the edge of the wood.

Having evicted the enemy from Cheriton Wood Hopton saw that he could fall upon the flank of their main position without much difficulty. Had this been on the Hinton Ampner ridge (the position described in John Adair's *Cheriton 1644*) it would have involved Hopton in a longish ride across the open valley, whereas from the top of the wood he had an almost perfect covered approach.

Harley's statement that the hills were not a whole culverin shot apart does not rule out the generally accepted positions of the two horseshoe ridges, for these are about 1,700 yards from each other. The Hinton Ampner–south ridge positions would be around 1,400 yards apart, but the intermediary ridge is only 650 yards from the south ridge, which would seem to be too close for that description to fit. Harley's village is a more difficult problem, and seems to point to the Hinton Ampner valley, where Hinton Marsh definitely existed, although Little London (a mere cluster of houses) probably sprang up later and received the name as a result of the battle. There could not have been a village in the horseshoe, unless Cheriton had outlying cottages in those days.

Turning to local tradition, there is the site (still marked on some maps) of Gunners' Castle. This is just beyond the north-east end of Cheriton Wood, and seems an extraordinary place to site a battery of guns, wherever the battle was fought. It is said that ghosts haunt the Hinton Ampner valley, but more important local evidence comes from a farmer with seventy years' experience of the valley, who told the writer that even now with modern drainage the fields are often waterlogged in parts at the end of March. No contemporary account mentions water, or heavy ground for cavalry to manoeuvre on. The valley where the battle was fought is referred to as a heath – a description unlikely to fit ground that contains the headwaters of the Itchen.

John Adair's site is preferable to the one hitherto generally accepted (the two ridges of the horseshoe); but somehow it doesn't seem quite right and there are too many serious snags for the present writer to be entirely satisfied. Admittedly the site here suggested of the south ridge (Parliamentarian) and the intermediate ridge (Royalist) is too cramped for comfort, but this might have been the cause of the confused dog-fight into which the battle developed and it is an arena scarcely, if at all, smaller than that of Marston Moor, in which larger armies were involved. There is also the question of Cheriton Wood. If it was the same shape and size (and this seems doubtful) as it is now, both the generally accepted site and the one I myself favour have the difficulty of Hopton's left wing, which would have been partly masked by the south-west end of the wood. Nevertheless, it seems to be the site that fits in best with the few important known facts.

CHAPTER 5

Marston Moor

2 July 1644

The Battle of Marston Moor was fought on ground immediately to the north of the Tockwith–Long Marston road, these villages forming respectively the flanks of the opposing lines. Long Marston is situated about five miles west of York on the B1224 road leading to Wetherby. The Tockwith road runs north-west from the crossroads in Long Marston, and the obelisk commemorating the battle stands on the north side of the road about one mile from Long Marston (Ordnance Survey one-inch map, sheet 97).

Easily the best view of the battlefield is obtained from the high ground to the south of the road in the vicinity of Cromwell Plump. The ground rises gently from the road to this feature, which is crowned by a few trees. However, there is no track to it, and during the summer months the ground is likely to be under corn and permission could not be obtained to walk it until after harvest. But the visitor can walk up Moor Lane (which runs almost due north from the obelisk) and in just over 400 yards, where there is now a pond, the line of the great ditch can be faintly traced. The lane continues for another half-mile until it comes to a cross-lanes. By taking the left of the four lanes and continuing to its end the visitor arrives at what was White Syke Close, where Lord Newcastle's Whitecoats made their last stand – and where they were mostly buried. The site is probably just to the south of the lane's end. This walk takes one round that part of the battlefield where some of the fiercest fighting took place.

The year 1644 began badly for the Royalist forces in the north when the Earl of Leven, at the head of a large Scottish army, marched across the border on 19 January in support of the Parliamentarian cause. On the 25th of the month Sir Thomas Fairfax inflicted a crushing defeat on Lord Byron's troops, who were besieging Nantwich, capturing seventy-two officers and 1,500 men, of whom more than half subsequently joined the Parliamentarian army (see p. 34). Indeed, the Fairfaxes proved irresistible in the early months of the year: Sir Thomas cleared the West Riding of Yorkshire, and then with his father took Selby on 11 April, making another large haul of prisoners.

The Marquess of Newcastle, with a totally inadequate army, could do nothing but fall back before the Scottish invasion and was in Durham when Selby fell. Finding himself squeezed between the Scots and the triumphant Fairfaxes, he retired on York. By 22 April the Scots and the Fairfaxes had joined forces and York, that aristocrat among cities with its massive walls, enchanting medieval houses and narrow streets, prepared itself for a long siege. At first the city was only partially invested and Newcastle was able to occupy the suburbs; but on 6 May Lord Manchester at the head of the Eastern Association's army took Lincoln, and by 2 June he had arrived before York to join the investing force. Constant attacks made the outlying areas of the city untenable, so Newcastle destroyed the bridges over the rivers, withdrew to the centre and played out time as best he could with spurious offers to treat, but fighting pugnaciously to repulse any enemy attempt to breach the walls.

After his success before Newark in March (see p. 34) Prince Rupert had retired to Shrewsbury to build up his army. From here he was summoned to Oxford and was in consultation with the King between 25 April and 5 May. Rupert held firmly to the view that York must be relieved as soon as possible, and he put forward a plan based on maintaining the strengths of the garrisons around Oxford with a striking force sufficient to occupy Essex and Waller, while Prince Maurice made an all-out effort in the west and Rupert himself concentrated on the relief of York. But the dust had scarcely settled on the hoofmarks of Rupert's horse before those in conclave with the King set about altering his plan, with nearly fatal consequences to the King's 'Oxford Army'.

However, Rupert remained constant to that part of his plan which allowed for the relief of York. With only 6,000 foot and 2,000 horse he had not the strength to engage the formidable host of some 27,000 men now before the city, so on 16 May he marched from Shrewsbury to win Lancashire and gain recruits. His progress was mainly one of triumph, although his successes were not gained without some loss, and the captured towns and garrisons suffered the barbarities usually inescapable when men are engaged in ruthless internecine quarrel. Such losses as there were were made good by the acquisition of the Lancashire regiments and troops brought in by Lord Derby, whose countess had put up such a gallant resistance to the Roundheads at Lathom House. Moreover, on 1 June Rupert was joined by Lord Goring and Sir Charles Lucas at the head of 5,000 cavalry and 800 infantry. Lord Newcastle

Alexander Leslie (above left), who as the Earl of Leven led a large Scottish army across the border on 19 January 1644 in support of Parliament. The Marquess of Newcastle, who had been created a duke by the time this portrait (above right) was painted, Prince Maurice of Nassau (below left) and Lord Goring (below right) were all Royalist commanders

had sent these troops to him, for cavalry were more of a hindrance than a help in a closely beleaguered city.

While at Liverpool Rupert received a letter from Sir Thomas Glemham, Governor of York, outlining the critical situation of the besieged. There was no time to lose and now, at the head of 7,000 horse and probably as many foot, he set out across the Pennines, marching via Skipton, Denton, Otley and Knaresborough, which town he reached on 30 June. He had wisely spent three days at Skipton resting, reorganizing and training his new recruits for the coming battle.

The generals commanding the allied army (Scots and Parliamentarians) were determined to maintain the pressure on York and had firmly resisted messages from the Committee of Both Kingdoms that they should detach a force to intercept Rupert in Lancashire. However, when information reached them that the Prince was at Knaresborough with an army of 18,000 men – for it was wrongly assumed that he had been joined by Sir Robert Clavering with 3,000 men – their task was clearly to prevent this relief force from getting into York. Accordingly on the morning of 1 July they raised the siege and marched to Long Marston in order to bar the Knaresborough–York approaches.

This was a wise move, for the allied commanders had learned that the expected reinforcements under the Earl of Denbigh and Sir John Meldrum could not be with them for a few days, and thinking Rupert to have more men than he had they felt unable to detach a part of their army to deal with him. Rupert's military reputation was now at its height. The story of his exploits in the field had become a heroic apologue of skill and daring. From his next manoeuvre the legend could only gain strength. The direct route to York was barred by a superior force, so the Prince having thrown out a cavalry screen to deceive the allied army on Marston Moor, struck north and marched via Boroughbridge, where he crossed the Ure, then to Thornton Bridge and over the Swale, through the district known as Galtres Forest and down to Overton, a small village on the Ouse opposite Poppleton. Here he scattered an outpost of Manchester's dragoons and seized the bridge of boats that they were guarding. In the course of a long day Rupert had marched his men twenty-seven miles. That evening York was relieved.

Exactly what happened in the Royalist camp on the evening of 1 July is no longer known. Lord Goring certainly rode into York to report to Newcastle, his military chief, but Rupert for reasons of protocol may have remained with his troops on the outskirts of the city. Late as was the hour, and tired though they would have been, a cavalry reconnaissance force would almost certainly have ridden out that evening to observe the enemy, for Rupert was determined on battle. Newcastle, and his veteran chief of staff General King (recently made Lord Eythin), were for waiting. It seemed to be the more sensible course: the allied army outnumbered them by about 8,000 men, all of whom were presumably in better shape than Rupert's 14,000, who had just completed a strenuous march, and the York garrison of some 4,000 foot which had undergone the rigours of a long siege.

Reinforcements were expected under Clavering, and possibly Montrose; and more importantly, Newcastle thought – with some reason – there were cracks in the allied army which might soon become a cleavage. A case could also be made for the commander-in-chief spending a day or two integrating his and Newcastle's armies. But caution seldom played much part in Rupert's reasoning: he firmly believed that in war courage and resolution cast aside all veils and disguises and became the only arbiters of success.

Although Newcastle probably did not meet Rupert on the evening of 1 July, he sent him a letter which ended with the words: '. . . neither can I resolve anything since I am made of nothing but thankfulness and obedience to Your Highness's commands.' These courtier sentiments were taken at their face value by Rupert, who sent peremptory instructions for Newcastle to join him with his army at dawn the next day. However, it was not until 9 a.m. on 2 July that the two men met. Only then did Newcastle and Eythin inform the Prince of their reasons for not wishing to fight. By this time Rupert's army was getting into position on Marston Moor, and the matter was closed when Rupert told Newcastle about a letter (which he did not show him) that he had received from the King ordering him to fight.

This letter, which Rupert was to carry with him for the rest of his life, was written from Worcestershire on 14 June when the King's fortunes were at a low ebb. The relevant passages were, 'If York be lost I shall esteem *my crown little less*'; and again, '*But if* York be relieved, and *you beat the rebels' army* of both kingdoms, which are before it; then (*but otherwise not*)* I may possibly make shift (upon the defensive) to spin out time until you come to assist me. Wherefore I *command and conjure you,* by the duty and affection I know you bear me, that all new enterprises laid aside, you immediately march, according to your first inten-

* Inserted by Lord Wilmot.

tion, with all your force to the relief of York.' Crystal-clear orders that at all costs York must be relieved, but no direct mandate to engage the enemy in battle afterwards. However, Lord Colepeper appears to have known Rupert better than his uncle did, for on learning that the letter had been sent he exclaimed to the King, 'before God you are undone, for upon this peremptory order he will fight, whatever comes on't'.

Meanwhile, there was some disagreement in the allied camp between the English and Scottish commanders. The English favoured giving battle at once, but the Scots – curiously more cautious, for their plan would have led them further from home – favoured withdrawing to prevent Rupert breaking through to the south, which seemed to be his most likely course. They won their point, and in the early hours of 2 July the army marched for Selby led by the Scottish infantry. The cavalry rearguard was not clear of the high ground south of the Long Marston–Tockwith road before Rupert's army commenced deploying to the north of the road. The head of the allied army was now within a mile of Tadcaster and the whole force was dangerously strung out along several miles of a narrow road. Fairfax at once sent messengers to recall the foot and artillery, for it was obvious that Rupert intended to give battle.

It is arguable that Rupert now missed his best opportunity of gaining a victory. For several hours the allied army, striving to regain the open ground and deploy for battle, was hopelessly vulnerable. The man who had been prepared to throw caution overboard a little while earlier now seemed content to wait upon events and hazard all on a set-piece battle for which he appeared to hold no advantage. But this is to look at only one side of the coin: Rupert had his problems. He was outnumbered anyway, and unless victory was certain – and in battle there is no such thing as certain victory – it would have been most inexpedient to attack without Newcastle's army; his own troops were not yet fully concentrated; and he himself probably did not arrive at Long Marston before the middle of the morning, by which time the chances of success had sensibly diminished. Knowing the man as we do one cannot help thinking that had it been possible to gather up his army for a quick swoop he would have done so. Admittedly Rupert was not a good commander-in-chief, but he never lacked the offensive spirit.

It was about 4 p.m. on a sultry afternoon, with the first thunder clouds gathering in the distance, before the whole of the allied army was back between the villages of Tockwith and Long Marston and in some sort of formation. An hour or so earlier they had established their artillery on the high ground south of the road and fired one or two rounds of defiance at the enemy, causing the loss of one Cavalier officer. But this cannonade and any skirmish there may have been on the Tockwith flank was of short duration.

The allied army was originally drawn up on the slope that descends gently from the low ridge on which stands the feature now known as Cromwell Plump – the command post of the allied generals. Immediately in front of the army was a field of rye and then came the Long Marston–Tockwith road (known as Marston Lane), which although then little more than a trackway followed the same line as the present road. North of the road the land was probably cultivated for about 400 yards up to the deep ditch that originally connected Atterwith Dyke (which used to run east of Atterwith Lane) with the Syke Bek that runs through Tockwith. The ditch had a hedge on most of its southern side and was partly filled in at its western extremity. Beyond the ditch the ground was at that time open moorland, and except for a number of gorse bushes that offered some protection to the Royalist left there was little cover between the ditch and Wilstrop Wood – which may have been larger in 1644. The only exception to this was Moor Lane, which runs north of the road from the site of the obelisk and was much as it is now, flanked by a hedge and shallow ditch.

The Royalist order of battle, numbers and dispositions were fairly accurately assessed and plotted on a plan (now in the British Museum) made at the time by Sir Bernard de Gomme. He gave a total of 11,000 foot and 6,500 horse, which may not have included officers, and if anything errs on the low side. Rupert probably commanded 18,000 men, which included 7,000 horse and an artillery train variously estimated as between sixteen and twenty-five guns. The strength of the allied army is less easily computed. Major-General Sir James Lumsden, who fought with the Scots army, has left a plan of the battle and an estimated strength of just over 21,000 men, which included 8,000 horse. Brigadier Peter Young, whose research on the battle has been more thorough than that of any other modern writer, does not dismiss this figure but thinks it may be too cautious. In his admirable book, *Marston Moor 1644,* he agrees with the generally accepted figure of 27,000 plus for the allied army assembled before York after Manchester had arrived, but the disparity between this number and Lumsden's figures for the battle is not precisely accounted for.* The total

* Pp. 68, 106 and 109.

89

was probably nearer 27,000 than 22,000, and the allies may have had a few more cannon than the Royalists – but little use was made of artillery in this battle.

Both armies drew up for battle in the conventional style of the time with their cavalry on the flanks and infantry in the centre. The Royalist right was under Lord Byron, who had Sir John Hurry, major-general of Rupert's horse, with him.* It comprised 2,600 horse and 500 musketeers interposed between the cavalry, and was drawn up in two lines, with one regiment of 200 horse under Colonel Tuke positioned in the right rear of the leading right cavalry regiment to prevent that flank being turned. The cavalry on the left was under Lord Goring, with Sir Charles Lucas to assist him. This wing too was drawn up in two main lines and again the flank was 'refused', this time by Sir Francis Carnaby's regiment. Goring would have ridden in the front line leaving his second-in-command with Sir Richard Dacre's brigade, which comprised the second line. This wing had about 2,000 horse and, like the right wing, 500 musketeers.

The infantry in the centre, probably under the overall command of Lord Eythin, was drawn up in three lines with the regiments six ranks deep, pikemen in the centre and musketeers on the flank. Their right front was somewhat advanced as a brigade under Colonel Napier had been placed to cover the gap between the centre and Byron's horse on the right. Sir William Blakiston's small cavalry brigade, probably no more than 800 strong, reinforced the infantry, taking position between the second and third lines. Newcastle's famous Whitecoats did not arrive on the field until the middle of the afternoon, and no doubt for this reason were placed on the right of the second and third lines under Sir Francis Mackworth. The centre comprised some 10,000 infantry and Blakiston's cavalry. Behind the infantry Rupert took personal charge of a small reserve of about 700 horse. The guns were mostly interspersed among the main body of the infantry, but four drakes were placed forward on the line of the ditch. The Royalist line stretched from about the Syke Bek in the west to just beyond Atterwith Lane in the east. The main position was some 200 yards north of the ditch, but the ditch and the hedge bordering Moor Lane were lined with musketeers. The men in the ditch had been

* Sir John Hurry had deserted from the Parliamentarian army in July 1643, but was back with them a few months after Marston Moor. He turned his coat yet again in 1646, was taken in the north of Scotland during Montrose's ill-fated expedition and, like Montrose, was executed in Edinburgh.

Right: Prince Rupert

given the unenviable task – even for a forlorn hope – of checking the advancing troops before withdrawing onto the main body.

The allied army was drawn up in something of a hurry and nationalist niceties had to be sacrificed to expediency, with the result that brigades were strangely intermingled. The cavalry and dragoons of Lord Fairfax's army, with the first line under his son Sir Thomas, were on the right opposite to Lord Goring. These troops, like the rest of the allied army, were drawn up in three lines, and like the Royalist cavalry were supported by musketeers. Oliver Cromwell, who was Lord Manchester's lieutenant-general of horse, commanded the first line of cavalry on the left wing. There were three Scottish regiments of horse (whose mounts were not comparable to those of the English) placed on each wing, and Sir David Leslie commanded those on the left. On the extreme left wing were 500 dragoons under Colonel Hugh Fraser. It is probable that the allied artillery was concentrated in the rear of the left wing.

The infantry in the centre were organized in fourteen brigades. In the first and third lines the English and Scots were intermixed: General Baillie commanded the Scots and General Crawford the English (part of Manchester's army) in the first line; General Lumsden's Scots occupied the second line; and according to a report submitted after the battle by the Parliamentarian generals, Lord Fairfax (he and Lord Manchester may have commanded their own brigades) had his foot on the right of the third line next to the cavalry. The same report* speaks of two Scots brigades in reserve. The cavalry wings each contained rather more than 5,000 troops, and with the reserve the centre may have had as many as 15,000 men. Lord Leven was in command of the centre, and Cromwell and Thomas Fairfax took charge of their respective wings.

When, at about 4 p.m., Lord Eythin eventually made his appearance at Long Marston it is alleged that he brought onto the field 3,000 of Newcastle's troops, most of whom were disgruntled over arrears of pay, and some of whom were slightly inebriated from plundering the abandoned allied camp before York. If this is true they soon forgot their troubles, for of all those who fought at Marston Moor none stood their ground so bravely as these men. It is to be feared that the most disgruntled man among them was Eythin himself – a veteran of many battles, but a commander with no spark of genius, and a man with a chip on his shoulder so far

---

* *A Full Relation of the Late Victory.* But Lumsden's plan shows Fairfax's men on the left and only one brigade in reserve.

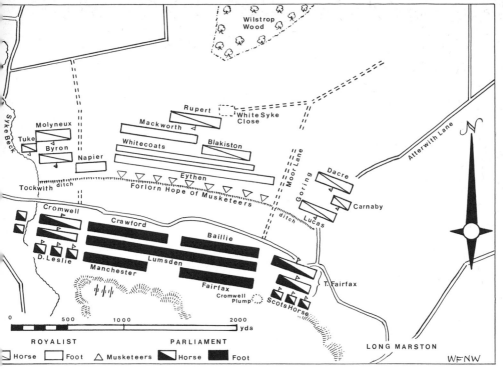

Above and overleaf: Battle of Marston Moor

as Rupert was concerned, dating from a continental battle sixteen years earlier. On being shown the dispositions he was not only disapproving but positively rude to Rupert, declaring that the army had been drawn up too close to the enemy. However, he told the Prince – who had probably already decided not to attack until the morrow – it was too late to make any alteration. By this time the allied army, which on their return from Tadcaster had been hastily deployed on the slope of the high ground south of the road, had advanced to a position perhaps only 250 yards from the ditch. This was necessary because from the area of the road most of the ditch is in dead ground, and is the position that seems to fit Scout-master-General Lion Watson's report.*

Rupert appears to have discounted the possibility of the enemy attacking that evening, as it was very unusual in those days for an army to attack with less than four hours of daylight (although Newcastle was not so sure), and having decided to await the dawn for his own attack he allowed the men – in modern parlance –

* *A More Exact Relation of the Late Battell.*

93

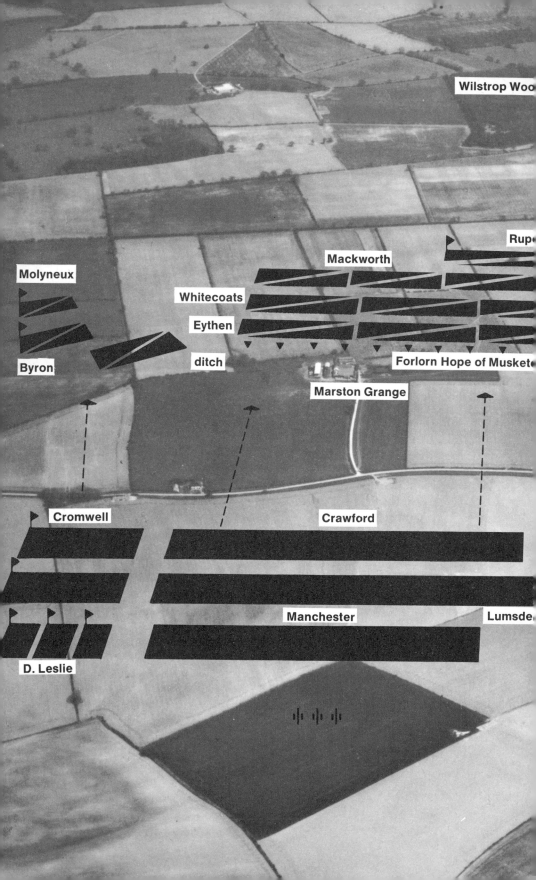

Wilstrop Woo[d]

Rup[ert]

Mackworth

Molyneux

Whitecoats

Eythen

Byron

ditch

Forlorn Hope of Musket[eers]

Marston Grange

Cromwell

Crawford

Manchester

Lumsde[n]

D. Leslie

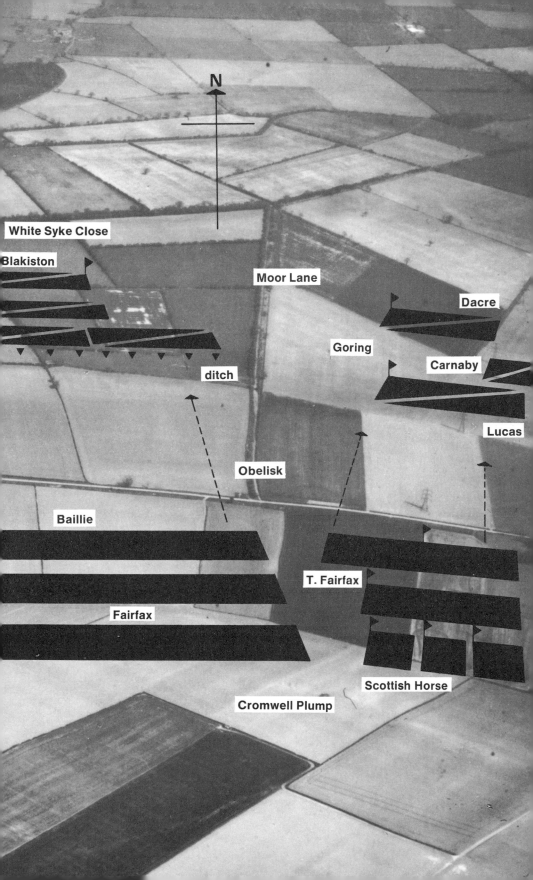

White Syke Close

Blakiston

Moor Lane

Dacre

Goring

Carnaby

ditch

Lucas

Obelisk

Baillie

T. Fairfax

Fairfax

Scottish Horse

Cromwell Plump

to stand down. He himself rode off to get his supper and Lord Newcastle retired to his coach for a smoke. This was surely a most unwise move on the part of a commander-in-chief, with the enemy almost rubbing noses with his forward troops and still nearly three hours of daylight left. Lord Leven seized his opportunity. At about 7 p.m., as the first few heavy drops of thundery rain began to fall, the unsuspecting Royalists looked up from their suppers to see the allied army bearing down upon them.

The clash of arms was almost simultaneous along the whole front, but the battle may be more easily understood if the account is split into the three sectors of the line. That on the allied left, where Cromwell and Leslie engaged first Byron's cavalry and then the reserve under Rupert, eventually driving them from the field; the cavalry fight on the Long Marston flank, where, although Fairfax himself won through, Goring routed the majority of his cavalry; and in the centre, where the infantry of both sides remained sternly embattled through the dusk and under a harvest moon, until the Whitecoats, forced back by Cromwell's triumphant cavalry, surrendered the ground only with their dead bodies. Thus a simple outline of a somewhat complicated battle.

As Colonel Fraser's dragoons began their task of clearing the hedge and ditch on Cromwell's immediate front the rain became heavy, and lightning from glowering clouds accompanied by peals of thunder replaced the noise of cannon as a backcloth to the battle. Cromwell owed his initial success, certainly in part, to the good work of Fraser's men and those of Crawford, whose infantry drove in Napier's advanced brigade, but also perhaps to the impetuosity of Lord Byron. It seems that instead of allowing Cromwell's troopers to pass over the difficult terrain of the ditch and then attacking them at a disadvantage, Byron adopted the normal cavalry tactics of immediate advance, which lost him the benefit of the musketeers that Rupert had given him. Be that as it may, he was beaten back, although his second line in some hard fighting – during which Cromwell received a flesh wound in the neck – temporarily stemmed the onslaught.

Prince Rupert, whom we have noted was eating his supper in the rear of the army when the battle began, lost no time in getting to horse and joining the reserve cavalry. It would not have been long before he realized the difficulties that Byron was in – though Goring on his left was making some headway against Fairfax. No doubt the proper place for Rupert was in control of the whole battle at his command post, while another led the reserve into battle, but when it came to action Rupert was never one for self-restraint. Moreover the chance to have a tilt at Old Ironsides, as he was to call Cromwell, was too good to be missed. Hence Rupert himself galloped off to the right at the head of Widdrington's brigade and his Lifeguard.

Almost certainly Rupert's wish to join battle with Cromwell was fulfilled: although the latter may have retired to Tockwith to have his wound dressed while David Leslie took command of that wing, the struggle there lasted for well over an hour and before the end Cromwell was undoubtedly back. This was no fast-moving cavalry action, but a battle of attrition with men hacking and thrusting at each other's limbs with their swords. Gradually the Royalist cavalry gave ground, until first one regiment and then another bent and finally broke before the storm. Lord Newcastle, upon the scene somewhat later than Rupert, tried in vain to check the headlong flight of horsemen towards and beyond Wilstrop Wood. And amid all this mayhem Prince Rupert, evidently horseless, contrived to escape capture by hiding in a bean field until the tide of battle had passed him by.

On the Royalist left flank matters fared somewhat better. The ground between Sir Thomas Fairfax's and Lord Goring's cavalry was not the neatly cultivated fields which now stretch east of Moor Lane to and beyond Atterwith Lane, but rough, wet ground liberally sprinkled with tough gorse bushes. The allied ranks advancing to the charge through this difficult country necessarily became somewhat disorganized, and Fairfax tells us that Goring's musketeers inflicted a number of casualties. This is understandable, but what is not so easy to believe is Captain Stewart's account in *A Full Relation* in which he tells us that Fairfax could only cross the ditch by advancing up Moor Lane and that his men, as they debouched in threes and fours, suffered the most heavily from Royalist musketeers. Undoubtedly the musketeers lining the ditch took some toll, but probably the Scots infantry on the cavalry's left suffered the most casualties. In fact there was little opposition until the ditch had been crossed, but thereafter the trouble began and only Fairfax, at the head of 400 men, achieved a breakthrough. His troops routed a small portion of Goring's cavalry and pursued them for at least two miles.

Goring, ably seconded by Lucas, in a hard fight that can be described in seconds but probably lasted the better part of an hour, eventually pushed back Fairfax's second line under Lambert and third under Eglinton, and pursued them through and beyond the Parliamentarian baggage lines. Some of the allied regiments (almost certainly Sir Hugh Bethell's was one) panicked and in doing so rode down the Scottish infantry on their immediate left, which added to the confusion. Fairfax reckoned that in the cavalry fight on this wing the allies had as many casualties 'as in the whole army besides'. Certainly his own family and that of the Montgomerys suffered severely.

Eyewitness accounts of this part of the battle are sparse, so it is difficult to be sure of the role played by individual regiments. But it seems that while some of Goring's first line were pursuing the enemy towards Tadcaster (thereby giving rise prematurely to rumours of a Royalist victory) others were plundering the baggage wagons, and some time elapsed before Goring could collect them up. Meanwhile Sir Charles Lucas had still to drive Eglinton's and Balgonie's Scottish horse from the field – and they fought most stubbornly – before setting upon the now unprotected flank of the Scottish infantry and causing grave damage. Fairfax, unable to rally his 400 men, returned from the pursuit almost alone to find most of his command gone and himself inextricably involved in the mêlée. Taking off his white Parliamentarian emblem he rode through the Royalist ranks, unscathed save for a sword slash in the face received during the charge, to join Lord Manchester's triumphant cavalry under Cromwell.

In the centre the infantry fight was as stubbornly contested and every bit as confused as it was on both cavalry wings. Crawford, as already mentioned, met with almost immediate success on the allied left centre, but elsewhere matters did not go so well for the Parliamentarians. Lord Newcastle, together with his brother Lord Charles Cavendish, fought with great valour (killing three men with his page's half-leaden sword) at the head of Sir Thomas Metham's troop of gentlemen volunteers. At the same time, and possibly with the help of Metham's troop, Blakiston's cavalry drove a wedge right through the middle of the allied line, routing Lord Fairfax's foot and a Scots brigade, whom they chased up the ridge south of the road. Lumsden did what he could to plug the gap, but prisoners had been taken and men killed as far as the third line, and the Scots generally had received a tremendous pounding, having been assailed from in front by Newcastle's Whitecoats and charged in the flank by Lucas's cavalry.

Incredibly, it was at this grave crisis in the battle, when the allied infantry appeared to be crumbling irretrievably, that all three allied commanders left the field. Lord Leven scarcely drew rein until he reached Leeds; Lord Fairfax made for his castle at Cawood, where finding no fires or candles he wisely went to bed; but Lord Manchester, more courageously, retired only a short distance and soon re-entered the fray to lead his men to ultimate victory. Total disaster was averted by the stout-hearted resistance of Lord Lindsay's and Lord Maitland's regiments – the latter commanded by Lieutenant-Colonel Pitscottie. Lining their musketeers with pikemen, they withstood three cavalry charges and held their ground while many around them fled, finally unhorsing Sir Charles Lucas and taking him prisoner. Generals Baillie and Lumsden never tired in their efforts to present some semblance of order among the allied infantry, but as the daylight departed and the thunder clouds dispersed to reveal a harvest moon the scene was one of the utmost confusion. Some men were in headlong flight, others managed to preserve their existence by the narrowest margins and chances. Arthur Trevor, arriving on the field at this time with dispatches for Rupert from the Duke of Ormonde, later commented, 'The runaways on both sides were so many, so breathless, so speechless, and so full of fears, that I should not have taken them for men, but by their motion which still served them very well.'

Such was the situation as the battle entered upon its closing stage. Both sides were without their commander-in-chief; the Royalist cavalry had been worsted on their right flank, but Goring had managed to rally many of his men on the left and was now occupying the position held by Sir Thomas Fairfax before the fighting began; in the centre the Royalist infantry was virtually intact. But the threat posed to their right flank would shortly develop into a thrust at the heart. In the brief lull before the final trial of strength, neither side could be confident that victory would crown its efforts.

Scoutmaster Watson (Parliamentarian) tells us that the battle was over and the field clear of the enemy by 9 p.m., but almost certainly he got his timing wrong, and anyway Royalist cavalry under Sir Philip Monckton remained on the field until midnight. The numbers engaged at the Battle of Marston Moor were larger than in any other battle fought on British soil with the exception of Towton, and although events moved with remarkable rapidity the various actions described above could not have been accomplished in much less than two hours. It is more likely that it was ten o'clock before the fighting ended under a moon that threw long shadows of horsemen across the carnage of the field, presenting to those onlookers who had come for the entertainment a strangely ethereal scene.

By the time Sir Thomas Fairfax had made his way through the enemy lines to the allied left wing Cromwell and Leslie had disposed of the Royalist cavalry and Prince Rupert. Fairfax, although fighting his first major battle, had given proof in smaller affairs that he was a most competent captain, and it was probably at his bidding that Cromwell's cavalry rode round between the embattled troops and Wilstrop Wood to come in on the left of the Royalist line. Fairfax would have seen enough of the battle in his wanderings to realize how precarious the allied position was, and he had sufficient tactical sense to grasp that if Goring's cavalry could be routed as Rupert's had been seeming defeat might be turned into victory.

The cavalry on the Long Marston flank were in exact reverse to their original positions; that is to say, Goring's men were coming down the slope from the area of Cromwell Plump, while Fairfax and Cromwell occupied the ground formerly held by Goring. There were other Royalist cavalrymen milling around the battle area, but with Lucas and Porter (Goring's major-general) captured and Sir John Hurry riding hell-for-leather for York there was only Sir Philip Monckton left to round them up, and this proved beyond

him. Goring's men were, therefore, hopelessly outnumbered and after a short, sharp fight, in which Sir Richard Dacre was mortally wounded, they were driven from the battlefield. The allied cavalry, which had been kept superbly under control, were then free to charge the rear of the by now hard-pressed Royalist infantry.

Lord Manchester was no general, but he was a good fighting soldier, who after a momentary lapse had returned to the field to lead his men, together with the thrusting Crawford, against Newcastle's Whitecoats and Major-General Tillier's and Colonel Broughton's Greencoats, who still stood unbroken and defiant. The weight of the attack, coming in as it did on the right of the Royalist infantry, had the effect of swinging the whole line round so that the axis of advance was west to east instead of south to north. The fighting here was the most stubborn of the whole battle, as the Royalists saw victory eluding them. Some contemporary accounts speak of the Greencoats (probably under Tillier, who was

The Battle of Marston Moor

captured) being the last troops to withstand the double onslaught of infantry and cavalry, but it is generally agreed that this honour rightly belongs to the Whitecoats, of whom it was said, 'they brought their winding sheets about them into the field'.

The pressure on the Royalist infantry became intolerable when the hammer of Cromwell and Fairfax began to pound on the anvil of Manchester and Crawford; nor were Baillie's and Lumsden's Scots standing idle, for recovering from wounds inflicted by Lucas's cavalry they now joined the pack for the kill. At the northernmost edge of the battlefield there was a field, partially enclosed by ditches, called White Syke Close. Pressed slowly back by the weight of the triple attack upon them, and now almost alone of the Royalist army still capable of fighting, it was said to be in this enclosure that the last glorious phase of the battle took place. Having caused considerable casualties to the Parliamentarian cavalry and foot before running out of ammunition, these Whitecoats disdained surrender and fought furiously with butt and pike, holding all at bay, until at last Colonel Fraser's dragoons pierced an opening through their ranks. The dam once broken, torrents of steel poured in. Then came the butchery, cruel and merciless.

It was said at the time that out of almost 3,000 men who took part in this last desperate stand, all but thirty lay dead on the field. But records of officer survivors known to have fought at Marston Moor indicate that the casualties in White Syke Close may not have been quite so great. Nevertheless, seldom in the annals of the British infantry have there been more indomitable soldiers than those amazing Whitecoats, who came grudgingly to the battle yet remained upon the field until the very end.

As with almost all these battles the casualties cannot be accurately assessed. The usual computation made by Parliamentarian scribes is between 3,000 and 4,000 Royalists killed and 1,500 made prisoner. Their own losses are often put as low as 300. Perhaps about 3,000 Royalists perished in fight or flight, but the losses in the allied army must have been more than 300. Fairfax's cavalry alone probably lost that amount or more, and in the early stages, and again at the end, both the Scottish and the English infantry took considerable punishment. It would seem more realistic to put the allied losses at approaching 1,500. The Royalists lost their entire artillery train, a great quantity of arms, powder and baggage, and enough colours 'to make surplices for all the cathedrals in England, were they white'.

The retreat in the dark towards York was an appalling shambles.

Only Lord Eythin appears to have made any attempt to rally some men in order to stave off pursuit, which continued with much bloodshed to within two miles of the city. The governor very wisely would admit only those troops known to have been part of the garrison. Even so the narrow streets were cluttered with the debris of battle – men suffering from terrible injuries, seared, wearied and in some cases dying. Prince Rupert, having lost his horse and his white poodle 'Boy', had remained hidden until dark and arrived in the city at about the same time as Newcastle, who had abandoned his coach in which were papers of some value to the enemy. The next morning, to the obvious distress of the inhabitants, Rupert gathered up the remains of his army and made off for Lancashire in the vain hope that fresh successes might retrieve the disaster of the battle. Newcastle, who had spent much money and effort in King Charles's cause, seems to have lost heart completely. He and Lord Eythin, abandoning Sir Thomas Glemham and York to their fate, made for Scarborough and took ship to Hamburg.

Among the generals the principal heroes of the battle were undoubtedly Thomas Fairfax and Oliver Cromwell. Rupert's stock suffered a severe setback. The legend of invincibility was gone; the victor of so many battles had lost the north for the King. As commander-in-chief he was the natural scapegoat and it must be admitted that after his brilliant manoeuvre to relieve York his performance as a commander was disappointing, although some allowance should be made for the froward Newcastle and Eythin. It has been truly said that the Royalists lost Marston Moor not so much through the prowess of their enemy as through their own mistakes.

Sir Thomas Glemham surrendered York on 16 July: with Newcastle's army demolished and Rupert's army away in the north he had no chance. Rupert had positive orders to save York, and yet he left it to its fate. But given the circumstances prevailing at the time it could never have held out for very long; it was better that he and his cavalry should be spared for other battles. After the fall of York the allied army split up. The Scots became preoccupied with Montrose in their own country, and Fairfax set about reducing the Royalist garrisons in Yorkshire. Manchester, with the Eastern Association's army, did practically nothing until the Second Battle of Newbury almost four months later (see p. 35), a contributory factor in the ever-widening breach between him and his more famous lieutenant-general of horse, Oliver Cromwell.

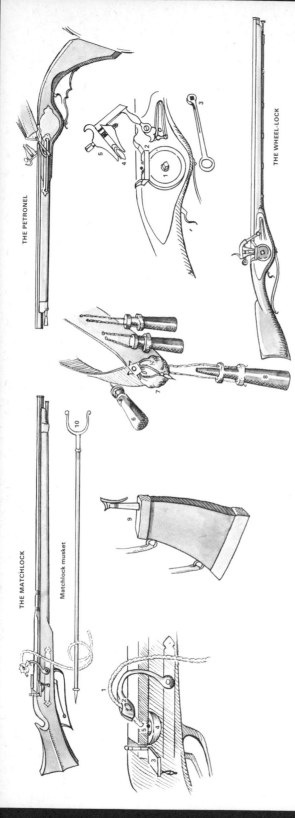

THE MATCHLOCK

Matchlock musket

THE PETRONEL

THE WHEEL-LOCK

Arquebus or matchlock musket

The matchlock musket or arquebus (like 'hackbut', derived from hakenbüchse) was in use from the end of the 15th century. It was the musketeer's weapon throughout the Civil War and was borne by at least one regiment at Sedgemoor in 1685. The slow match (1) of cord soaked in saltpetre is held in the serpentine (2). The pan-cover (3) being rotated outwards, the pan (4) is uncovered. When the trigger is pulled the serpentine carries the lighted match to the pan, igniting the priming powder there, which in turn, via the touch-hole (5), fires the charge. Charges of powder were made up and carried in wooden bottles (6) ('twelve apostles', usually eight in front and four behind) suspended by

cords from a bandolier which also bore a bullet-pouch (7) and a larger wooden bottle of fine-grained priming powder (8). Additional powder was carried in a powder horn or flask (9). Because of the length of the matchlock and its weight of up to 20 lbs, a forked rest (10) was used as a support

The wheel-lock

The wheel-lock musket and carbine were much used by officers and mounted troops throughout the Civil War. A wheel (1), the upper edge of which protruded up through the bottom of the priming-pan (2), was turned with a key or wind-ing spanner (3) against the pressure of a strong V-spring until it engaged with a sear, which

cocked the mechanism. When released by pres-sure on the trigger, the wheel spun sharply back, grating its serrated rim against a piece of iron pyrites (4) held against it in the pan by the lowered cock or doghead (5). The sparks thus produced fired the priming and thence the charge

The petronel

The petronel (French: poitrine) was a very large pistol or short carbine, with a sharply down-curving butt which was held against the chest rather than the shoulder, hence the name. Used by horsemen, it was supported by a shoulder-sling attached to the top or side so that it could be held in the aim and fired with only one hand, leaving the bridle-hand free

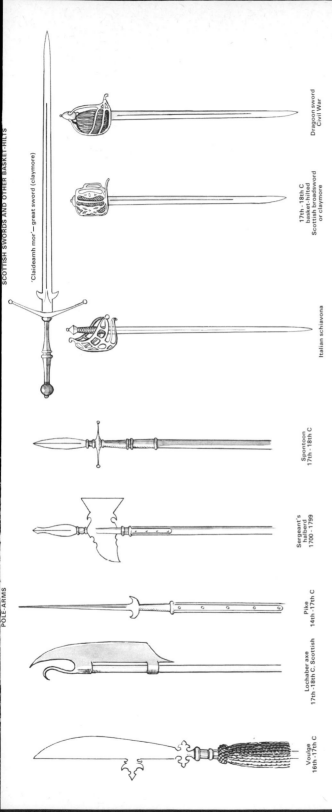

'Claideamh mor'—great sword (claymore)

Dragoon sword
Civil War

17th - 18th C
basket-hilted
Scottish broadsword
or claymore

Italian schiavona

Spontoon
17th - 18th C

Sergeant's
halberd
1700 - 1799

Pike
14th - 17th C

Lochaber axe
17th -18th C. Scottish

Voulge
16th -17th C

Pole-arms

Pole-arms continued in use during the 17th century. Companies of pikemen with 18-foot-long pikes, halberds and similar weapons not only protected the musketeers during the lengthy process of reloading, but also advanced to the attack 'at push of pike'. Improved muskets and the advent of the bayonet in the early 18th century ended the usefulness of these pole-arms, though some were carried by officers and sergeants for another 100 years as a mark of rank

Scottish swords and other basket-hilts

The claymore (claidheamh mor—great sword) was properly the 6-foot-long two-handed broadsword of the 14th-16th century Scots. The single-handed basket-hilted broadsword of the 17th-18th centuries, often called a claymore, may have been developed from the Italian Sciavona. The basket-hilt was usually lined with leather (the liner), and this type of broadsword was also much used in England, especially by cavalry and dragoons

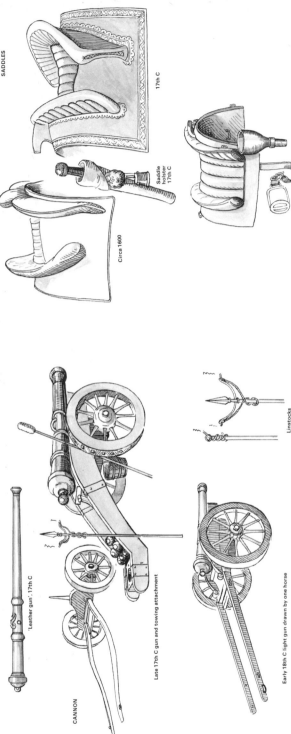

SADDLES

17th C

Saddle
holster
17th C

Circa 1600

18th C saddle and furniture

CANNON

'Leather gun', 17th C

Late 17th C gun and towing attachment

Early 18th C light gun drawn by one horse

Linstocks

Cannon

Originally made of welded iron bars, cannon barrels were later cast, first of brass and then, from the mid-16th century, normally of iron. By the 17th century muzzle-loading cannon had assumed more or less the form they were to retain until the introduction of quick-firing breech-loaders in comparatively modern times, though a variation was the 'leather gun' of the Civil War, a lightweight, easily manoeuvrable copper or brass barrel bound with leather, on a light carriage. Cannon were fired by means of a slow match fastened to a portfire or linstock. According to their size and shot-weight pieces of ordnance received distinctive names such as cannon royal, firing a 48 lb shot and needing a team of up to twenty draught horses in tandem: the culverin 18 lb shot, with a team of nine horses: demi-culverin, 9 lb shot: falcon, 6 lb, and saker 5¼ lb

Saddles

By the 17th century saddles were beginning to assume a shape more familiar to modern eyes, though still retaining higher cantle and pommel until the 18th century, and still keeping a raised and padded front plate, presumably for comfort and support rather than for protection

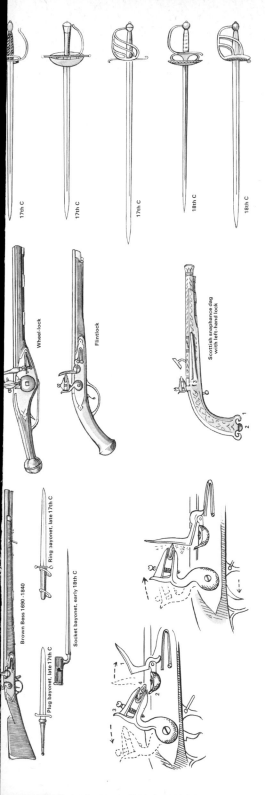

The flintlock

The flintlock musket, known as Brown Bess, was in use from 1690 until 1840. When it had been muzzle-loaded with powder and ball from a paper-wrapped cartridge, the top of which had to be bitten off, the frizzen (1) was raised to uncover the pan (2) for priming, and then lowered again, and the cock (3) holding the flint (4) was drawn back. When the trigger was pressed, the cock fell, and the flint scraped hard against the frizzen. This produced sparks and at the same time forced back the spring-loaded frizzen, thus allowing the sparks to ignite the priming powder in the uncovered pan, which via the touch-hole fired the charge in the breech. The snap-hance lock was a late 16th–early 17th century fore-runner of the flintlock. It worked on the same principle except that pan-cover and frizzen were separate, so that the pan-cover had to be opened before the frizzen was lowered into the firing position

Pistols

The invention of the wheel-lock made pistols a practical proposition and thus provided a fire-arm suitable for use by horsemen, which the matchlock certainly cannot have been. Scottish pistols or 'dags', snap-hance or flintlock, were made with all-metal stocks. They were often supplied as a pair, one with a right-hand lock, the other with a left. The butt, at first fish-tailed, was by the 18th century the so-called 'ramshorn' butt (1) with a ball (2) screwed into the base. This held a pin, the pricker, used to clean out the touch-hole. The dag usually had a ball-type trigger and no trigger-guard, and was fitted with a long belt-hook (3) along the plate, being worn suspended by this hook from a shoulder belt

Swords

The trend towards swords suited for thrusting as well as cutting continued during the 17th and 18th centuries. The increasing popularity of fencing at about the beginning of the 17th century led to the development of swords and rapiers more and more devoted to the thrust, with hilts of which the loops, bars, shell-guards and cups added to the quillons are too varied to be enumerated. Military swords retained greater weight than did dress rapiers, and cavalry swords still had weight and edge for effective cutting

CHAPTER 6

Naseby

14 June 1645

Naseby is some six miles south of Market Harborough and eleven miles north-west of Northampton. The battle was fought about one mile north of the village and the opposing lines overlapped the present Naseby–Sibbertoft road, the Royalist position being on Dust Hill and that of the Parliamentarians on the forward part of the broad Mill Hill–Red Hill Farm ridge (Ordnance Survey one-inch map, sheet 133).

There are no convenient footpaths crossing the battlefield, but a good view can be obtained from the undulating Naseby–Sibbertoft road – from the area of the monument for the Royalist position and the entrance to Prince Rupert's Farm for the Roundhead one. For those anxious to view from some special angle, the local farmers are most cooperative and will usually give permission for their fields to be crossed.

In the spring of 1645 King Charles and his advisers found themselves, not for the first time, uncertain as to which was the wisest course to pursue. The position was by no means hopeless, for although the north had been virtually lost as a result of Marston Moor (see p. 35 or chapter 5 for full details) the King had an army at Oxford and another under Lords Goring and Hopton in the south-west, while Sir Charles Gerard commanded a considerable force of Welsh levies that could be called upon. Plymouth proved unassailable and Weymouth had been lost, but Bristol was a valuable port and although Gloucester and Taunton continued to hurl defiance at their attackers almost the whole of Cornwall, Somerset and Dorset was held for the King. In Scotland Montrose was working through his year of miracles and Charles had thoughts of going north to join him. But events overtook him and divided counsels, so often disastrous, prevailed.

Parliament could put into the field greatly superior numbers to the King, and by now their cavalry – or at least a good part of it – was more than a match for the Cavaliers, but their latest fighting machine, the New Model Army, was still in the process of being formed, and in April was hardly ready. The other troops were scattered: Brereton was besieging Chester, Massey was at Glou-cester, Poyntz was in the process of taking over from Lord Fairfax (who was subject to the Self-Denying Ordinance) in Yorkshire, and Leven was on the borders, fearful of coming too far south while Montrose was scourging the Covenanters in Scotland. This wide dispersion of their forces, with Sir Thomas Fairfax's New Model still not completely formed, offered Charles his last chance of gaining an important, possibly decisive, victory. But it required concentration of effort, undivided loyalty, resolute leadership and, as always in war, a good deal of luck. None of these was to be found in the Royalist camp. Indeed on both sides there was much muddled and confused thinking and manoeuvring in the six weeks prior to the Battle of Naseby.

Prince Rupert, although nominally commander-in-chief of the Royalist armies and principal adviser in military matters, was finding the King increasingly convinced of his own military ability and the officious Secretary of State Lord Digby arrogating to himself the role of sole adviser. However, Rupert's plan that the King should march from Oxford with his army and artillery train to join with him and Prince Maurice in an attempt to relieve Chester, and then thrust northwards, was adopted. But before it could be put into operation Oliver Cromwell had thwarted it.

The Committee of Both Kingdoms, anxious to keep matters static until the New Model was ready, ordered Cromwell, whose extended period of grace allowed by the Self-Denying Ordinance had not yet elapsed, to keep the Oxford army contained. This, with only a cavalry force, he did to such good intent that the King found himself without the necessary draught horses to move his guns, and instead of being able to carry out the sensible plan of joining Rupert he had to send for him and Goring, who was almost – but never quite – into Taunton. Cromwell continued his successful raiding tactics until the end of April, meeting with only one setback when Faringdon Castle repulsed his attack with loss on the 29th. But back in the Oxford area in early May he was unable to prevent the King, together with Goring, from leaving the city on the 7th, and indeed suffered the painful humiliation of allowing himself to be surprised by Goring at Burford and having two colonels taken prisoner.

Meanwhile, at the end of April, the New Model Army was thought to be ready to take the field, and its first task – an un-necessarily ponderous one for so large a force – was to march to the relief of Taunton. Something has already been said about this army (pp. 28–9), and it will be remembered that to begin with it was not up to establishment. More importantly, over half the infantry were pressed men – raw material with no battle experience who needed, and eventually got, good disciplinary grounding. But when it took the field at Naseby it had the advantage of being almost twice the size of its opponents, and in Fairfax and Cromwell it had two commanders whom the Royalists with all their talent were totally unable to match. Fairfax marched from Windsor on 30 April and had reached Blandford by 7 May, when he received orders to detach six regiments for the relief of Taunton and return with the rest of the army. He arrived at Nuneham, just south of Oxford, on 19 May at the head of some very weary, footsore infantry, and here he was joined by Cromwell, who with General Browne had been marching around the Midlands keeping a watchful eye on the King. This, for the moment, completed a series of meaningless manoeuvres, the penalty of remote control by committee, and Fairfax settled down to invest Oxford.

At the same time as Fairfax was starting his return to Oxford, the King – now with an army of 6,000 horse and 5,000 foot – was at Stow-on-the-Wold. Here he held a council of war, the consequences of which proved fatal to his last chance of winning the war. The choice before the council was to go north, broadly following Rupert's plan, or with a force equal in numbers and superior in·cavalry to attack Fairfax and smash what the Royalists firmly believed was a very inferior army before it had a chance to get into its stride. Almost certainly the latter plan, strongly supported by Digby and Goring, was the better; but the northern venture, which was favoured only by Rupert and Sir Marmaduke Langdale, had its merits, for Leven's army had been weakened through having to send troops into Scotland, and a move to the north must have drawn Fairfax in pursuit. So long as one or other course was pursued with vigour and with the whole army the chances of success were considerable, but Charles agreed to a miserable compromise whereby Goring (whose principal anxiety was to retain an independent command) with his 3,000 horse returned to the south-west, while Charles and Rupert headed north.

On his march northwards the King drew off all available garrisons in order to swell his now diminished army. He was at Droitwich on 11 May, and left it on the 14th. When he reached Market Drayton he received the welcome news that Brereton had raised the siege of Chester – so at least the first part of his plan had been successful. But now he was again undecided and, uncertain of the situation at Oxford, he was loath to head north at once. Instead he marched through Staffordshire with a view to going north by

Oliver Cromwell

the Vale of York, or moving south if Oxford became seriously threatened. The King was now once more at the head of about 11,000 men and had summoned Goring, Charles Gerard and the Newark garrison to join him in the Market Harborough area. While he waited he decided to occupy the army by taking Leicester.

Prince Rupert was almost as happy storming a fortified city as he was leading a cavalry charge, and he made short work of Leicester. Summoned to surrender on 30 May, the city, with only 1,500 defenders and in poor shape to resist, nevertheless did so, and for over two hours its garrison and inhabitants put up a fine fight in the breaches made by Rupert's siege guns and then in the streets and market place. Eventually laying down their arms, not all of the garrison received quarter, and the sack that followed was appalling.

The King's progress through the Midland counties, and his apparent intention of going further north, had caused a considerable rift between the Scottish and English members of the Committee of Both Kingdoms. The attempt to form a northern army with Leven's troops as the principal component had proved a failure: the news of Auldearn (see pp. 131–2) had persuaded Leven that he could not stray far from the borders, and only 1,500 English troops had found their way to the appointed rendezvous in Lancashire. The Scots' desire to send the New Model after the King, instead of besieging Oxford, had been narrowly defeated in the Committee, and as a compromise Colonel Vermuyden with 2,500 horse was detached and sent north. But the news from Leicester brought the Committee to their senses; at last they saw their duty clearly. Fairfax was ordered to raise the siege of Oxford and on 5 June he marched towards Stony Stratford. Four days later his earnest request that Cromwell (who at the end of May had been sent to the Isle of Ely to raise men for the Eastern Association) should be made lieutenant-general of horse and second-in-command of the New Model, was approved by the Commons. And also on that day the Committee of Both Kingdoms, at long last, released Fairfax from their apron strings and gave him and his war council full operational control.

After Leicester there was once more divided counsel in the Royalist camp: the news that Oxford was no longer invested had not arrived, and Rupert was again in opposition to Digby and others when he strongly advised against marching to its relief, for he felt sure – rightly as it happened – that Fairfax would come to them. Not that they could have been very anxious for an immediate battle, because as a result of Leicester (casualties, the need for a garrison, and the temporary desertion of some loot-laden troops) the Royalist army was reduced to about 4,000 foot and 3,500 horse. Moreover, Langdale's Northern Horse were on the verge of mutiny when threatened with a southerly march, and Goring was making every possible excuse for not coming to join the King. By 7 June the Royalist army was at Daventry, and there they lingered for five days. Although they knew by now that Oxford was not beleaguered the King's council insisted on sending large quantities of meat on the hoof against a further siege, and it was necessary to await the return of the cavalry force that escorted this curious agricultural adventure.

Fairfax was at Newport Pagnell by 7 June and here Vermuyden, who had been recalled from Derbyshire, rejoined the army with his 2,500 horse.* On the 12th the army camped at Kislingbury, some eight miles east of Daventry, and late that afternoon cavalry patrols clashed with the Royalist outposts on Borough Hill. Surprise was complete, for Charles (who was hunting in Fawsley Park) and Rupert had no idea how near the enemy were; but it was too late for Fairfax to mount an attack, and the scattered Royalist troops were hastily summoned to take up a strong position on Borough Hill. In the early hours of the 13th, Scoutmaster Watson brought information of a Royalist withdrawal, and also a captured letter from Goring which clearly established that Fairfax had no need to worry about his army, for it was still before Taunton. Just as the Roundheads were preparing to pursue the retreating Royalists their already soaring spirits were raised still further when, to a rapturous welcome, the newly appointed lieutenant-general of horse rode into the camp. Cromwell had been urged to make all speed, and although he had only had time to collect 600 horse his presence among the troops was worth a whole brigade. Fairfax now had an army of more than 13,000 men.

The King and his advisers wished to avoid battle until they could draw on reinforcements, and when they marched from Borough Hill they took what precautions they could to conceal their direction from the enemy and made for Market Harborough en route for Belvoir Castle. In spite of their anxiety to break away their progress was insufficiently rapid to shake off the pursuing Roundheads, and Fairfax (whose army camped the night of the 13th at Guilsborough), with two probing antennae under Major

* Vermuyden was the son of Sir Cornelius Vermuyden, a distinguished Dutch engineer. At Newport Pagnell he obtained leave to resign his commission and depart to Holland. His regiment was commanded by Major Huntington at Naseby.

Henry Ireton (left) and Thomas
Fairfax (right) were two of
Parliament's leading generals

Harrison and Colonel Ireton, was always in touch. Indeed, Ireton
came upon a rearguard left at Naseby and captured these unsuspecting men as they were at supper. The King had intended
spending the night at Lubenham, but when news reached him of
Ireton's coup he hastened to Market Harborough for a midnight
conference with Rupert and others of his council. All were agreed
that a further withdrawal with the enemy cavalry hard on their
heels would take on the aspect of a flight, which would be demoralizing and dangerous. Rupert was therefore ordered to draw
up the army early on the morning of the 14th along the commanding high ground that runs from East Farndon towards Great
Oxendon. This ridge, rather less than two miles south of Harborough, was an excellent defensive position, and there is reason
for thinking that Lord Astley, who commanded the infantry, was
anxious to await the enemy there. But later developments caused
Prince Rupert to take the offensive.

There is very little argument about the course the Battle of
Naseby took: it has been well documented, and on the whole it

was a fairly straightforward fight which lasted for about three hours. The same cannot be said about the initial manoeuvring for position. Contemporary accounts are apt to be confusing, and although the final dispositions of both armies are known with some accuracy the question of how they arrived at them and whether the Roundheads conformed to the Royalists (as is generally thought) or vice versa (as the present writer thinks) is not easily solved.

The early part of June had been very wet, but the morning of the 14th dawned bright and sunny with a north-west wind. Visibility was good and from their first position the Royalists would have had a view uninterrupted by trees and woods (which is no longer the case) to the higher Naseby ridge some four miles to the south. The ground between these two prominent ridges is very undulating and at that time was almost completely open. The shallow dales could hold water – even in summer – for there were many springs and the river Welland rises close to Naseby. In a letter written two days after the battle the writer describes the ground as 'some ploughed, some champion', and a 1630 map clearly shows strips of cultivated land leading from the Royalists' final position towards the low ground known as Broad Moor. The same map also indicates that at that time there was only one road worthy of the name in the area: the one leading from Naseby village past the present New House Farm to Kelmarsh.

Fairfax left Guilsborough in the early hours of the morning of Saturday 14 June, and by sunrise the whole army would have been established on the Naseby ridge, probably in the area of the road junction north of the obelisk on the present Clipston road. Fairfax could not be certain at this time that the Royalists would stand and fight, so the army may have advanced below the ridge. But it is more likely that at about 8 a.m. Fairfax and Cromwell, with a suitable escort, rode forward to reconnoitre the ground for the most suitable position. On either side of the Clipston road the ground slopes steeply from point 631, and even now the fields in that bottom hold water. Cromwell quickly realized that to attack with cavalry over such a rough, waterlogged area would be a hazardous operation such as might determine the Royalists to refuse battle. Turning to Fairfax, and pointing to the high ground a little way to the west of where they were, he said, 'Let us, I beseech you, draw back to yonder hill, which will encourage the enemy to charge us, which they cannot do in that place without absolute ruin.' Fairfax saw the wisdom of this and the army marched to its left.

The position eventually taken up by Fairfax stretched from the area of Red Hill Farm in the west to beyond where Paisnell Spinney now stands. From Streeter's engraving in Joshua Sprigge's *Anglia Rediviva** we have a pretty accurate plan of the Roundhead order of battle, although his positioning of some of the Royalist regiments is slightly suspect. Just before the battle, Cromwell had persuaded Fairfax to make Ireton commissary-general, or second-in-command of the cavalry, and he had charge of the cavalry on the left wing. On this wing the horse was formed up in two lines: each regiment had two 'divisions' (squadrons as we would call them) and each squadron three troops drawn up in line and in three ranks. The infantry in the centre was under Sergeant-Major-General Skippon and drawn up with five regiments forward and three in the second line. On the right Cromwell's cavalry was not only cramped for room, but had difficult ground in front of it: he drew it up in three lines, with two squadrons in the third line and Colonel Rossiter's 400 horse, who only arrived from Lincolnshire just before the battle began, squeezed in between the first and second lines.

The total strength of the army was about 13,500 men, the cavalry numbering 6,500, the infantry 6,000 and Colonel Okey's dragoons 1,000. There is a tendency to give this formidable force a frontage of only one mile, but without going into details as to how much room is needed in the ranks it is difficult to see how an army with a large cavalry component, and musketeers needing at least four feet, could do with less than 2,500 yards. To get even this their left must have rested on a very thick boundary hedgerow (part of which still stands) called Sulby Hedges, and indeed we are told that this was so, although it would have meant the left of Ireton's cavalry being off the hill on flat ground. It would also have meant that Okey's dragoons, whom Cromwell ordered to line the hedges, must have been firing into the right of the Royalist cavalry at almost point-blank range – yet it is not apparent that they did great damage.

At about 7.30 a.m., while the Royalist army was still on the East Farndon ridge, Rupert had sent his scoutmaster forward to discover the enemy's position. For some reason that is not easy to understand, even allowing for the undulating ground, this man returned with completely negative information, and so Rupert decided to go himself. He had reached the neighbourhood of Clipston when he saw the enemy's army at about the time they were

* Sprigge was Fairfax's chaplain at the time of the battle.

116

Sergeant-Major-General
Skippon, commander,
Parliamentarian
infantry, at the
Battle of Naseby

beginning their march to the Red Hill position. He was too experienced an officer to think that they were withdrawing, but he
realized that there was a chance to attack them while they were
unbalanced. Sending a galloper back to the King, requesting that
the army should be brought forward at once, he rode on to reconnoitre a position. This he found on a ridge known as Dust Hill,
which is now bisected by the Sibbertoft–Naseby road at point 555.

When the army arrived he drew it up with its right in the area
of the present Prince Rupert's Farm and its left at the eastern edge
of what is now Long Hold Spinney. The Royalists were outnumbered by nearly two to one. Clarendon gives a total of 7,400
with only 2,500 infantry, although other accounts indicate that
there were slightly more infantry and about 4,500 cavalry. If the
foregoing suggestion of events and their timings is agreed, then it
would seem that Rupert was doing his best to conform – with a
very thin line – to the Parliamentarian position, and although he
might have liked to get to windward of the enemy the Sulby
Hedges prevented this. Even though the King was in the field it
seems clear that Rupert had the overall command, and it would
have been better had he let his brother Prince Maurice lead the
right wing of the cavalry instead of doing so himself. The left

wing was under Sir Marmaduke Langdale, who had 1,600 not entirely reliable cavalrymen, while Rupert had more than 2,000. Lord Astley commanded the infantry and Streeter's plan shows three brigades (those of Sir Bernard Astley, Lord Bard* and Sir George Lisle) forward, and Colonel Howard's horse behind in support. A reserve of about 1,300 men consisted of the King's Lifeguard under the Earl of Lindsey, Prince Rupert's infantry regiment and – according to Clarendon – the King's Horseguards under Lord Bernard Stuart.

Shortly before the Royalist army advanced to the attack – which was a little after ten o'clock – Fairfax had withdrawn his entire army, less a forlorn hope of 300 musketeers, to the reverse slope of the ridge. He probably did this to ease the pre-battle tension of his many raw recruits, for he advanced the whole line into the forward position again as the enemy were almost at the attack – which in itself was no mean feat. Presumably what few light cannon he had remained forward, because we learn that they fired one totally ineffectual round at the advancing Royalists and that that was the only part played by artillery in the battle.

The Royalist line advanced at a steady pace, with the cavalry of the right wing slightly in advance, but battle was joined almost simultaneously along the whole front. Rupert's cavalry were caught in Okey's cross-fire, which probably accounted for their quickening pace, but except for Okey's own rather confused account in a letter to a friend in London we do not hear of many empty saddles. It seems that on this wing the cavalry of both sides halted for a short space of time when within a few hundred yards of each other. Ireton may still have been organizing his squadrons as they came forward, and Rupert, who halted first, may have wanted to give his horses a breather before the charge which he now initiated. The two right-hand squadrons of Ireton's broke the Royalists to their immediate front, but the centre squadron failed to press its charge and on the extreme left the Roundhead horse was – in less than half an hour – put to flight.

Both commanders now committed understandable errors. Prince Rupert, at the head of his triumphant 'divisions', pursued the fleeing enemy up to their baggage train, which was a little way to the south-west of Naseby. Ireton, whose fault was even more forgivable, saw that the infantry brigade on his immediate right was in peril and so turned his two squadrons inwards instead of

* Sir Henry Bard was not in fact made a peer until a month after Naseby.

118

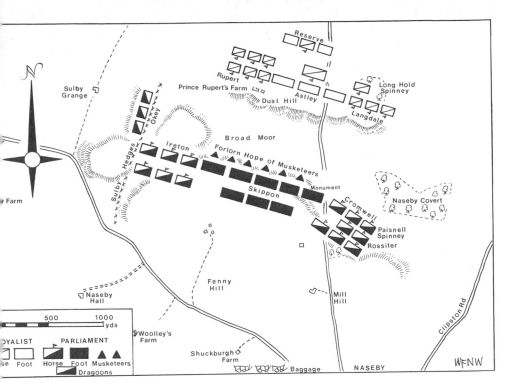

Above and below: Battle of Naseby

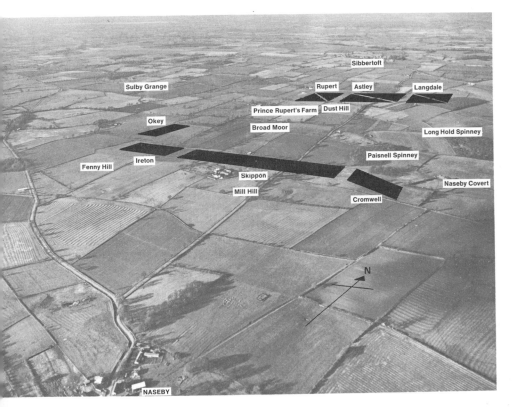

attending to the cavalry battle. The result was disastrous: his troops were badly mauled and he himself received two nasty wounds and was, for a short time, a prisoner. Soon most – but not quite all – of Ireton's cavalry were out of the battle.

The Royalist infantry in the centre, although heavily out-numbered, soon showed the value of battle experience. As the Roundheads came over their hill only a short distance separated them from the enemy. There was time for just one volley before the opposing ranks clashed and the battle became one of musket butts and push-of-pike. On the Parliamentarian right Fairfax's regiment held (they do not appear to have had much opposition), but on the left Skippon's regiment, commanded by Lieutenant-Colonel Francis who was killed, and even the more experienced troops under Colonels Montague and Pickering, were pushed back up the hill by the determined onslaught of the Royalist foot, led by that stout-hearted veteran Jacob Astley. Soon the Parliamentarian front line was in complete disorder, with colours fallen and officers striving in vain to rally their retreating men, who were scrambling to the comparative safety of the reserve lines.

We are told that the main fight in the centre lasted a good hour, and it was probably about half-way through it that Fairfax, returning from the extreme right of the line, saw the sorry state of his centre, for by now Ireton's intervention would have failed – probably worsted by Colonel Howard's supporting horse. Fairfax reacted swiftly. He and Skippon brought up the reserve and it was while the latter was leading Colonel Pride's men into the battle again that a musket ball pierced his armour and passed through his side. Fairfax, himself without a helmet, which had been lost in the cavalry action on the right, begged Skippon to retire, but the tough old soldier replied that 'he would not stir so long as a man should stand'. With the reserves committed the battle in the centre still remained in the balance. The Royalist troops strove magnificently against odds that were too great. Had it been a purely infantry encounter they might still have prevailed, but with Rupert still away on their right Colonel Okey saw his chance, and mounting his dragoons he thundered into battle against the right-hand ranks. At the same time a worse fate beset those on the left, for Oliver Cromwell, with several squadrons of his well disciplined cavalry, wheeled in to pulverize that flank.

Cromwell was enabled to do this because his cavalry on the Roundhead right had met with complete success. The ground on this flank presented problems for cavalry: the slope was steeper here and the hillside was dotted with gorse bushes, and there was

Defeat of Charles I at Naseby

also a fair-sized rabbit warren to be negotiated. Any idea that Cromwell's men swooped down on Langdale's Northern Horse in a whirlwind attack can be dismissed. Apart from the fact that a large part of Cromwell's 3,500 horsemen were well disciplined veterans – some belonging to his own Eastern Association – this fight had of necessity to be a much more controlled affair than the one on the other flank. Langdale was a brave and capable commander, and although the Northern Horse had recently been showing signs of disaffection they fought now with commendable courage. Nor is the criticism that Langdale failed to take advantage of the broken ground to scatter the Roundheads as they were descending the hill in loose formation valid, for the ground presented difficulties that were even greater for Langdale than for Cromwell. The plain fact is that the Royalists were hopelessly outnumbered – by more than two to one – and Cromwell was able to turn their flank with his right 'divisions'.

It was Whalley, on Cromwell's left, whose squadrons were the first to engage. Both sides discharged their pistols at virtually point-blank range and then fell to it with their swords. Soon the action had become general along the whole wing, with Rossiter's men in the fairly early stages starting to turn Langdale's flank. The two Royalist squadrons opposing Whalley were the first to break, but not until they had given a good account of themselves, and in less than an hour the whole of the Northern Horse was pouring back to behind their starting line. Sir Edward Walker tells us that 'four of the Rebel Bodies in close and good order' followed this defeated wing. The very nature of this controlled fight would have enabled Cromwell to keep a firm grasp on his squadrons, and he probably detached his first line to pursue the enemy with the limited objective of ensuring that they could not reform. Had Rupert been able to do something similar on the other wing he could scarcely have won the battle, but he might have saved his infantry from total surrender. But his attack was a much faster-moving and less well controlled affair.

At some stage in the battle, and it seems to have been as Langdale's men were streaming past him, the King took personal command of the reserves and advanced in an attempt to stabilize the line and aid his hard-pressed infantry. But the Earl of Carnwath is said to have seized his bridle exclaiming 'Will you go upon your death?', and prevented him from implementing this noble impulse. Then it was, Walker says, that the meaningless command 'March to the right hand' rang out, which was taken to mean 'everyone to shift for himself', and the reserves 'turned about and ran on the spur almost a quarter of a mile, and there the word being given to make a stand we did so, though the Body could never be rallied'.

Meanwhile, the wretched infantry were left on their own. Besides Cromwell's thrust on their left and Okey's on their right, some of Ireton's men had rallied and were in their rear. One brigade won the ungrudging admiration of its opponents by its stubborn resistance to every form of attack. Eventually it was practically ridden and trodden down when Fairfax brought up his own regiment of foot, which was still quite fresh having been only on the fringe of the battle, and led a concerted attack in conjunction with his Lifeguard under Captain Charles Doyley. It is probable that the heaviest infantry casualties were suffered by this brigade in the last minutes of the battle. Most of the other regiments laid down their arms and formed the greater part of the huge haul of prisoners – not very far short of 5,000 men in all.

While all this was happening Rupert was gradually gathering up what men he could to return to his duty on the field of battle. He had been rudely repulsed by the guard on the baggage train.

The commander had at first mistaken him for Fairfax, for both generals were wearing the same red headdress, called a *montero,* but on realizing his error he greeted him and his men with a hail of shot. Rupert's return to the battlefield was too late to be of any assistance to the .Royalist infantry, and in any event his horses were by now in no state to endure another fight over heavy ground. He therefore rode back to where the King and the reserves – most of whom had never been committed, but would have been had Rupert remained in overall command of the battle – were making that half-hearted stand mentioned by Sir Edward Walker.

Here, briefly, they faced the New Model, hastily reformed for a final thrust to victory. It was never made, for in spite of all that the officers could do what was left of the Royalist troops had had enough. One volley from Colonel Okey's dragoons and the field was deserted. This time the pursuit, although for the most part under control, was not limited as to distance and, attended by considerable slaughter, it continued for twelve miles, until at Great Glen, just short of Leicester, Lord Bernard Stuart with the King's Lifeguard managed to check it.

It does not appear that the Roundheads lost much more than 150 men, but the Royalist casualties are harder to assess. Contemporary accounts are confused and contradictory, but probably about 400 soldiers were killed in battle, and Langdale's cavalry may have lost as many as 300 in the pursuit. There was a most unpleasant incident when, unknown to Fairfax, some of his more licentious soldiery got among the Royalists' mobile brothel. These whores, 'who were full of money and rich apparell', were thought to be Irish, but were most probably Welsh. At least 100 were massacred and many more had their faces slashed, or noses slit, which was the unpleasant treatment meted out to such women in those days.

Virtually the entire Royalist commissariat fell to the victors: 200 carriages and sumpter-wagons, forty barrels of powder, a good quantity of much needed cheese and biscuit, the entire artillery train, 8,000 arms and a rich haul of colours. But more damaging by far than all of these was the King's cabinet, in which were his private papers that included copies of the most damning correspondence between himself and the Queen, outlining his plans for bringing over Irish papists and his efforts to secure foreign mercenaries and money from continental princes. As was to be expected, Parliament wasted little time in publishing these papers.

The King paused for a short while in Leicester and then rode on to spend the night in Ashby-de-la-Zouch. He displayed his usual calm in the wake of defeat and even then his unbounded optimism could not be suppressed. When Gerard's Welsh levies eventually joined him he had the makings of a fresh infantry force and he still had about 4,000 horse, and Goring's army was intact in the south-west. But in July Goring was brought to battle at Langport in Somerset by the powerful combination of Fairfax and Cromwell, and decisively beaten (see p. 36). The First Civil War was to linger on for another year until the capitulation of Oxford in June 1646, but it was the clamant disaster of Naseby that sounded the death knell of the King's military machine.

'When did you last see your father?' Painting by W. F. Yeames. The battles have all been fought and the hunt for the surviving Royalists is on

Cromwell, in his letter to the Speaker written on the same day as the battle, says that it lasted for three hours and was for much of the time 'very doubtfull'. This was perhaps a pardonable half-truth. The issue in the centre could for a short time be said to have been in some doubt, but the Parliamentarians were never in real danger of total defeat. Heavily outnumbered, outgeneralled and with the advantage only of a better infantry arm, Charles could have had little hope of victory. Battle should have been avoided until Goring had been hanged and Hopton had marched his army to the King. This is perhaps too simple a solution which does less than justice to a man who, until he became unstable, unprincipled and dissolute, had displayed considerable courage and powers of leadership. Nevertheless, it is difficult to avoid the conclusion that Goring lost the King his last chance.

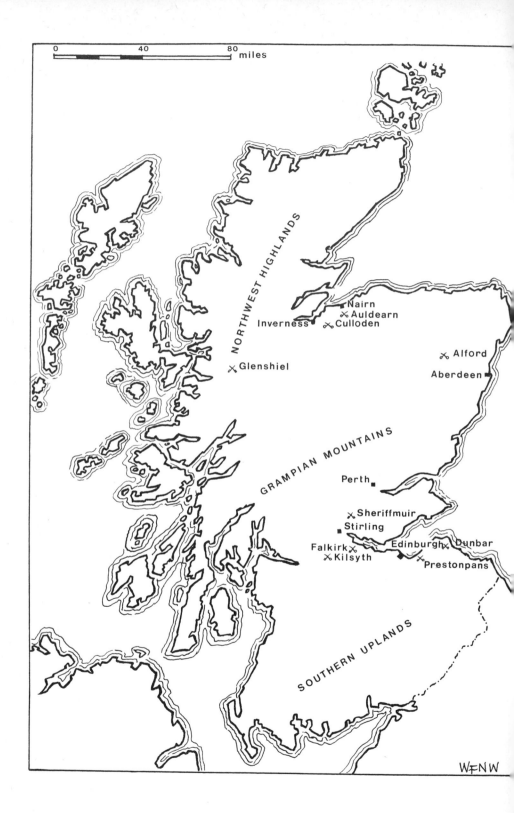

0   40   80 miles

NORTHWEST HIGHLANDS

Nairn
✗ Auldearn
Inverness ✗ Culloden

✗ Alford
Aberdeen ■

✗ Glenshiel

GRAMPIAN MOUNTAINS

Perth ■

✗ Sheriffmuir
Stirling ■

Falkirk ✗   Edinburgh ✗   Dunbar
✗ Kilsyth   ■ ✗ Prestonpans

SOUTHERN UPLANDS

WFNW

CHAPTER 7

Montrose's Battles
Auldearn, Alford and Kilsyth

9 May 1645, 2 July 1645 and 15 August 1645

Of the three battlefields the most rewarding, from the visitor's point of view, is Auldearn. This small town lies just over two miles south-east of Nairn on the A96 road. The National Trust for Scotland have put an excellent plan and description of the battle at a viewpoint (Boath Dovecot) just to the west of the church. From here it is possible to see almost the whole of the battlefield and follow its course from the narrative. The church stands on the site of the 1645 one, but then the village consisted of just a few houses running north and south along the ridge due south of the church.

Alford (pronounced Arfud) is some thirty miles north-west of Aberdeen. At the time of the battle the village was a mile to the west of the present town, and the local inhabitants will point out the site of the church, smithy and shoeshop, which stood on the hill where now there are only farmsteads at a tiny place called Ardgathen. Looking north from this hill (with Gallowhill just in the left rear) the visitor gets an excellent view of the battlefield.

Kilsyth lies about fifteen miles north-east of Glasgow on the A803 road. The fields in which Montrose had his camp have now been flooded for a reservoir, but the west end of the reservoir can be reached by a very rough track that leads off the A803 road just by the entrance to the public park half a mile east of Kilsyth. From this end of the reservoir an excellent view of the battlefield, with the hill (near Banton) up which Macdonald attacked, can be obtained. The ridge immediately north of the reservoir is the one that Baillie was trying to reach so as to outflank Montrose.

No account of the Civil War, however brief, would be complete without mention of at any rate three of the battles in the remarkable series of victories gained, against great odds, by James Graham, fifth Earl and first Marquess of Montrose. Auldearn, Alford and Kilsyth were not large-scale affairs, but the first two were tactical gems. History has endowed Montrose with an aura of romantic heroism, for he was a much adored and courageous leader, a poet and a patriot, but he combined these qualities with

James Graham,
Marquess of Montrose,
the man who almost
succeeded in gaining
Scotland for the King

political foresight, and he was also a superb guerilla leader, who
at times displayed a military genius far in advance of most of his
contemporaries.

Montrose was born in 1612 and started his military career in
1638 in the Covenanter army commanded by Alexander Leslie –
later Earl of Leven – that tough veteran of the Thirty Years' War,
who commanded the Scots' army at Marston Moor (see p. 35 or
chapter 5 for a full account). During the next four years he made
a big reputation for himself, but soon became disillusioned with
the Covenanters. In signing the Covenant Montrose did not feel
that he was joining in an act of rebellion, but that the Covenanters
offered the best chance of redressing the grievances of the Scottish
nation without coming into conflict with the constitutional
authority of the crown. But what had started as an honest attempt
to resolve a religious problem became the means whereby a small,
self-appointed authority could gain political ascendancy in Scotland in opposition not only to episcopacy and the Prayer Book,
but also to the King. The man who stood at the head of this cabal
of diehard Presbyterians was Archibald Campbell, Earl of Argyll.
He and his cronies, while outwardly supporting the original aims
of the Covenant, were using them to gain sovereign control of
Scotland.

Argyll was a most unpleasant man, cowardly, cruel, dishonourable in his dealings and entirely without compassion. Nevertheless he was a shrewd and capable politician, and full of cunning. He was jealous of Montrose's popularity with the people, and annoyed when he became the leader of a moderate party that in 1639 drew up a Bond in which they asseverated their loyalty to King as well as Covenant. By the time King Charles unfurled his standard at Nottingham in 1642, Montrose was ready to break with the Covenanters. His soul flamed within him as he watched the ugly turn that events were taking in Scotland; but on the few occasions that he attempted to warn Charles of the dangers that were impending he was most coolly received. The King preferred to rely on the insidious advice of the Marquess of Hamilton, who in a court bedevilled by cabals of favourites was the interpreter of Scottish affairs.

It was not until the autumn of 1643 that Charles realized the extent to which he was being duped, and belatedly turned to Montrose as the man upon whom he could best count not only to counsel but to act. After he had been sent from Oxford to gain Scotland for the King there were to be disappointments and hardships before the tide began to turn in Montrose's favour. The Earl of Antrim had been sent to Ireland to raise his Macdonalds and land them on the west coast of Scotland by 1 April 1644, and Lord Newcastle was ordered to provide Montrose with cavalry. But Leven's army was well into England, which prevented Newcastle from sparing any troops, and when Montrose crossed the border at the head of 1,300 militiamen from Cumberland and Northumberland there was no sign of the Irishmen. He waited some days at Dumfries – during which time his English levies started to desert – before withdrawing into England, where he routed the Covenanter garrison at Morpeth and took the town. But he arrived too late to assist Prince Rupert at Marston Moor, and after that disaster was prevailed upon to hand over his small force to the Prince.

Many commanders bereft of all troops would have returned to headquarters, but failure never affected the buoyancy of Montrose's courage. The knight errant side of his character drove him on to pursue glory irrespective of reward. He determined to 'invade' Scotland with just two companions: Colonel Sibbald, who was later to abandon the Royalist cause, and William Rollo. Travelling in disguise, with Montrose posing as the two gentlemen's groom, these three journeyed to Tullybelton on the edge of the Highlands, where news was received that the Macdonalds (only about 1,100 of them) had arrived at last under Alasdair Macdonald, a man of action and a warrior of huge stature and great strength. Montrose ordered them to meet him at Blair Atholl. When he arrived there he found the men of Atholl on the point of fighting the strangers from Ireland, but the immense personal force of Montrose soon had the two parties agreeing to become allies against the enemies of the King. Now Montrose had the nucleus of an army. It comprised scarcely 2,000 men, ill equipped with primitive weapons and short of ammunition, but it justified the unfurling of the royal standard. On 28 August 1644 the precious piece of silk that had been so carefully concealed in Montrose's saddlebag was raised above his little force amid a fanfare of trumpets.

There followed small battles or engagements at Tippermuir, Aberdeen, Inverlochy (see p. 35 for accounts of these three battles) and Dundee. These were conducted with great skill and élan. Always fighting with inferior numbers to his enemy, Montrose time and again would snatch victory from seemingly certain defeat, or lead his men safely out of the most cunningly set trap. His name became a legend in the Highlands, and although he constantly found himself at the head of only a few hundred soldiers – for the clansmen invariably made for home when they had garnered sufficient loot – men were proud to serve with him, for he never asked them to do what he himself could not do better. In spite of difficulties, desertions and inadequate support from those he had relied on, by the spring of 1645 Montrose had the King's enemies in Scotland thoroughly demoralized.

In April of that year Montrose had under command 2,000 infantry, and when Lord Gordon and many of his clan had at last joined the Royalist army (the Marquess of Huntly was never reconciled to Montrose after an unfortunate affair right at the beginning of the campaign) he could muster some 250 cavalrymen. The Covenanter commander in the north was that Colonel Hurry whom we saw fighting for the Royalists at Marston Moor. He was determined to defeat Montrose and put to shame those less fortunate commanders – Argyll, Elcho, Balfour of Burleigh, and Baillie – who had tried and failed. He decided that his best chance of doing this was to lure Montrose into a part of the country where he had no friends; he therefore adopted the tactics of *reculer pour mieux sauter* and kept falling back in front of Montrose from Elgin nearly to Nairn. Close to Auldearn he turned upon his pursuer, hoping to surprise him by a night march. But as he advanced some of his men discharged their muskets to clear them of damp powder, and Montrose's sentries being on the alert heard them. Montrose had little time in which to make his dispositions, but he made them with boldness and skill.

The village of Auldearn then comprised just a few cottages that ran north and south along a low ridge. On the western slope of the ridge, which stretched down towards a burn, were the cottage gardens and outbuildings, and below them rough scrub extending to boggy land near the burn; this bog and a small hill protected the ridge from the south. Montrose placed his Irishmen, under Alasdair Macdonald, just to the north of the village, and the bulk of his troops to the south of the cottages, where they were hidden from view by the hill, and on the reverse slope of the ridge. He had no centre, save for a few men whom he placed among the cottages with orders to keep up a steady fire to give the impression that the village was strongly held. Macdonald was given the royal standard, and Montrose hoped that Hurry would attack him in mistake for the main body. Montrose would then fall upon the Covenanters' flank.

On the morning of 9 May Hurry marched headlong into the trap, but the plan nearly miscarried through the fiery impetuosity of Macdonald. He had been given too few troops with which to guard the standard – only 500 out of Montrose's total of 2,250 – and Hurry could put against him 3,500 foot and 400 horse. Never one to stand on the defensive, Macdonald probably thought that his best chance in the circumstances was to rush down the hill and attack Hurry as his men struggled through the marshy burn. It was a gallant gesture in the face of huge odds, but it nearly lost Montrose the battle. As the Macdonalds, badly mauled by Hurry's leading regiments (Lawers's, Lothian's and Buchanan's), tried to regain the high ground, Alasdair could be seen swinging his great broadsword and slicing off heads like artichokes from their stalks, but it was the coolness of Montrose that won the day. From his viewpoint he could see all too well how badly the battle was going. Turning to Lord Gordon and his men behind the ridge he loudly exclaimed, 'Why are we lingering here, my dear lord, when our friend Macdonald is driving the enemy before him? Shall all the glory of the day be his?'

The Gordons needed no further spur. They charged as cavalry should, no longer being so weak in numbers as to need supporting fire, but with sword in hand and with all the dash and fury of Cromwell's Ironsides. They rode straight at the Covenanters' flank and soon scattered their cavalry under Major Drummond, who crumpled into their own infantry. Confusion was made worse when Montrose and the rest of the Gordons followed in support, and Macdonald once more rallied his Irishmen. Isolated pockets of Hurry's army fought bravely, and he himself was almost the last to leave the field, but the victory was complete, and the slaughter savage. It is estimated that between 2,000 and 3,000 Covenanters perished in the battle and the rout, and large quantities of ammunition, money and stores were captured.

Auldearn successfully disposed of Hurry's army, but General William Baillie – the recently appointed commander in Scotland – and Lord Lindsay of the Byres were still in the field, each with a sizable army, and Montrose needed time before taking on another battle. He consequently avoided a fight with Baillie by one of those fascinating games of hide and seek in the hills at which he and his tough Highlanders were so adept, but having given Baillie the slip he felt strong enough to attack Lindsay in Atholl. However, before he could do so a messenger arrived from Huntly recalling his clan. Lord Gordon refused to obey the summons, but Montrose forbade him to put pressure on his clansmen as he wished to do. With the departure of the Gordons Montrose lost his cavalry arm, and he could not offer battle until he had built up his strength. Accordingly Alasdair Macdonald and Lord Gordon were sent off to recruit, while Montrose spent the time prowling round the skirts of his enemy. He found Baillie too firmly entrenched in Strathbogie, so he drew him southwards and lured him into unfavourable ground at Alford on the south bank of the Don.

Lord Gordon had managed to persuade about 200 Gordon troopers to join, or rejoin, the army, but Alasdair Macdonald was still away, which was a matter of considerable comfort to the Covenanters. Nevertheless, when Baillie saw Montrose's position he was loath to attack, but his every movement was subject to approval by the Committee of the Estates, and they ordered him to proceed. The upper reaches of the Don were a more formidable obstacle in those days, but near the present town of Alford there was a ford. It is difficult now to be quite certain of the exact location of this ford, but it was probably at, or close to, the present Bridge of Alford. Montrose had drawn his army up on the Gallowhill ridge overlooking the ford and the marshy ground surrounding it. The cavalry was divided and placed on the flanks, with Lord Gordon commanding on the right and Lord Aboyne on the left. Nathaniel Gordon commanded the infantry on the right and Colonel O'Kean (Macdonald's second-in-command, whose name is sometimes spelt O'Cahan) that on the left; in the centre John Drummond of Balloch and Macdonnell of Glengarry commanded

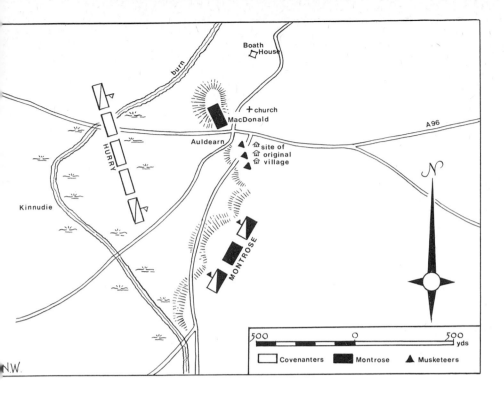

Above and below: Battle of Auldearn

the Highlanders and the Master of Napier was behind the hill with the reserve.* Both armies were almost equal in infantry with about 1,800, but Baillie had twice as many horse as Montrose.

The battle began on the Royalist right. No sooner were the Covenanters over the river than Lord Gordon was upon them with his handful of cavalry. As at Auldearn his shock tactics paid off, but not quite to the same extent. In Lord Balcarres he had a stout opponent, and a fierce cavalry fight ensued until Nathaniel Gordon came to his kinsman's rescue. He instructed his infantry not to fire at random among friend and foe, but to concentrate on hamstringing the enemy's horses. This completed the dis-comfiture of Baillie's cavalry, who were soon off the field, leaving the Gordons to turn against his centre. For much of the time that the right wing was so hotly engaged Aboyne and O'Kean remained motionless, but as soon as they saw the enemy left begin to crumble they advanced to the attack, and before long Baillie found both his flanks enveloped and Glengarry coming down the hill at his centre. Defeat was now certain, and when Napier appeared over the brow of the hill it became a rout. The Covenanter losses were not far short of those they suffered at Auldearn, while Montrose lost comparatively few officers and men considering the tough fighting on his right. But in the pursuit Lord Gordon was killed by a stray bullet. The death of this one man turned the victory sour: the Royalist army had lost a capable and courageous leader, and Montrose a devoted and irreplaceable friend.

Alford was fought on 2 July 1645, a little over a fortnight after the Royalist disaster at Naseby (see p. 35 or chapter 6 for a full account). Montrose realized that if he was to save the King he must cross the border, but before he could do this he needed to collect a sizable army. This took time, and while he was waiting for his 'recruiting sergeants' to do their work he baited Baillie by fleeting appearances in the neighbourhood of Perth. By the beginning of August Montrose had collected the largest army that he had yet commanded. Lord Aboyne (Huntly's second son) brought in 200 horse and 120 mounted infantry, Alasdair Macdonald and his Irishmen were back again, and the chiefs of Glengarry, Clan-ranald, the Macleans and the Atholl Stewarts were present with a

* Mark Napier in his *Memoirs of Montrose* (Vol. II, p. 527) puts a completely different construction on both Montrose's and Baillie's positions immediately before the battle. But having carefully examined the ground the writer agrees broadly with most other accounts. The site cannot be fixed with absolute certainty without knowledge of the exact spot where Baillie forded the Don, and this can no longer be established.

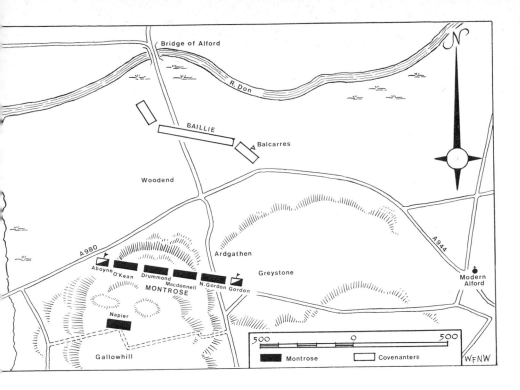

Above and below: Battle of Alford

good following. In all Montrose probably mustered around 4,400 infantrymen and 500 cavalrymen. Against this the Covenanters, when they had been joined by the Fife levies, numbered 6,000 infantry and 800 horse, but their new recruits were a raw, ill disciplined lot.

On about 10 August Montrose moved south. Slipping past Perth, he made for Stirling and crossed the Forth two miles upstream. Baillie, as was to be expected, came in hot pursuit. Montrose knew that Hamilton's brother, the Earl of Lanark, was marching towards Baillie with substantial reinforcements, and he decided to offer the latter battle before the two forces joined. By the night of the 14th the rival armies were within three miles of each other, but Baillie was anxious to wait for Lanark before attacking. However, he still had the incompetent committee round his neck, and they not only insisted on his attacking but actually altered his dispositions and plan of attack.

Montrose halted his army in some meadows a mile north-east of Kilsyth. These low-lying fields formed as it were a basin, and on the rim to the east Baillie drew up his men. He had what seemed a commanding position with a rough, rugged slope between him and Montrose; within this stern amphitheatre Montrose was soon to fight his most savage battle and gain his most decisive victory.

The fifteenth of August gave promise of being a scorching hot day, and Montrose, partly for comfort and partly to aid recognition, ordered his men to fight in their shirts. This strange sight seemed to goad Argyll and his committee colleagues into more damaging indiscretions than usual. They were firmly convinced that they had Montrose in a trap, and their only anxiety was that he might try to escape to the north. With this in mind they overruled Baillie's insistent objections and ordered him to carry out a flank march in full view (for it never occurred to anyone to use the cover of the hill) and almost within musket shot of their formidable foe. The result was soon a shambles – but not all of it on the Covenanters' side.

Montrose had sent some men forward to occupy a number of buildings on the lower slopes of the hill, and one of Baillie's officers could not resist the temptation to charge these men. This in its turn was too much for Alasdair Macdonald, who without orders launched the Macleans and the Macdonalds against these troops. The clansmen raced up the hill after their retreating foe and a fierce fight ensued on the hilltop. The Covenanter army was cut in two, for Baillie's advance guard had almost reached the height to Montrose's left. The Gordon foot and horse attempted

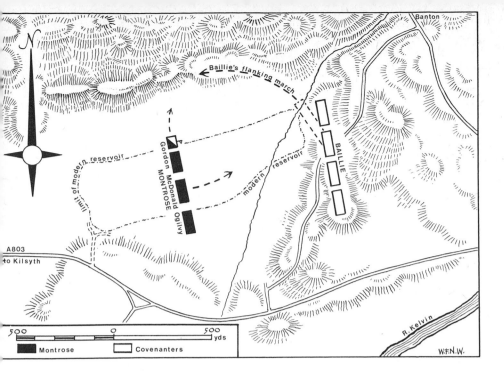

Battle of Kilsyth

to break this dangerous threat to their flank, but were out-numbered and before long in grave peril. Montrose dispatched Lord Airlie and the Ogilvys to redeem the situation, and this gallant man, now in his sixtieth year, led his troops with such spirit that even before Nathaniel Gordon reinforced him with more cavalry the battle on that flank was won. Macdonald's private war, undertaken at considerable risk, was also paying off, and Baillie turned in desperation to his reserve – the Fife levies. But he turned in vain: these gentlemen, seeing how matters stood, had wisely decamped towards their homes.

The day for Baillie was well and truly lost. When Montrose was trailing his coat round Methven Wood a few days before the battle, some female camp followers of the Irishmen had been captured and butchered; now no one could stop these men from taking their revenge on the defeated army. The well mounted senior officers made good their escape, as did most of the cavalry, but it is said that of the 6,000 infantrymen who saw the sun rise that August day, scarcely 100 were alive to see its going down.

In the short space of eleven months Montrose had defeated an enemy superior in numbers on six different occasions. He was now the master of Scotland. No Covenanter army remained in the country to oppose him; Argyll had fled to Berwick, and many other leaders were in exile. The principal cities made their humble submission, and vied with each other in their endeavours to please the victor. Royalist prisoners were liberated, but no revenge was permitted; both in Glasgow and Edinburgh the troops were kept strictly in hand. Undoubtedly this was the principal cause of Alasdair Macdonald – knighted by Montrose after Kilsyth – taking most of his Irishmen off to plunder Campbell country. These were halcyon days; but there was to be another battle, exile, return, capture (some say betrayal) and execution before the story of the Great Marquess was over.

At Philiphaugh on 13 September 1645 Montrose suffered his first major defeat at the hands of David Leslie, a much younger and possibly more able general than his kinsman Alexander, under whom he had fought at Marston Moor. As usual Montrose was short of men: the Earls of Home and Roxburgh had allowed themselves to be captured, and on the very eve of the battle the Earl of Traquair, who had almost certainly sent word to Leslie on the whereabouts and weakness of the Royalist force, ordered his son Lord Linton to march his men out of Montrose's camp. Nevertheless Montrose was taken unawares, even to the extent of being at breakfast some way from his army when Leslie approached through the morning mist. Heavily outnumbered, at first without their commander, and not drawn up for battle, their defeat was a foregone conclusion. Montrose fought furiously, but the odds were too great. He wanted to die on the field, but his officers persuaded him to escape. His troops surrendered on promise of quarter from Leslie, which promise was overruled by the Committee of the Estates, and a hideous slaughter ensued. The days of success were over; dark clouds loomed large on the horizon.

For the next few months Montrose strove, with only limited success, to build up another army, but little could be accomplished that winter beyond a minor success at Callander and some guerilla warfare on Speyside. However, by the spring of 1646 matters were beginning to go his way again, when quite suddenly he was faced with what was probably the bitterest moment of his life. On 31 May Montrose received a letter from his king ordering him to disband his army and leave the country. At the beginning of that month Charles had escaped from Oxford in disguise and sought refuge with the Covenanter army, who at once made it clear that he was to be little better than a prisoner. Almost their first demand upon the King was that he should issue this vindictive order.

Four years later, and in the service of a new king, Montrose landed once more in his beloved Scotland. There crossed in April

Charles I imprisoned in Carisbrook Castle, from a broadsheet of 1648

1650 from the Orkneys to Caithness a curiously mixed assortment
of men: 500 Danes, 1,000 Orcadians, and a small cavalry arm of
fifty gentlemen – all soldiers of fortune and many of them officers
who had served with Montrose in the past. No one knew better
than Montrose what a desperate, even forlorn, venture it was:
Charles II was not such a weak man as his father, but he was
young, ill advised and determined to regain his crown. He did not
deliberately send Montrose to his death, but if there was a chance
of success through double dealing it had to be taken. If Montrose
could successfully dominate Scotland and allow Charles to break
the promise he had made to the Covenanters, well and good; but
if he could only come to Scotland on Covenanter terms then
Montrose might have to be sacrificed. It was a piece of duplicity
not uncharacteristic of the Stuarts.

   The expedition, which might have succeeded beyond all expec-
tations had Montrose gained a foothold in the Highlands, where
many thousands would have joined him, was dogged by ill fortune
from the start. Before Charles's last letter ordering him to lay
down his arms ever reached Montrose, his small force had been
brought to battle at Carbisdale at the head of the Kyle of Sutherland and utterly routed. Montrose, who was wounded several times

The execution of Montrose in Edinburgh in 1650

in the battle, was again prevailed upon to escape. After days of wandering across tracts of barren land, often draped in wetting mist from bog and river, he was captured on 30 April and taken to the castle of Ardvreck on the banks of Loch Assynt. Here the laird of Assynt, Neil Macleod, delivered him to the Covenanters.

On 5 May Montrose left Ardvreck for the long journey to Edinburgh. He was led through towns and villages mounted on a Highland pony, his feet fastened under its belly, suffering from his wounds and an incipient fever, with a herald proclaiming him traitor. Such foolish, cruel treatment miscarried in its purpose, for where there was meant to be hostility his courage and dignity drew forth pity and admiration. And so it was at the journey's end. He was met at the watergate of Edinburgh, where the grisly sentence of hanging, drawing and quartering was pronounced. Then, with arms pinioned, they transferred him to the hangman's cart and paraded him through streets lined by a wild mob specially worked upon to jeer and throw filth at their fallen foe. But his cool, resolute, almost debonair bearing conquered their steely hearts. They looked up at him not in anger, as his tormentors had hoped, but in the silence of sorrow and respect, for in every way Montrose was a man uplifted above the crowd.

CHAPTER 8

Charles II's Civil War

1650–51

The best way to view the sites over which the Battle of Worcester was fought is to approach the town from the south, starting at Upton-upon-Severn. Here eighteen gallant Parliamentarians held out in the church against 300 Royalists. The present A440 and A4021 roads north from Upton follow roughly the course taken by General Fleetwood's troops after they had won the fight at Upton, and at Powick the church tower still has the bullet marks of the brief encounter there. At Powick Bridge one gets some idea of the battle for the river crossing, but the area is now very built over and one cannot quite see the confluence of the rivers Teme and Severn from the new bridge.

Almost the only viewpoint worthwhile in Worcester itself is the cathedral tower, which Charles himself climbed to see how the outlying battle went. The verger will unlock the door leading to the steps. But it is a long, steep climb not to be recommended for the elderly unless they are absolutely fit. Once up at the top a perfect view can be obtained, and the various tactical features, such as Red Hill, Perry Wood, Fort Royal and the confluence of the rivers, can be picked out easily by those who have made themselves familiar with the course of the battle and possess a copy of, or have memorized, the plan of the city as it was in 1651.

The Commandery, which is situated in Sidbury just west of Fort Royal Hill, is open to the public and is of interest in itself, for it is still very much as it was at the time of the battle. It was in this building that the Duke of Hamilton died of his wounds a few days after the battle. It leads straight onto the site of Fort Royal – now an open grassed mound.

When Charles I was executed in January 1649 his son was almost immediately proclaimed Charles II by the Scots. But it took them eighteen months to get him to Scotland on the terms that they exacted. Eventually, by an agreement signed at Breda on 1 May and reaffirmed by oath on board ship just before he landed in Scotland on 23 June, Charles agreed to take the Covenant, to embrace Presbytery himself, to enforce it upon his English subjects

FAC-SIMILE OF THE WARRANT FOR THE EXECUTION OF CHARLES I.
A.D. 1648.

Right: Charles II, after Lely

and to root out episcopacy. In order to gain a crown he was prepared to dissemble, as Henry IV of France had done some fifty years earlier when he observed, 'Paris is worth a mass'. It was a piece of hypocrisy practised more by the Presbyterians than by the King, for they well knew that they were imposing upon Charles a condition that he could not in full sincerity accept.

The Council of State in London had realized some time before Charles arrived in Scotland that it would have to send an army north to bring the Scots to heel. Thomas Fairfax was still nominally commander-in-chief of the English army, but he was not found willing to conduct what would obviously be a strenuous campaign. Oliver Cromwell had been home only a few weeks from excoriating the Irish Catholics, and was the natural choice to succeed Fairfax. He set off for Scotland on 28 June and crossed the border on 22 July at the head of just over 16,000 men. He had with him Generals Lambert, Whalley and Fleetwood and his army was well disciplined, well trained and homogeneous – almost everything that his opponents were not.

In June 1650 the army in Scotland was less than 6,000 men, and it became necessary to levy a large number of troops very quickly.

Broadsheet of 1651 satirizing the tough conditions laid before Charles II by the Scots before they would support his cause

General George Monck (left), one of the leading Parliamentarian generals, played an important part at the Battle of Dunbar, where the Scots army of David Leslie (right) suffered a crushing defeat

When the two armies eventually met in battle the Scots under David Leslie had some 22,000 men, while the English army had been reduced by sickness to less than 12,000. However, the advantage of superior numbers was sadly offset by the quality of both the officers and the men that Leslie had to command. Power rested firmly with the Kirk and many of the Scottish Cavaliers, especially those who had been engaged in the disastrous Battle of Preston in 1648, were excluded from further command, preferment being on religious rather than military merit. For this and other reasons very few Highlanders were among the newly raised raw levies.

During August Leslie was content to avoid battle and watch the English army suffer the hardships of a particularly wet Scottish summer without tents and short of rations. At the beginning of September Cromwell, who had fallen back on Dunbar, was becoming desperate: to return across the border would be difficult and demoralizing, while to stay to face the winter with a rapidly diminishing army seemed likely to be disastrous. Leslie, who had been hustling the English along the coastal road in a march that closely resembled a retreat, took up a position on 2 September above the sick and weary English on a feature called Doon Hill at the very edge of the Lammermuir hills. Here he was virtually unassailable, and he sent a force to block the road to England at the Cockburnspath defile. He must have thought that he had

144

brought Cromwell to the brink of catastrophe. But the English were out of artillery range, and had a fleet behind them; to crush them Leslie had to come down from the heights and give battle on the low ground – albeit with a superiority of nearly two to one.

On 3 September 1650, between the dead hour of 4 a.m., when a waning moon was just piercing the clearing rain clouds, and two hours later when a rising sun was warming the darkly purple hills, Oliver Cromwell won what was undoubtedly his greatest victory. Leslie, some say advised by an ever-watchful Committee of Estates, but more likely himself anxious to have done with the business, had left his hillside position on the previous evening. Cromwell and Lambert saw their opportunity and General Monck, with perhaps more experience than either of them, concurred in their plan. In essence this was to be a frontal attack, supported by artillery, under Lambert and Fleetwood, who would engage the Scottish line from across the ravine that protected them, while Cromwell would lead three of his best foot regiments and one of horse over the Brox Burn lower down and to the right of the Scottish position, and come in on their very restricted flank.

With such stealth was the attack mounted that the Scottish host was caught not fully prepared for battle. Nevertheless, they fought with determination and for some while their long pikes kept the English centre at bay; nor did Cromwell's flank attack make immediate headway. However, it was on this cramped right wing that the battle was won: after desperate work at push-of-pike, the English horse came through the infantry in one further furious clash which sent the Scottish cavalry scattering among their foot. Their army was soon hopelessly wedged between the ravine and the steep hills; great numbers were now a hindrance and merely fodder for darting pikes and flailing swords. It is said that 3,000 perished and as many as 10,000 were made prisoner. It was indeed a disaster of the greatest magnitude.

This crushing defeat inflicted upon the Kirk's army at Dunbar was no disappointment to Charles and the Royalist faction, who saw that the Kirk must needs turn to them if a new and more efficient force was to take the field. Stirling was the key to the Highlands, for the only serviceable road to the north crossed the Forth there. If Stirling could be held Cromwell could do what he liked in the south, but an army from the Royalist north could be assembled. As it happened Cromwell could not do exactly as he liked, for although Edinburgh yielded the governor of the castle continued defiant, and the English had to weaken their army still further by leaving garrison and siege troops in Edinburgh.

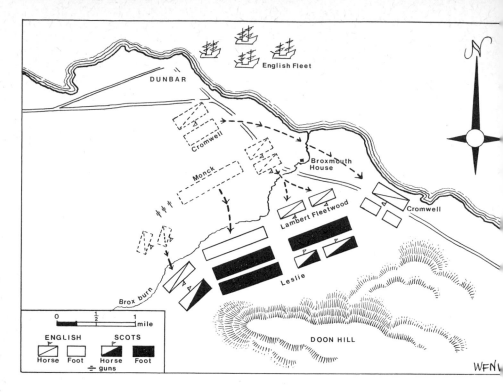

Above: Battle of Dunbar
Below: Cromwell at Dunbar – undoubtedly his greatest victory

During the autumn and winter months, while the Scots were building up a strong defensive position in and around Stirling, Cromwell marched and counter-marched between Edinburgh, Linlithgow and Glasgow without achieving very much. On 24 December the garrison of Edinburgh Castle surrendered upon honourable terms, but even with this obstacle removed Cromwell was not able to attempt anything against Stirling, and in February he became seriously ill. Meanwhile, Charles's personal position had sensibly improved. It is true that an attempt to break away from Argyll's steely clutches in October had been foiled, but as the latter became more and more dependent on the Royalists he was forced to treat Charles with greater respect. On 1 January 1651 Charles was crowned at Scone and made nominal commander-in-chief of the new army. Leslie, who was his second-in-command, retained operational control: Middleton was made lieutenant-general of the horse and Massey (who had defended Gloucester so stoutly for the Roundheads in the First Civil War) now had command of Charles's English contingent.

Cromwell's illness, watched with considerable anxiety by the Council of State and with pleasurable anticipation by the Royalists, lingered on throughout the spring of 1651, and it was not until June that he seemed to shake it off. By then changes in the command of the English forces had been made. Fleetwood was back in England organizing troops needed to meet any Royalist advance into the country: Harrison was in Cumberland with about 5,000 men: Lambert was in command of the horse in Scotland: Richard Deane (now a general but soon to be employed at sea as an admiral with Blake) had charge of the infantry, and Monck was also in Scotland with Cromwell. The problem was how to shift Leslie from his inexpugnable position around Stirling onto ground more favourable to the smaller English army.

For most of the summer Leslie relied upon Fabian tactics, and although at times he advanced to Torwood and showed signs of offering battle he would not allow himself to be caught at a disadvantage again, and Cromwell had to be content with the occasional skirmish. To turn his right flank by crossing the Forth in its upper reaches would be useless, but if Cromwell could cut off his supplies from Fife by crossing the Forth in the Queensferry area the Scots would be forced to shift from their commanding position and either give battle or head for England. Cromwell was well aware that they were likely to take advantage of a moderately clear run into England and for this he was well prepared (having summoned Harrison to Linlithgow for consultation on this very contingency), and indeed desirous of it. Accordingly on 17 July Colonel Overton crossed the Forth with a force of less than 2,000 men. Fortunately Lambert felt sure that Cromwell had under-estimated the numbers necessary to ensure success, and he took personal command of a further 2,500 troops. It was as well, for on learning of this threat to his left flank and supply line Leslie sent Sir John Browne with 4,000 men to drive the English back across the Forth. In a short, sharp battle near Inverkeithing Lambert smashed the Scots, killing some say as many as 2,000 and taking their commander prisoner.

On learning of Browne's defeat Leslie determined to march his whole army against Lambert, but Cromwell was too close to him. The Scots were only a few miles beyond Stirling before Leslie realized the danger, and quickly swinging back on his tracks just regained his former position in time, for Cromwell and Deane had already reached Bannockburn. Still unable to force an issue with Leslie, Cromwell now transferred the bulk of his army across the Forth at Queensferry, leaving only a few regiments to keep watch on the enemy at Stirling. On 24 July the English had got the island of Inchgarvie and on the 29th Burntisland. Cromwell then marched on Perth, which surrendered to him on 2 August.

We do not know what Leslie would have done if left to his own devices. It is possible that he would have interposed his army between Cromwell's army at Perth and Edinburgh, accepting battle on ground of his own choosing with a numerically superior army. But matters were taken out of his hands by Charles and the Royalists: confident of massive support from loyal Cavaliers they determined on a march into England. On 31 July Charles, who was beginning to assume more than nominal command of his army, broke camp and headed for the border, which the army numbering some 14,000 men crossed on 6 August. Leslie, whose subsequent action at the Battle of Worcester was to make defeat doubly certain, had no confidence in the army or the venture. He is alleged to have said to Charles that 'he well knew that army, how well soever it look'd would not fight'. Nor was the Duke of Hamilton much more encouraging with his written comment: 'We are all now laughing at the ridiculousness of our condition. We have quit Scotland, being scarce able to maintain it: and yet we grasp at all, and nothing but all will satisfy us, or to lose all.' There were others, such as Argyll and his kinsman Lord Loudoun, who deemed it inexpedient to leave Scotland.

Cromwell was in no great hurry to pursue the Royalist army: he had laid his plans well. His army recrossed the Forth on 4

August and Lambert was sent off independently with about 4,000 horse with orders to join Harrison and to harass the Scottish army, but not to risk a serious engagement, while Monck was to be left in Scotland with some 6,000 men to besiege and take Stirling. In England Fleetwood was collecting a force north of London: the Council of State had been advised of the plan and requested to summon the militia, and Cromwell himself wrote to the Northern and Midland County Committees instructing them to raise troops and remove their animals from the advancing Scots. Recent arrests of prominent Royalists throughout England had further strengthened Parliament's chances of concluding the forthcoming business successfully.

Cromwell with the bulk of the infantry left Leith on 6 August and marching rapidly he crossed the Tyne on the 13th. That same day Lambert and Harrison joined forces south of Preston and together they fell back before the Scottish advance and joined the Cheshire militia on the south bank of the Mersey at Warrington. Their combined force numbered at least 9,000 horse and 3,000 infantry, so they were not greatly, if at all, inferior to the Royalists, who had had a most disappointing march through the northern counties gathering remarkably few recruits. They might therefore have disputed the crossing – even though the Royalists had gained the bridge before they could destroy it – but it was not part of Cromwell's plan that Charles should be brought to battle before the full force that he was so carefully assembling could be concentrated. And so Lambert and Harrison withdrew to Knutsford. From there they marched to Warwick, where on 24 August they were joined by Cromwell, whose troops had averaged sixteen miles a day since leaving Leith.

The Royalist 'success' at Warrington was scarcely sufficient to raise their flagging spirits. Lord Derby joined them there from the Isle of Man, but he had with him only 250 foot and sixty horse, and everywhere the militia were responding to Parliament's orders. Any attempt to march on London with hostile forces ringing them round was no longer feasible – but might there not be some hope from the Welsh border and the western counties? It was therefore determined to leave Lord Derby to rally the Lancashire loyalists and Massey, himself a Presbyterian, to try to gain recruits from his own sect, while Charles and his weary Scots continued towards Shrewsbury. Here the governor refused a summons to surrender, and the army moved on south. At Worcester Charles was slightly more fortunate: the Parliamentary Committee had determined to oppose the Royalist entry, but with the approach of the army the mayor and citizens of this consistently loyal Royalist city turned against the committee, and on 23 August Charles entered Worcester unopposed.

It seemed as good a place as any in which to rest his tired troops, who after 300 miles had had more than enough marching. Food and forage were fairly plentiful and Worcester commanded the approaches to Wales and the south-west, from where Charles still hoped to draw reinforcements. The fortifications had fallen into a sad state of disrepair, but men were hastily pressed for what repair work was possible in the time. Particular attention was paid to the earthwork, known as Fort Royal, just outside the city wall at the south-east, and connected to the walls by a rampart. When Massey rejoined them from his abortive attempt to rally the apathetic Presbyterians he was sent with a small force to destroy bridges at Powick, Bransford and Upton. Only the one across the Severn leading from the city to St John's suburb was left intact, allowing troops to be positioned in that suburb and to the south, where the meadows adjoined the Teme at its confluence with the Severn. When this was done Charles probably considered he occupied a fairly strong defensive position – but rivers are seldom a reliable barrier, a fact that he was soon to realize.

Meanwhile, Cromwell was drawing the net round Worcester ever tighter. He was in no particular hurry and had taken every conceivable precaution even down to ordering tools for a siege should this become necessary – though with an army that when finally assembled was almost double the size of that of his opponents he would not have allowed his mind to dwell too long on siege warfare. Colonel Lilburne had been ordered to deal with Lord Derby during the march south, and afterwards to position himself in the Bewdley area to intercept any Royalist retreat. Fleetwood had moved to Banbury and was now marching to join Cromwell, as was Lord Grey of Groby with 1,100 horse, and General Desborough was advancing from Reading with further troops. Cromwell was at Evesham on 27 August, and by the time that Fleetwood and the other commanders had joined him he had amassed an army of about 28,000 men.

His general plan, like all good plans, was simple. The attack was to be made on both sides of the river Severn. Fleetwood was to cross the river at Upton with about 11,000 men and march up the west bank, while Cromwell took the rest of the army via White Ladies Aston and Spetchley to occupy the Perry Wood – Red Hill heights above Worcester with his left on Bund's Hill, above the confluence of the rivers Teme and Severn. Contact between the

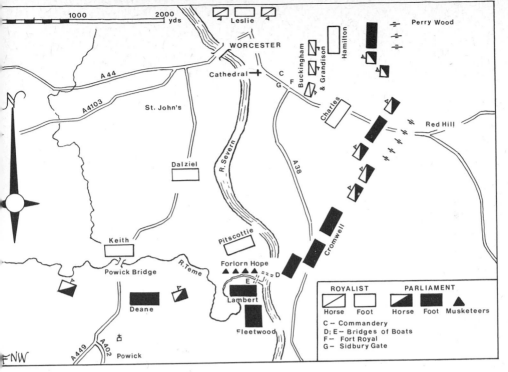

Above and overleaf: Battle of Worcester

two wings was to be effected by means of two bridges of boats – one across the Teme and the other just above it across the Severn.

Back in Worcester the enthusiasm with which Charles had been proclaimed king was not matched by any great desire to join his army. It is doubtful if as many as 2,000 had rallied to his standard since the army crossed the border, and it cannot now have numbered any more than 16,000 men. Their morale was far from high and their commanders did little to inspire them. The Duke of Buckingham had been sulking ever since Charles sternly rebuked him for his temerity in suggesting he should be given command of the army; Leslie continued to maunder over the poor fighting quality of his troops, and to make matters worse he was hardly on speaking terms with the capable General Middleton. It could not, therefore, have been a very harmonious council of war that met in the Commandery on the afternoon of 29 August.

At this council it was decided to mount an attack that night against the battery on Red Hill, which had just started bombarding the city, and also upon a post above the river. General Middleton and Colonel Keith led 1,500 men altogether on these sorties, but surprise was lost through the plan's being betrayed by a Puritan tailor called Guise (who was hanged next day), and both parties

151

Leslie

St. John's

Keith

Dalziel

Powick Bridge (new)

Deane

R. Teme

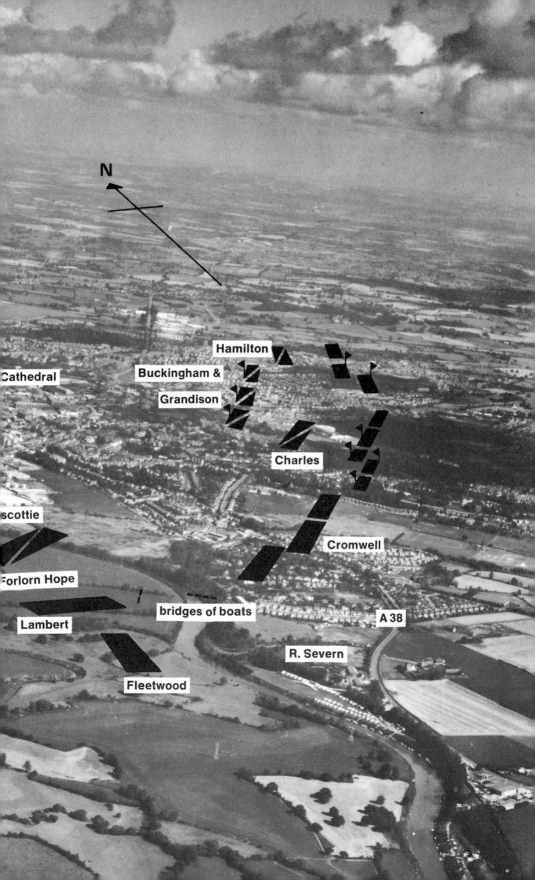

N

Cathedral

Hamilton

Buckingham &

Grandison

Charles

scottie

Cromwell

Forlorn Hope

Lambert

bridges of boats

A 38

R. Severn

Fleetwood

were repulsed with loss upon reaching their objectives. To add to Charles's discomfiture, three days later Lord Derby arrived wounded in the mouth and with thirty men, almost the only survivors of the 1,200 who had been routed by Lilburne near Wigan on 25 August.

It is difficult to know why General Massey was sent to Upton-upon-Severn with only 300 men. Some rudimentary defences had been constructed around Wick just north of the river Teme, so it looked as though the Royalists considered an attack west of the Severn feasible, and if so Upton was an important outpost, for here the river would most likely be crossed. It was even more surprising that such an experienced soldier as Massey should have been caught napping, and the river crossing forced through the gallantry of eighteen men.

The bridge that spanned the Severn at Upton in 1651 was a little way downstream from the one there now, and a little further down still (just below the present Swan Inn) the river was found to be fordable. This was not known at the time and General Lambert, who was spearheading Fleetwood's army, on finding a plank over the partly broken bridge chose eighteen picked dragoons to carry out the unpleasant crossing high above the swirling water in the early hours of 29 August. It was still dark as the daring eighteen straddled rather than walked the single plank, and scrambled across unseen by a negligent enemy. Once across, however, their presence was quickly discovered and there followed a fierce fight, first in the churchyard and then the church itself,* into which the men barricaded themselves and for some time held out against the 300 Royalists.† To reinforce the eighteen from across the broken bridge was quite impossible, but in desperation Lambert ordered more dragoons, this time mounted, to try the crossing lower down. Half fording and half swimming, they struggled over, and taking the enemy in the rear forced them back against their improvised entrenchments. Massey, who was spending the night at the Lechmeres' house, Severn End, was quickly on the scene and fought bravely, suffering two severe wounds. But soon Lambert hopelessly outnumbered his small force, and Massey broke off the engagement and made for Worcester.

By the next day the bridge was repaired and Fleetwood's army,

* The church exists no longer, but the tower still stands and the churchyard is kept up.
† Most accounts refer to the men of the Upton outpost as Scots, but as Massey commanded Charles's small English contingent they were more probably English.

reinforced by two regiments of horse and two of foot under General Deane, crossed over to the west bank. Now the task was to collect boats and planks for the two bridges, and this did not prove too difficult. By 2 September everything was ready, but the Lord-General had decreed that the attack should not be made until the next day. It was no coincidence that it therefore occurred on the anniversary of his great victory at Dunbar, for Cromwell was becoming increasingly superstitious and it seems almost certain that the auspicious day was predetermined. What could be considered a coincidence, however, was that the first engagement of the Civil Wars, in 1642, and the last, in 1651, were both fought around Powick Bridge. Furthermore, the date of his victories – 3 September – was seven years later to be the date of Cromwell's death.

At about 5 a.m. on Wednesday 3 September Generals Fleetwood, Deane and Lambert began their advance up the west bank of the Severn. It was slow going, for with them they hauled twenty 'great boats' for nearly eight miles against the current – and no doubt there were plenty of mishaps. In the early afternoon they were held up for a short while by an action fought around the church at Powick, but the river Teme was reached at some time between two and three o'clock. We cannot be certain of the exact sequence of events in the fighting west of the river, and it seems incredible that two bridges could be constructed (according to one source* in only half an hour) in the face of a determined enemy. The general plan was for Deane to try to force the bridge at Powick, while Lambert made use of the bridge of boats; meanwhile the batteries on Red Hill and Perry Wood were to keep the Scots in Worcester fully occupied. The bridges were to be thrown across the rivers within pistol shot of each other, the one across the Severn being just to the north of the confluence.

Major-General Robert Montgomery was in charge of the Royalist troops in the Powick meadows, and he had ordered Colonel Keith's brigade to hold the bridge, while Colonel Pitscottie's Highlanders were on the right bank of the Severn in the meadow above the confluence. In reserve was Major-General Dalziel's brigade on the higher ground between Powick and Worcester. Powick Bridge had not been completely destroyed: planks had been left for patrols, and for the rearguard that had held up the advance by the church, but it was a formidable task to force it and certainly the cavalry could cross only by a ford higher up the river.

The fighting all along the river Teme front was very bitter. A

* Henry Cary, *Memorials of the Civil War,* London, 1842, Vol. II, p. 357.

forlorn hope was put across the river (presumably in boats) to cover the construction of the floating bridges. No doubt this made the operation possible, but it nevertheless remains an incredible feat of ingenuity and it is a pity that we have so few details. General Deane could make no headway against Powick Bridge and when Lambert's advance troops did get across their pontoon the Highlanders at first drove them back. It only needed one of the two attacks to succeed and the other brigade would be forced to retire. Charles had been watching the fight from the top of the tower of Worcester Cathedral, and was soon galloping to the river to give personal encouragement. Also watching from the high ground east of the Severn was Cromwell, and now his foresight in throwing the bridge across became apparent. Seeing what little headway Fleetwood's men were making he personally led three brigades across the river.

Pitscottie's Highlanders, tough and desperate, beat off the superior numbers of their opponents for a little while: but attacked in front by Lambert and in the flank by Cromwell they gradually gave ground, fighting every inch of the way with discipline and fury. But these men were at a disadvantage when it came to hedge fighting, and the fields round Powick were much enclosed. The English had considerable experience of this type of in-fighting and pressed the Scots back remorselessly. Their forced withdrawal left Keith's brigade with its left flank in the air, and becoming discouraged by this development they quickly broke, leaving their commander to be captured. Dalziel either could not or would not stem the rapidly accelerating retreat and General Montgomery was severely wounded and out of action. Soon the retreat became a rout and the Scots were streaming back through St John's and across the bridge into Worcester, the English not far behind them.

This river battle lasted for a full two hours, and Charles is usually credited with being personally responsible for the Royalist attack on Cromwell's right. This is quite possible, even though he must have been kept busy riding between Worcester and Powick. Certainly Leslie had nothing to do with it, for neither he nor his large cavalry force stirred from the Pitchcroft just north of the city all day. In crossing the river Cromwell had seriously weakened his position, for although he had great numerical superiority some of the troops left on Red Hill were inexperienced militiamen. Charles was operating on interior lines and had the opportunity of launching an attack on the enemy's right wing while his army was unevenly divided. It was a brilliant conception and executed with a resolution that nearly succeeded.

156

The attack was two-pronged: Charles commanded the right thrust against Red Hill and the Duke of Hamilton the left against Perry Wood, while the Duke of Buckingham and Lord Grandison were in support with cavalry. Leaving the city by the Sidbury Gate and covered by the guns from Fort Royal, both wings met with success, and Hamilton's men were soon among the enemy artillery at Perry Wood. The Parliamentarian foot gave way all along the line in a battle that lasted for three hours. Had Leslie's cavalry not refused to fight, Cromwell's position east of the river might have become desperate. He still had on that side some of Lambert's cavalry and those from Whalley's and Harrison's brigades, who came to the support of the militia, but the issue continued in doubt until Cromwell had recrossed the river ahead of his three brigades and taken personal command. Meanwhile, the Royalist attack was almost spent and Hamilton's men were running short of ammunition, while Hamilton himself was seriously wounded in the leg. The arrival of Cromwell's brigades finally turned the tide and the Royalists were driven back into the city in considerable confusion. It had been a bold attempt that deserved to succeed.

The last phase of the battle was an untidy shambles. From out of the imbroglio there emerged several instances of individual gallantry, but there was no time to organize any proper defence of the city and little desire on the part of the troops to become further involved in the bloody, bewildering business of street fighting. When the Royalists were forced back from Red Hill, they were closely pursued right up to the Sidbury Gate, where the confusion was appalling. Charles, who had displayed great courage throughout the fighting, now found his way blocked by an ammunition wagon whose leading ox had been killed. He was forced to dismount and squeeze through the gate with the enemy close behind him. Discarding his heavy armour and taking a fresh horse he joined with such stalwarts as the Earl of Cleveland, Sir James Hamilton and Colonel Wogan in trying to rally some of the broken regiments and induce them to continue the battle.

Their combined efforts met with only partial success, for by now the enemy were hemming them in on all sides. There had been no time to destroy the bridge across the river from St John's, and Dalziel's brigade, which might have held up the advance on the west for some time, laid down their arms without firing a shot: Leslie's cavalry continued supine on Pitchcroft: and when Sir Alexander Forbes refused to surrender Fort Royal the Essex militia stormed and captured it with great élan, and then proceeded to turn its guns onto the tortured city. There was by now only one gate by which the defeated Royalists could hope to escape: the Bridge Gate was in the hands of Fleetwood's men: the Sidbury and Friars Gates were also held by the enemy, and the Foregate had been blocked up. Everyone converged upon St Martin's Gate and the road to the north. Some panicked, but most were fighting their way at push-of-pike and the slaughter in the city was considerable. On Castle Mound, Lord Rothes, Sir William Hammond and Colonel Drummond continued to hold out until offered terms by Cromwell personally, and the courage of men like Cleveland and Hamilton, and a small party of English Cavaliers, enabled Charles to make his escape from the doomed city. As he started upon what was to be the most thrilling adventure of his life the sound of explosions and the faint patter of musketry were still ringing in his ears.

It was a total disaster: of the 15,000–16,000 men who began the battle – mostly Scots – only a very small proportion made good their escape. Somewhere between 2,000 and 3,000 were slain in battle, and about 10,000 were captured either on the battlefield or as they vainly tried to make their way north, including 640 officers. Save for Charles himself hardly a single officer of consequence survived the battle a free man. The Duke of Hamilton was carried back to the Commandery after the Red Hill sortie and died there

Ier.50.5. Come let us joyn ourselves to the Lord

i 6   a Solemn   4 3

in a perpetuall Cov that shall not be forg

LEAGVE AND COVENANT,
for Reformation, and defence of Religion, the Honour and happinesse of the king, and the Peace and safety, of the three kingdoms of ·

ENGLAND, SCOTLAND, and IRELAND.

We Noblemen, Barons, knights, Gentlemen, Citizens, Burgesses, Ministers of the Gospel, and Com of all sorts in the Kingdoms of England, Scotland, and Ireland, by the Providence of God living one king, and being of one reformed Religion, having before our eyes the Glory of God, and the adv ment of the kingdome of our Lord and Saviour Iesus Christ, the Honour and happinesse of the king iesty and his posterity, and the true publique Liberty, Safety, and Peace of the kingdoms, wherein e ones private Condition is included, and calling to minde the treacherous and bloody Plots, Consp cies, Attempts, and Practices of the Enemies of God, against the true Religion, and professors reof in all places, especially in these three kingdoms ever since the Reformation of Religion, ar how much their rage, power and presumption, are of late, and at this time increased and cised; whereof the deplorable state of the Church and kingdom of Ireland, the distressed te of the Church and kingdom of England, and the dangerous estate of the Church and ki dom of Scotland, are present and publique Testimonies; We have now at last, (after oth means of Supplication, Remonstrance, Protestations, and Sufferings) for the preservation selves and our Religion, from utter Ruine and Destruction; according to the commendab ctice of these kingdoms in former times, and the Example of Gods people in other Natio After mature deliberation, resolved and determined to enter into a mutuall and solemn Le und Covenant; Wherein we all subscribe, and each one of us for himself, with o hands lifted up to the most high God, do sweare;

· maii · 22   1643

on 12 September: the Earls of Derby and Lauderdale were captured in Cheshire – Derby was executed and Lauderdale was a prisoner until 1660. Generals Massey, Montgomery and Sir Alexander Forbes were wounded; and Keith, Pitscottie, Grandison and many others joined those taken in Worcester and herded into the cathedral, whose nave formed a temporary prison. Leslie was caught in Yorkshire and, like Lauderdale, remained a prisoner until 1660. The English army is said to have lost only 200 men. This is probably an underestimate, but there was seldom a Pyrrhic victory in the Civil Wars so it may not be very far out.

In his letter to the Speaker on the day after the battle, Cromwell wrote of it: 'The dimensions of this mercy are above my thoughts. It is, for aught I know, a crowning mercy.' For those who favoured Parliament his words proved true. This battle ended the Civil Wars, and it was the last serious attempt to reinstate the lawful King of England by force of arms – other small risings, such as Penruddock's in 1655, were easily dealt with. The battle is also notable for the spotlight it throws upon Oliver Cromwell. The strategical and tactical brilliance of the Worcester campaign is often compared to the best endeavours of the great masters of war. Certainly the means by which Cromwell dislodged Leslie from an impregnable position at Dunbar, and then organized the pursuit in such a way as to bring the Royalist army to battle at a considerable disadvantage, displayed military talents of the highest capacity. But it must be remembered that in the fight which ensued Cromwell outnumbered his opponents by nearly two to one, and the morale of his army was much higher than that of Charles's. This overwhelming superiority enabled him to violate one of the first principles of war: he not only divided his force, but divided it by one of the largest rivers in England. It was a calculated risk, which had Leslie's cavalry shown any inclination to fight might easily not have come off: it was the measure of the man that he took it.

After Worcester Cromwell sheathed his sword. He had risen from the humblest to the greatest position in the military hierarchy through his own genius, and he had created and trained an army that at that time had not its peer in all Europe. For this and much else he deserves his place in the hall of fame. But it is less easy to number him among the great captains, for his battles were fewer and more restricted in scale than men like Gustavus Adolphus, Turenne, Marlborough, Wellington and Napoleon. If he had less opportunity than those men to display his strategical and tactical skill on a broad canvas, he can proudly fall in beside that other great creator and trainer of a modern army, Sir John Moore.

Left: The Solemn League and Covenant accepted by Parliament and imposed on the British people, 1643

CHAPTER 9

'Let Monmouth Reign!'

Sedgemoor

6 July 1685

The battlefield is still in unspoilt country, although it presents a very different picture from what Monmouth knew: where there were areas of only partially drained moorland, there are now orderly well drained and cultivated fields. But the landscape itself has changed little and the visitor walking the ground has no difficulty in appreciating what a stupendous task Monmouth had in marching an army in absolute silence across this land at night.

The Battle of Sedgemoor was fought about three-quarters of a mile to the north of Westonzoyland church. Westonzoyland is some three miles south-east of Bridgwater on the A372 road. If the visitor wishes to follow Monmouth's line of march on foot it is best to work off the 2½-inch Ordnance Survey map (sheet ST 33). It is not possible to follow the whole route from Bradney to Westonzoyland along public footpaths, but so long as one is prepared for a rather muddy walk (except in mid-summer) a great deal of it can be followed in the first instance by walking down the drove leading south-east from Peasy Farm, and then by driving to Chedzoy and walking down a drove that starts near Parchey and joins the public footpath by the King's Sedgemoor Drain. This was not there at the time of the battle, but may in part mark the line of the Black Ditch. The public footpath follows the drain, and to get to Westonzoyland one has to leave it and strike south across a small field that leads to a drove in which is situated – somewhat obscurely – the memorial stone, which stands about 200 yards to the south of the site of the chief burial pit. This pit was excavated at the end of the last century. Coming from Westonzoyland the route to that part of the battlefield is fairly well signposted.

James Scott, Duke of Monmouth, was born in Rotterdam on 9 April 1649. His mother was Lucy Walter, and despite what was often said to the contrary, both then and later, it is almost certain that Charles II described him accurately in the Duke's marriage contract with Anna Countess of Buccleuch as *'Filio nostro naturali et illegitimo'*. Unfortunately for Monmouth, Charles proved a weak

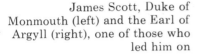

James Scott, Duke of Monmouth (left) and the Earl of Argyll (right), one of those who led him on

and over-indulgent father, who seemed more concerned to heap honours upon the boy than to further his education, which was lamentably neglected. Already transformed from James Crofts to Baron Scott, Earl of Doncaster and Duke of Monmouth, Charles made him Duke of Buccleuch and Earl of Dalkeith on his wedding day (20 April 1663), and conferred upon him the Order of the Garter. Henceforth Monmouth took precedence over every man in the country after the King, the Duke of York and Prince Rupert – small wonder that we find him acting as though he were Prince of Wales, and making sumptuous progresses into the West Country and the north. Nor can we fail to understand the grave displeasure that all this caused the Duke of York.

Monmouth was in many ways an attractive young man. He was a much better-looking edition of his father, with all of Charles's charm; but although often amusing and gay he quickly gave way to flaccid despair whenever anything went wrong. He was a loyal friend, though an unfaithful husband, and a courageous fighter who hated cold-blooded cruelty. Perhaps his greatest fault, which was in the end his undoing, was his weakness and vacillation. He seemed unable to make a decision, and his uncle James spoke the truth when at the end, having granted him an interview at which he refused to pardon him, he said of his victim, 'Poor Monmouth, he was always easy to be imposed upon'.

There was no more obvious choice than the popular 'Protestant Duke' as the fugelman for that growing party of discontented

161

Whigs and Dissenters who were determined that Catholic James should not ascend the throne. Monmouth, with cries of 'A Monmouth! A Monmouth!' and 'Let Monmouth reign!' still ringing in his ears from his triumphant progress through the western counties, was not averse to being set up as an alternative to James. He became a willing tool in the hands of Shaftesbury, and later of even more dangerous plotters. As a member of the Council of Six he was closely involved in their nefarious schemes to extort from the King, by force if necessary, the summoning of a parliament and an end to what they considered his arbitrary rule, but he never countenanced the designs of the extremists in connection with the Rye House plot. The rejection by the Lords of the second Exclusion Bill in 1680 caused consternation in the City, where Monmouth was given a rapturous reception. This and much else angered James almost beyond endurance. He had every reason to mistrust his nephew, and whether Monmouth was in exile, in Scotland, or in London James laboured for his downfall – and as Charles was determined that the lawful succession should be upheld, James was bound to triumph in the end. Banished from the court, pardoned by a devoted father (although not by a cold, unforgiving uncle, to whom he had made an abject apology), and finally advised to leave the country for a time, Monmouth was at the Hague when on 5 February 1685 Charles died.

His position now was most unenviable: his wisest counsellors had recently perished on the scaffold, he had no friend of importance at court and his uncle wanted him home – but in chains. Monmouth, like the Earl of Argyll and a number of other political agitators, was in exile. Nor could he stay in Holland, for the Prince of Orange found it expedient ·to placate his father-in-law, although he proved extremely negligent in keeping watch on the movements of his erstwhile guest. At this we are not surprised, for William had all to gain from any attempt on the throne by Monmouth. If he succeeded, which the Prince felt quite certain he would not, there would be a Protestant ally in his quarrels with Louis XIV, and if he failed the succession of the Princess Mary became less complicated. It seems certain that by now Monmouth had no wish to become King of England. He was just beginning to enjoy domestic life with his devoted mistress Henrietta Wentworth (the Duchess was still in England), and they had plans to summer in Sweden – but we know that he was easily imposed upon.

The Earl of Argyll; that arch-plotter and turbulent priest Robert Ferguson; the reprobate Lord Grey of Warke, Monmouth's *eminence grise*; Heywood Dare, a goldsmith from Taunton with

A.Blooteling fe et

ƷVS EBORACENSIS ET ALBANIÆ DVX, COMES ULTONIÆ ꝛꞔa

immense influence in the West Country, and others were urging Monmouth, against his better judgement, to head a rebellion in the west that would synchronize with Argyll's landing in Scotland. He knew the difficulties, and although aware that there was a genuine fear for Protestantism, especially in the western and northern counties, he was not so certain that the gentry would rally to him. Moreover, James had begun his reign with caution and summoned a parliament – the first for three years – which was entirely loyal; money was short with which to buy arms and equipment; and above all Monmouth knew, from his own not inconsiderable military experience, the value of a standing army, and that a rabble could never defeat disciplined troops. However, he allowed himself to be overruled. Argyll sailed for the western Highlands on 2 May and a month later Monmouth, in the 32-gun frigate *Helderenburgh,* with two other small ships and eighty-two companions (including some Dutch gunners), left the Texel for the south coast of England.

Finding the money for the hire of the frigate (£5,500) and the purchase of arms and equipment had not been easy. Monmouth had pawned his Great George* and all his jewels, and Henrietta and her mother had added theirs; his friends in Holland had also contributed, but money expected from London had not been forthcoming. He bought four light cannon, about 1,500 back and breast plates (most of which were never used; the money would have been better spent on additional muskets) and a fair quantity of small arms, ammunition and powder. All this left him with very little cash with which to pay his volunteers and buy provisions.

On 11 June, after a voyage of twelve days, the tiny expedition dropped anchor off Lyme Regis. The landing was unopposed, although it seems that had powder been readily available the mayor and at least one loyal citizen would have been prepared to fire upon the small boats bringing Monmouth and his party to the shore. Soon the green standard, inscribed with the words 'Fear nothing but God', was unfurled and it was not long before the eighty-three invaders were joined by a band of eager recruits. Shouts of 'A Monmouth! A Monmouth!' and 'The Protestant religion' greeted the reading of the rebel declaration. This scurrilous document – even for those days when it was customary to use powerful, and often libellous, words to conjure up real or imagined wrongs – was mainly the work of Robert Ferguson.

Not long after the landing there was an unpleasant incident at

* Monmouth received the Garter in 1663.

Lyme that had serious consequences for Monmouth. Andrew Fletcher of Saltoun and old Heywood Dare quarrelled over a horse, and Fletcher killed Dare. The latter's son demanded justice and Monmouth was forced to send Fletcher off to sea. Both these men were a grievous loss, Dare on account of his local standing, and Fletcher because he was a young man with recent battle experience. This unfortunate beginning was followed by a most unsatisfactory affair against the Dorset militia at Bridport. What could have been a successful joint infantry and cavalry operation against a very half-hearted enemy came undone when Lord Grey and his horse turned tail after one volley had been fired at them. Colonel Venner had already been wounded in some house fighting and a complete shambles was only saved by the steadiness of Nathaniel Wade, who was to prove himself Monmouth's most reliable officer.

Although the landing had been unopposed there were those in Lyme ready to speed the news: the local militia commanders had it within the day, and Whitehall knew by 13 June. The King at once despatched Lord Churchill with six troops of horse and dragoons and five infantry companies to keep a close watch on the rebels. Monmouth had no time to lose if he was to avoid being boxed in at Lyme. On Monday 15 June the rebel army, now about 3,000 strong, marched for Axminster. The original plan had been to rally at Taunton on the first stage of a march to Bristol, Gloucester (where it was hoped to link up with the men from Cheshire) and then London. But this plan was to undergo many changes. In addition to a small, shaggy cavalry force under Lord Grey, there were now four regiments: the Duke's (Red) commanded by Nathaniel Wade, the White (Colonel Foukes), Green (Colonel Holmes) and Yellow (formed by Major Fox and later commanded by Colonel Matthews). A fifth regiment, the Blue under Colonel Basset, was added later. There was no shortage of volunteers (a notable newcomer being Daniel Defoe), but many had to be turned away for lack of arms, and some went to war carrying a scythe blade at the end of an eight-foot pole – a formidable weapon at close quarters.

Albemarle's militiamen were encountered at Axminster. Although they outnumbered the rebels by at least a thousand they had no stomach for fighting, and many of them joined Monmouth. The rebel army then went on its way undisturbed to Chard, Ilminster and Taunton. Not taking Exeter at this point was perhaps Monmouth's first mistake: personally brave and popular with his troops, he was not, however, a good general, and although his strategic planning was often sound he was seldom capable of taking a daring decision. Above all he frequently failed to maintain the momentum of success – so essential for an insurgent army. Exeter could have been taken without any difficulty, and with it much needed arms, money and ammunition. A similar opportunity to revitalize the cause was later to be lost before Bristol.

They reached the outskirts of Taunton on 18 June, and the next day Monmouth entered the town to a tumultuous welcome. It was here at the market cross that he was first proclaimed king. Ferguson and Grey had been urging this step upon him ever since the landing, but Monmouth was almost certainly sincere when he said that he wished to leave the matter open for the time being, although he had hinted that he would accept the wishes of his followers. The great majority of these were eager to have him king, and for two principal reasons he agreed: he had become seriously alarmed by the failure of the gentry to enlist, and he was assured that many were holding back because they feared another Commonwealth. This was not the whole truth, but it was a slightly more plausible reason for assuming kingship than the belief that in the event of defeat his followers would be in a more favourable legal position because they were serving a king – if only a *de facto* one – rather than a rebel leader. Treason could not be thus deceitfully veiled.

Leaving Taunton on 21 June Monmouth marched to Bridgwater at the head of almost 8,000 men. But his heart was heavy, for there had been no encouraging sign from London or the north and still the local gentry held back. His objective was Bristol, the second richest city in the country, and could he but capture it the tide might yet flow in his favour. The Duke of Beaufort, in command of the Gloucestershire militia, held the town and Lord Feversham, who had superseded Churchill in command of the royalist forces, was at Bath with some 2,000 troops. Bristol was vulnerable from the Gloucester side and a more determined commander than Monmouth would have taken it. The rebels repaired the bridge over the Avon at Keynsham and crossed the river. Coming back to the town for rest and provisions they were surprised by a body of enemy cavalry, but managed to drive them off after suffering some casualties. However, Monmouth, fearing that he might be caught between Churchill's force, which had been constantly harassing him, and the main royalist army, abandoned the assault. The sunshine days were now gone; the long grey aftermath of disappointment, dejection and defeat lay ahead. And Monmouth knew it.

166

King James's men – dragoon, gunner and grenadier

His occasional flashes of unbounded optimism were now crowded out by long periods of gloomy pessimism. Indecision had cost him Bristol; now, uncertain of his reception and fearful of Churchill's harassing operations on his slow-moving, badly shod army, he discarded the plan to march north. Instead, as an act of bravado born of despair, he decided to summon Bath to surrender. When the unfortunate herald who was sent upon this forlorn mission was killed, Monmouth bypassed the city and with no apparent plan in mind marched to Philips Norton (now Norton St Philip). As it was in this village, which lies a few miles south of Bath, that on 27 June the first engagement of any consequence was fought between the King's army and his nephew's rebel host, we should briefly turn our attention to the troops that James was able to bring against Monmouth.

At the Restoration Charles II was careful to retain a small standing army, although there were certain alterations to the system. It was an ironical touch that in 1678 Monmouth should have become this army's captain-general. In 1685, when James succeeded, the cavalry comprised three troops of Life Guards, with Grenadier dragoons (mounted infantry) attached to each troop, the King's Regiment of Horse (later the Royal Horse Guards) and the Royal Dragoons (recently the Tangier Horse). On the English establishment there were two regiments of Foot Guards and five other regiments of foot – of which one was called the

Admiral's Regiment and served mainly at sea. In addition there were six regiments (three raised in England and three in Scotland) which were maintained by the Dutch and served in Holland, but they could be recalled if needed. The militia had been remodelled shortly before the Restoration, and gentlemen were liable, according to the value of the land they held, to equip and pay a horseman, a pikeman or a musketeer. Under the King the lords lieutenant held the command in their counties and the men could be called up for periods not exceeding fourteen days in one year. It was estimated that the total militia force was around 130,000 men.

With the exception of the 3rd Regiment of Foot (the Buffs) the Admiral's Regiment and some cavalry units, Feversham had under his command the whole of the regular army and sixteen light guns. Companies of the 3rd Guards (who were then on the Scottish establishment) were ordered to join him, but did not arrive until after the rebellion had been quashed. The Prince of Orange was asked to send his six regiments over and offered to lead them himself, but they took no part in the fighting. Weapons and equipment had not changed greatly since the Civil War. The soft hat had replaced the cavalryman's helmet, but troopers still wore the cuirass and in addition to sword and pistol they now carried a carbine. The pikemen no longer wore armour, and indeed by now the infantrymen had been given the long red or blue coats. In most regiments the flintlock had replaced the matchlock, but bayonets issued in 1673 had been withdrawn again. Each regiment of foot now had a Grenadier company, but these played no part in this campaign. Out of a total standing army of about 4,000 all ranks,* Feversham had 1,800 infantrymen and 700 horse. If we discount the militia regiments, which took little part at Philips Norton and none at Sedgemoor, he was inferior in numbers to what Monmouth could bring against him, but in training, discipline and firepower his infantry and artillery were immeasurably superior; while Monmouth's troopers, mounted on country hacks completely unaccustomed to the noise of battle, only added to the incalculable hazards of the battlefield.

* The total number of men serving in the standing army at the time of Monmouth's rebellion cannot be accurately given. There are no muster rolls extant for this time, and the annual pay rolls vary enormously. These can be studied in the Public Record Office (War Office Class 24, pieces 7 and 8 and 25/3206). The pay roll for 1 January 1685 (W.O. 24/8 Pt 3) shows a figure greatly in excess of the one given here, but many regiments existed only on paper, and that of 3,617 for the standing army of 1684 (W.O. 24/7) is probably fairly accurate for both that year and the next.

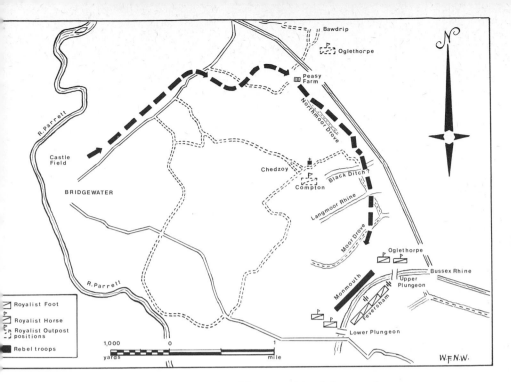

Above: Battle of Sedgemoor, showing Monmouth's night march
Overleaf: Battle of Sedgemoor

The rebel army arrived at Philips Norton on Friday 26 June and Monmouth spent the night in the Old House – now the George Inn. The long drought had at last broken and the rain was pouring down as the infantry sought what shelter they could in fields adjacent to the town; the cavalry took up positions in the town itself. The troops were not alone in their dejection; Monmouth's spirits were rapidly reaching their nadir. He had expected 500 horse to join him here under a Colonel Adlam, and had been confidently assured that many royalist soldiers would come over to him. In both events he was disappointed.

Wandering round the old parts of Norton St Philip now, it is not possible to be certain from contemporary accounts exactly where the fighting took place. There was a lane leading from a ploughed field that ran close to the courtyard of a fair-sized house – possibly near the site of the present house that stands back from the road north of the inn – and Monmouth had placed a barricade in this lane. Throughout the night of 26–7 June there had been alarms, but it was not until the morning of the 27th that Feversham, marching from Bath, made contact. He sent a party of Grenadiers, under Monmouth's half-brother the Duke of Grafton, against the barricade, but they came under sharp fire and Mon-

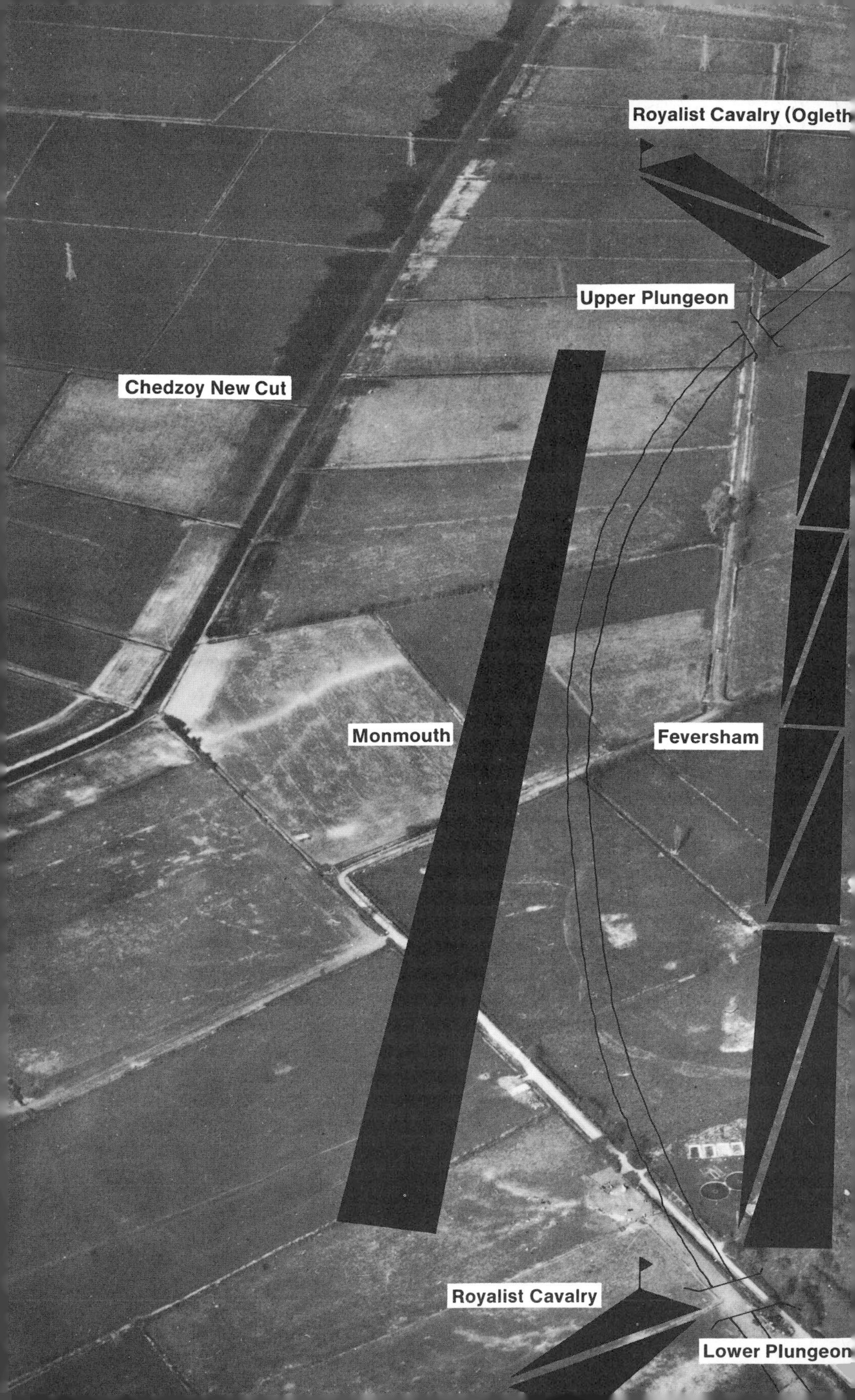

Royalist Cavalry (Ogleth

Upper Plungeon

Chedzoy New Cut

Monmouth

Feversham

Royalist Cavalry

Lower Plungeon

King's Sedgemoor Drain

Bussex Rhine

N

Oxford House

WESTONZOYLAND

mouth immediately led his own regiment through the courtyard of the house and took them in the flank. It was an ill conducted affair on Feversham's part, and although he sent strong reinforcements in support of Grafton they too came under heavy fire from rebels lining the surrounding hedges. Failing to achieve a breakthrough, he withdrew the attacking force, and for the next six hours both armies conducted a brisk cannonade which did no harm to anyone. Eventually Monmouth gave orders to attack, but the royalists did not wait: they withdrew to Bradford having lost about eighty men (some crawled into the standing corn to die, and were not found until the harvest) as against Monmouth's eighteen.

Monmouth had had the best of his first proper engagement with his uncle's army, but it did nothing to raise his morale or remove those bouts of melancholy; and many of his men, no doubt sensing eventual defeat, began to drift away. The army marched to Frome and here the situation was deemed so bad as to warrant a council of war. At this serious conclave it was suggested that the men should be allowed to take the benefit of the pardon offered by James to any who would desert Monmouth, and those exempt from this pardon (Monmouth and all who had come from Holland with him) should make good their escape. It must have been a difficult decision for Monmouth, who had just learned – to add to his other disappointments – that Argyll had been captured and executed in Scotland. But he probably knew that to abandon the enterprise now was to abandon it for good, and he had had experience of the way that James treated plotters and put no faith in his uncle's promises.

Undoubtedly the decision to fight on was the right one. It was decided to revert to the original plan and march north to join up with Lord Delamere in Cheshire; but discovering that Feversham was at Westbury Monmouth retired again on Bridgwater, from where he dispatched his chaplain Nathaniel Hooke to London to urge his supporters there to rise at once, and sent a detachment to Minehead to procure more horses and the guns from the quayside. Meanwhile, chiefly as a bluff, for he had determined to march north on 6 July, some steps were taken to fortify Bridgwater.

Lord Feversham, learning of Monmouth's movements, advanced on Bridgwater, reaching Somerton on 3 July. From here he carried out a personal reconnaissance as far as Middlezoy, where he intended to have his next camp, but when he learned that Westonzoyland, which was less than four miles from Bridgwater, was a much more favourable site, he left his 1,500-strong Wiltshire militia at Middlezoy and marched the rest of the army to Weston.

Between this village and the even smaller one of Chedzoy, less than two miles to the north, was an expanse of open, boggy moorland, which was partially drained by ditches taking the water to the river Parrett. Two of these ditches, known locally as rhines, were formidable obstacles, and even after a long dry spell were impassable to horse except by the recognized crossing places. Any force occupying Westonzoyland had the protection of one of these obstacles, the Bussex Rhine, which ran roughly in a crescent from just across the Bridgwater road at its southern end almost to where the King's Sedgemoor Drain is now situated. There were two crossing places, known as plungeons; one was immediately to the north of the Bridgwater road, and the other about 1,000 yards up the ditch.

The royalist army reached Westonzoyland on Sunday 5 July, and Feversham pitched his newly arrived tents between the village and the Bussex Rhine, leaving room for the infantry to deploy behind the rhine (for the royalist army's order of battle see page 180). Feversham was a naturalized Frenchman and nephew of the great Turenne. He certainly had not inherited his uncle's military talent, and his conduct of the campaign has often been criticized; and in particular he has been blamed for being taken by surprise at Sedgemoor. But in fact his tactics before and during the battle were almost beyond reproach. The outlying picquets may not have been as alert as they should have been, but the dispositions would seem to have been perfectly adequate. The infantry were encamped 100 yards behind the rhine, the cavalry were in the village and were ordered to remain saddled throughout the night, the cannon were on the left guarding the Bridgwater road. Colonel Oglethorpe, with a strong patrol of Life Guards, was sent to Bawdrip to watch the Bristol road, along which it was expected that Monmouth would march north; Sir Francis Compton, with a hundred horse and fifty dragoons, was positioned in Chedzoy; there were further outposts on the Bridgwater road, and to the rear at a ford over the Parrett. The only important place that appears to have been left unguarded was the upper – or right-hand – plungeon.

The Reverend Andrew Paschall, Vicar of Chedzoy, to whom we are indebted for a lively account of the proceedings, was a royalist and was largely responsible for keeping his flock out of trouble; but at least one of them, a farmer called Sparke, held rebel sympathies. And when Sparke, watching through his spyglass from Chedzoy church tower, saw the royalist army taking up position he sent his servant Richard Godfrey to inform Monmouth. Monmouth was painfully aware that his army stood no chance against the royalists in an open fight; but here perhaps was an opportunity for a surprise attack by night. One of the most hazardous operations of war, even with well trained, well disciplined troops, is an approach march over difficult country by night; but it often proves irresistible as a gamble in desperate circumstances. After some discussion it was decided to attempt it, provided Feversham was not dug in. Accordingly Godfrey, who knew every inch of the moor and was prepared to act as guide, was sent off to discover if the enemy were entrenched. He reported that they were not; but he apparently made no mention of the Bussex Rhine – no doubt assuming that everybody knew about rhines and he was only asked to investigate trenches. The night attack was to go forward and the Bussex Rhine would be its undoing.

Not long after the decision to attack had been taken news was brought to Monmouth – certainly exaggerated and probably untrue – that the enemy were in no state to resist, for most of the officers and men were sadly affected by the local cider. At least it pushed up the mercury in Monmouth's personal barometer: 'We shall have no more to do than to lock up the stable-doors, and seize the troopers in their beds' was the over-optimistic remark John Oldmixon tells us he made. No doubt he modified these views on hearing the latest reports of Feversham's outpost positions. These made it necessary for the rebel army to take a wide circuit of almost six miles from their camp in Castle Field, instead of a short three-mile 'approach along an easy road. The plan was daring, if perhaps dangerously simple, and displayed great confidence. Nathaniel Wade, who with Monmouth and Lord Grey was chiefly responsible for its conception, tells us that the horse were to break into the right flank of the enemy camp and engage the foot, keeping them from coming together before Monmouth's infantry and cannon could engage them from the front. The whole action was to be swiftly accomplished before the enemy's cavalry and cannon could become effective.*

It was 11 p.m. on the night of Sunday 5 July when Wade's regiment led the advance out of Bridgwater. The most savage orders

---

* Historians are totally unable to agree on whether Monmouth knew about the Bussex Rhine and the plungeons before leaving Bridgwater. Contemporary accounts are mostly silent on the matter, although King James asserts that Monmouth did not know of it. Almost certainly Godfrey made no mention of it, but before marching the presence of the Black Ditch and the Langmoor Rhine seems to have been known, so it is possible that the Bussex Rhine was too. The plan could fit either contingency, so long as the position of the upper plungeon was known.

The Duke of Monmouth is defeated at Sedgemoor

had been given to preserve silence; anyone breaking it was to be immediately stabbed by his neighbour. To avoid Sir Francis Compton in Chedzoy the army marched north-east up the Causeway (present A39 road), leaving the baggage wagons and one gun in the Knowle Hill area ready for the march on Bristol after the victory. From here they followed the route shown in the sketch map (p. 169), and somewhere in the area of Peasy Farm the horse passed through the infantry and took the lead.* It was here, too, that the ammunition wagons were parked, for the army was about to debouch onto the open moorland. The night was not completely dark; the moon was almost full, but a thick mist blanketed the moor, restricting visibility to a few feet and to some extent muffling sound. Even so it is difficult to understand how nearly 3,000 infantrymen and 800 horse could have passed within half a mile of Colonel Oglethorpe's patrol without being heard. Great credit must be given to Godfrey, who led the rebels unerringly over a narrow moorland track, and across the Black Ditch; only on reaching the Langmoor Rhine, more a morass than a ditch with one crossing place, did he falter temporarily and miss the ford.

Up till now the march had been carried out with a secrecy and skill that must evoke our admiration. Those who have been

* It is perhaps curious that horse should have led the way on a night march.

engaged in a night march will know how every eye seeks to pierce the darkness, and the strain that it puts upon any sensitive soldier when strange objects distort the vision and unbidden fears leap to the mind. Everyone is tense: any moment the deep silence may be broken by the crash of a volley, or the crack of a single shot. Directly Godfrey had managed to find the crossing place and got the army safely to the other side of the Langmoor Rhine the silence was shattered by that sound that every man had dreaded to hear – a pistol shot.

Almost certainly the pistol was fired by a vedette (a mounted sentinel – and not, as is sometimes asserted, by a traitor in Monmouth's army), who made all haste to Chedzoy to inform his picquet commander that the enemy were at hand and in strength. The Langmoor Rhine was about half a mile to the south-east of Chedzoy and almost exactly a mile from the royalist camp. It is immaterial whether the pistol shot was heard in either place, because it would have conveyed little without the vedette's information. In any event Sir Francis Compton at Chedzoy was not slow in despatching a trooper to inform the main camp, and it was clear to Monmouth that they had been discovered. There was nothing for it but to press on urgently, and hope that an attack might still be launched before the enemy were fully prepared. Lord Grey was therefore ordered to trot forward with his cavalry to engage the enemy in the flank as originally planned, while the infantry, still in column, followed as quickly as they could.

To go back in time an hour or two and to the royalist camp, we find Lord Feversham leaving Westonzoyland around 11 p.m. to visit most of his outposts. He rode first up the Bridgwater road and then struck north to Chedzoy, where he spent some time chatting with Compton. He was back in camp before 1 a.m., and when soon afterwards a messenger came in from Colonel Oglethorpe to say that there was no sign of any movement up the Bristol road and he was marching towards Bridgwater to investigate, Feversham felt fairly sure that there would be no night attack, so retired to his quarters in the village. He could hardly have got into bed when at about 1.45 he clearly heard the alarm being sounded, and pausing – very properly – only to dress himself correctly he was soon back in the camp. Battle had already begun, but Lord Churchill was on the spot and taking the necessary measures to meet the tactical situation.

In the fighting, although great courage was shown by most of the individual combatants, the rebel army as a whole and the officers who led it did not distinguish themselves: the odds against them were far too great. But no praise can be too high for the skill and discipline of their night march. After the Langmoor Rhine had been crossed Godfrey was either dismissed, or more likely left behind in the general scramble that followed the alarm, but the last mile was covered at speed with no guide except the light from the enemy's matchlocks* as they came close to the great ditch. The rebel army had covered almost six miles, much of it across extremely difficult country, in a thick mist, and maintaining absolute silence, in just under three hours. It was a remarkable achievement by any standard.

Before the night march ended and the enemy's main force could be engaged, Lord Grey had a brush with Sir Francis Compton's detachment of Blues and dragoons. As the latter rode from Chedzoy they met the rebel cavalry either by accident or design and a fierce and very confused skirmish took place in the mist. Compton was wounded by a bullet in the chest, but he and his men had given the royalist army time to deploy for battle, and most of the picquet (including Compton) got safely across the Bussex Rhine and took up position at the upper plungeon, which they held with considerable stubbornness against 300 enemy cavalry. For Grey had hit the rhine some distance below the upper plungeon, and split his force. He sent Captain Jones and 300 men up the rhine and they found the plungeon, while Grey with the remainder soon became engaged by the Grenadier battalions. It is not really surprising that these rustic men on their even more rustic animals, after a trying march and a sharp skirmish, should have shrunk before the destructive fire that flared and crackled at them out of the darkness. Cavalry to cavalry before the plungeon they showed some spirit, but Grey was quite unable to control the main body of his horse, who fled from the bullets in a disorderly rabble.

Monmouth, coming up with the infantry, was hampered by the retreating horsemen, but the Dutch gunners got their three remaining pieces into action on the left, and did some damage to the Grenadiers and Dumbarton's regiment. Wade tells us that the last part of the march had been so fast that the infantry arrived in some disorder, and the deployment from column into line was a rather ragged affair. Unfortunately his personal account of the

* James II would seem to have been mistaken in his statement that Dumbarton's regiment was the only one still using matchlocks at this battle. The equipment scale of the Sedgemoor army shows a distinct preponderance of matchlocks over flintlocks in all but the Grenadier companies and dragoons. What few muskets Monmouth's army had would have been mainly flintlocks purchased in Holland.

177

battle is confused, but there is no doubt that the rebel infantry halted some hundred yards from the enemy and stood, crowded together, firing their muskets at random. Those men lucky enough to be armed with a musket had had little training in its use, and although the weapon had a range of about 400 yards it was not noted for its accuracy; even trained soldiers found it difficult to hit a man at a hundred yards. Monmouth's men discharged a lot of shot – and their ammunition reserve was back at Peasy Farm – but we are told that they were firing high and doing little damage.

As soon as he saw that the rebel left extended beyond Dumbarton's right, Churchill switched Kirke's and Trelawney's regiments to strengthen that flank, and the artillery was hastily moved from the extreme left of the line. Many of the gun team (probably impressed civilians) had already left the field, but the militant Bishop of Winchester, Doctor Mews, who had had more experience with culverins than crosiers, quickly unharnessed the horses from his coach and personally assisted in the movement of the artillery to the right and centre of the line, where he continued to supervise the firing. As soon as he arrived on the scene Feversham issued strict and very sensible orders that no infantryman was to cross the ditch before daylight. Grey had reached the rhine a little

Monmouth pleading with James II

before 2 a.m. and the infantry battle probably started rather less than half an hour later. Not long after it started, and while it was still dark, Feversham led three troops of cavalry across the lower plungeon and positioned them on the rebel right flank with orders to envelop this flank as and when possible. On recrossing the rhine he was met by Colonel Oglethorpe and his Life Guards, who had ridden completely round the battlefield without having seen the enemy. Feversham immediately led these in the rear of the infantry to cross by the upper plungeon – now cleared by the Blues of enemy horse – and positioned them on Monmouth's left flank. At first light the frontal attack went in and the rebel army found itself being relentlessly squeezed on three sides. Nevertheless, perhaps out of desperation, they continued for a little to fight most courageously, even though their leader had fled the field.

As we have seen, it is in pursuit of a defeated army that the heaviest casualties are apt to occur, and this is especially true when that army is little better than an ill-organized rabble. Wade says that he 'made a kind of disorderly retreat to a ditch a great way behind us'. He was Monmouth's best commander and probably held his troops together longer than the others; the ditches and bogs did not help, and the royalist cavalry took a fearful toll of these misguided peasants. Rebel casualties have always been difficult to assess, for they often include those who were hanged out of hand after the battle by orders of the victorious commander, and even those who were the victims of the notorious Judge Jeffreys. Probably no more than 300 were killed in the battle and a further 1,000 in the pursuit. The royalist casualties are usually given at around 400, which is probably too high. Many rebel prisoners were taken on the field and 500 of them spent the night after the fight in Westonzoyland church.

Had Monmouth died on the battlefield he would have been a hero; but although in the heat of battle he always fought with great courage, he was not the stuff of which heroes are made. He knew that he could not save his army and when Grey (who accompanied him) and others suggested that he should try to save himself while there was still time he found it difficult to refuse. We may criticize him for deserting men still fighting his battle, and we may find ourselves unable to excuse him on the grounds that he himself had been deserted, but we can perhaps understand something of the agony of it all. But although in life Monmouth was never a king, in the Tower and on the scaffold he knew how to behave like one. And he died horribly at the hands of a bungling executioner.

Order of Battle for the Royalist Army at Sedgemoor

(Extracted from Viscount Wolseley's *Life of Marlborough,*
Vol. I, p. 319.)

Infantry

From the right of the line to the left:
5 companies of the Royal Regiment (Dumbarton's), now the
Royal Scots, under Lieutenant-Colonel Douglas: one company
was a Grenadier company.
7 companies, of which one was a Grenadier company, of the
1st Battalion of the King's Guards, now the Grenadier Guards,
under the Duke of Grafton.
6 companies of the 2nd Battalion of the King's Guards, now the
Grenadier Guards, under Major Eaton.
6 companies of the 2nd Regiment of Guards, now the Coldstream
Guards, under Lieutenant-Colonel Sackville.
5 companies of the Queen Dowager's Regiment, now the Queen's
or West Surrey Regiment, under Colonel Kirk.
Note: Wolseley places these troops on the extreme left. So does
Roberts (*Life of Monmouth,* Vol. II, p. 61), but Roberts
puts 5 companies (of which one was a Grenadier company)
of Trelawney's regiment, now the King's Own, under
command of Lieutenant-Colonel Charles Churchill,
between Sackville and Kirk.

Cavalry

150 men selected from the three troops of Life Guards, and 60
Horse Grenadiers, under Lieutenant-Colonel the Honourable
F. Villiers.
7 troops (about 400 men) of the King's Regiment of Horse, now
the Royal Horse Guards (Blues and Royals), under Sir Francis
Compton, who was senior cavalry officer in command of horse.
3 troops of Churchill's dragoons, now the Royal Dragoons (about
150 men under Lord Cornbury). The fourth troop of this regiment
was at Langport watching the passage over the river Parrett.

Artillery

Under the command of Mr Shere, helped by the Bishop of
Winchester, Dr Mews, 2 twelve-pounders, 8 demi-culverins,
4 six-pounders, 2 minions.

Totals given by various authorities differ slightly, but the
general consensus is that there were 1,800 infantrymen, 700
cavalrymen and with the artillerymen a total force of about
2,700 men.

CHAPTER 10

The First
Jacobite Rising

Preston, Sheriffmuir and Glenshiel

12–14 November 1715, 13 November 1715 and 10 June 1719

There is little to be gained from a special visit to Preston, for it has now spread almost to the bridge over the Ribble in the south and beyond the bridge (near the site of the old ford) on the Liverpool road. But a visitor to the town can still pick out some of the main features, which stand on or near the sites occupied in 1715. The parish church (rebuilt in the last century), the market place and the main street (now Church Street and Fishergate) are on their original sites, and the modern bridge across the river is not far from the old site.

Sheriffmuir, on the other hand, remains very much as it was more than 250 years ago. The battlefield lies about five miles north of Stirling between the two minor roads that run from Dunblane and Bridge of Allan to Blackford. It is difficult to be certain exactly where the fighting took place, because there were no recognizable landmarks, such as a road, village, wood or river to feature in the contemporary accounts, and there is more than one ridge to choose from. The site marked on the one-inch Ordnance Survey map (sheet 54) is probably about right. Argyll's line may have crossed the Dunblane road near the site of the MacRae cairn and stretched down towards the Wharry burn, while Mar – whose right overlapped Argyll's – would have had much of his force north of the road. The present Dunblane–Blackford road therefore runs through the site of the two positions at the outset of the battle, and from the Gathering Stone (just north of the cairn) a view of the battlefield, and the line of Mar's approach from Kinbuck, can be obtained.

Glenshiel is twenty miles west of Fort Augustus (twenty-five by road) in Ross and Cromarty. The A87 runs through the glen and the site of the battle is at the narrow pass immediately to the west of the present Forestry Commission plantations, almost exactly as marked on the one-inch Ordnance Survey map (sheet 35). The whole battlefield can be viewed from the main road, or one can climb the shoulder to the north of the road for a better view of the glen.

When James II died in exile in 1701, Louis XIV of France at once recognized his son, James Francis Edward, as James III of England and VIII of Scotland. Had not James II, and indeed his son too at a later date, refused to abjure his Catholic faith for a throne, the Prince would, in due course, have been recognized as James III in England as well. As it was this young man, who at the death of his father was only thirteen years old, was soon to be known to his supporters as the Chevalier de St George (a blatantly transparent pseudonym given to him when he embarked on his first attempt to regain the throne in 1708), and to his enemies as the Pretender.

By the Act of Settlement (1701) the crown was to pass on the death of Queen Anne to the Electress Sophia of Hanover (the granddaughter of James I) and her descendants, who were Protestants. The Electress died on 28 May 1714 (O.S.) leaving her very unattractive, narrow-minded son as the next in line. Queen Anne died less than two months later. The two men principally concerned with the government of England in the months immediately preceding the Queen's death were Robert Harley, Earl of Oxford, and Henry St John, Viscount Bolingbroke. Both had been secretly working for a Jacobite restoration while outwardly supporting the legitimate Protestant succession; both had realized that Jacobite prospects were gravely diminished, if not completely doomed, when they learned from James some five months before Anne died that he would not consent to change his religion – but Bolingbroke continued right up to the end to run with the hare and hunt with the hounds.

The Queen's death found Bolingbroke unprepared. Some say that he needed only six weeks more, but it is unlikely that he could ever have brought off a *coup de main*. He was not a forceful enough character; unpredictable and unprincipled, he failed to master events and was sadly lacking in drive or purpose. His Whig adversaries had the measure of him, and had taken every precaution to ensure that the Elector of Hanover was proclaimed king without disturbance.

At the time of Anne's death James was at Commercy, for under the terms of the Treaty of Utrecht Louis XIV had accepted the Protestant succession and James had been obliged to leave France for Lorraine. He was now twenty-six, tall, good-looking and almost as dark as his uncle Charles II. He was utterly humourless and inclined to be taciturn and withdrawn, but he was almost always courteous, rarely lost his temper and bore his many reverses with dignity. He was in an unenviable position, for any attempt to cross the Channel was bound to be obstructed. His visit to his

182

Queen Anne (above left), whose death in 1714 led the way to the first
Jacobite rebellion, and Prince James Francis Edward, the Jacobite
pretender. Both the Earl of Oxford (below left) and Viscount
Bolingbroke (below right), had been intriguing for a Jacobite
restoration even before Anne's death

King George I (left) and the Earl of Mar (right), principal supporter of the Jacobite cause after the summer of 1715

mother in France was soon discovered and he was ordered to leave that country at once. He could only issue a manifesto in which he cautioned his friends in Scotland to have patience, for no foreign help could be expected at present. On 18 September 1714 King George entered his kingdom, and soon the principal Scottish clans had sent a letter to the Earl of Mar (Secretary of State for Scotland) assuring the government of their loyalty. And yet the chances of a successful Jacobite rebellion were immeasurably greater than they were to be thirty years later. Had James been served by a capable commander in the coming months, the course of English history might have been quite different and certain disasters might have been avoided.

George I was little better than a puppet in Whig hands, and they had many personal scores to pay off. Bolingbroke realized at once that he could expect no favour under the new regime and quickly fled the country. The Duke of Ormonde, commander-in-chief of the army, had been too closely involved with Bolingbroke at the time of the Treaty of Utrecht not to expect dismissal, but he stayed on in England for a little while until the threat of impeachment drove him to join Bolingbroke in France. This left Lord Lansdown and Sir William Wyndham in charge of Jacobite affairs in England, where it had been intended to raise the standard of revolt in the summer of 1715. Bath was to be the centre, and it was planned that James should land at Plymouth. But their plans although well laid were ill concealed, and the government, acting on information and with considerable speed, stamped out this incipient revolt and arrested many of the leaders. This left the principal support for the Cause in the person of the Earl of Mar, whose surprising adherence came about when, in spite of many protestations of loyalty, he had had the seals of office taken from him in a most peremptory way.

John Erskine, sixth Earl of Mar, was a man perfectly prepared to turn his coat according to circumstances, and we may be fairly certain that in spite of a refusal by the Duke of Atholl to lead any rebellion Mar must have reckoned the chances of success to be good. Once he had decided where his interests lay he moved – almost for the only time – with speed. He summoned a number of prominent Scottish chieftains or their sons to what became known as Mar's hunting party, and they met him on 27 August. More than once James had warned him against acting precipitately, for he felt that with the collapse of the English rebellion the time was not opportune. However, at Braemar on 6 September 1715 Mar raised what was called the Restoration Standard, that symbol of hope intended to replace the constant round of intrigue and diplomacy in the council chamber with courage and skill on the battlefield.

Mar's original force at Braemar may not have numbered as many as 500, but it quickly snowballed and very soon almost all Scotland north of the Tay was under Jacobite control. He opened his campaign with a forcefulness that unfortunately was not maintained. An attempt to take Edinburgh Castle through an artifice was a dismal failure, but Lord Kinnoull's younger son John Hay secured Perth with a party of 200 horse, and King James was proclaimed with enthusiasm at Aberdeen, Montrose, Inverness, Forfar, Brechin and Dundee. By the time Mar arrived at Perth towards the end of September he had an army of some 5,000 men, which was increasing every day as more recruits came in from the Highlands. Most of these men lacked any experience, but they were malleable material given competent leadership. Having plunged precipitately into rebellion Mar seems to have thought that he could possess Scotland by sitting passively in Perth. He did not realize that if rebellions are to succeed they must be prosecuted with ruthless vigour. He possessed little military skill, and what he had was of the slow shuffling kind.

In the early autumn of 1715 the English government were rightly more apprehensive of the danger in the south-west, and although they recalled troops from Flanders* the order was rescinded when the French (now ruled by the Duke of Orleans as regent for Louis XV) assured them that they would not permit James to embark. However, in the Duke of Argyll the government possessed an able general whose intention was to block Mar's path to the south at Stirling, even though his garrison when reinforced numbered little more than 3,000. The spirit of rebellion was infectious, and in the Lowlands as well as in the north of England men of import-ance had come out in favour of the Jacobite cause. Mar held all the cards: had he been a man of action and played them with determination he might have gained the kingdom for his new master. With his superior numbers he could have swept Argyll's force, the only obstacle to his joining hands with the southern rebels, out of existence. But instead he stayed at Perth and sent Brigadier Mackintosh of Borlum with 2,000 men on a somewhat vague expedition to the south.

Mackintosh's adventures are a story of their own, which we can pick up only on his arrival at Kelso, where he joined two other Jacobite contingents. Ormonde's hurried flight to France and his subsequent signs of recreancy had produced an atmosphere of uncertainty, if not defeatism, among Jacobite supporters in the south and west of England. It was, however, different in the north, where men like the Earl of Derwentwater, Mr Thomas Forster (the Member for Northumberland) and Lord Widdrington came out in arms. Among the Lowlanders, too, the Cause received considerable support, and the third party now assembled at Kelso included Lords Kenmure, Nithsdale, Carnwath and Winton.

These three forces had united at Kelso by 22 October. A con-temporary chronicler† gives the total as 1,400 foot and 600 horse, but this is clearly wrong and must exclude Mackintosh's men, which even allowing for those he failed to get across the Forth and some subsequent desertions would have numbered a thousand or more. Mar had commissioned Lord Kenmure to command the Scots and Thomas Forster the English contingent. It was con-sidered that the Cause would be best served by giving the command to a Protestant, otherwise there could be no excuse for Forster's commission: he may have been a good Member of Parliament, but he had no conception of the military art.

* Two-thirds of a total army of 22,000 were at this moment serving abroad, and in Scotland there were only some 1,500 men.

† Peter Rae, *The History of the Rebellion rais'd against His Majesty King George I by the Friends of the Popish Pretender*, p. 268.

At a council to decide on the next move opinions were divided. The Englishmen under Forster, short of arms and without artillery, had already made a feeble attempt to take Newcastle, and a suggestion that they should try again with the much stronger combined force was ruled out through a quite unjustified fear of General Carpenter's strength. Dumfries was found to be too well guarded, but had there been any coordination by Mar the obvious course of a joint attack from north and south on Argyll at Stirling must have succeeded, and with Scotland secure the advance into England, which was finally decided upon, could have been more easily undertaken.

Thomas Forster was the moving spirit of a bold strike into north-west England. He promised that in Lancashire they would find overwhelming support for the rebellion. However, the Scots were very loath to undertake what they deemed a grave and almost desperate venture: eventually Forster overcame their reluctance, but 500 Highlanders turned for home, only to end their march in an Edinburgh prison. Lord Winton also would not at first conform to the agreed plan and led off a body of his men, but soon seeing where his duty lay turned back upon the road that was to lead him to the Tower. The small (less than 3,000 men) but reasonably well equipped army crossed the border on 1 November and spent that night at Brampton. A large rabble of mainly unarmed peasants had been hastily got together by Lord Lonsdale and the militant Bishop of Carlisle to bar the invaders' way north of Penrith, but on sighting their enemy they quickly dispersed. Thereafter Forster's march through Appleby, Kendal, Kirby Lonsdale and Lancaster was notable only for the few recruits who rallied to the Chevalier's standard. On the night of 9 November the Jacobite horse entered Preston. Two troops of Colonel Stanhope's dragoons, who were in the town, withdrew without offering any resistance.

On 10 November the foot also arrived in Preston, and Forster, who had been assured through his local intelligence system that he could expect ample warning of any enemy approach, intended resting his army for a day or two before proceeding to Manchester. It came as a considerable surprise to him, therefore, to learn on the 12th that General Wills, who commanded the royalist troops in Cheshire, was at hand with five cavalry and three infantry regiments. Moreover, General Carpenter, displaying an offensive spirit that went far to compensate for the inferior material at his disposal, was said to be closing in from the north-east. This information seems to have proved too much for Forster, who issued a series of orders and counter-orders then retired to his lodgings. When, a little later, Colonel Oxburgh and Lords Kenmure and Widdrington reported for orders they found their 'general' in bed.

Preston was a quite unprotected small market town, but a resolute commander could have put up a strong defence. The key point to be held was the bridge over the Ribble and John Farquharson of Invercauld had been sent there by Forster with a small force of picked men. Farquharson had plenty of courage and he and his men would have given a good account of themselves, but at the first hint of danger they were withdrawn to the town. Wills was so amazed at finding the bridge unguarded that he immediately suspected an ambush in the narrow lane with its high hedges that led from the bridge up the hill to the town. He therefore proceeded with caution, which enabled the Jacobites to perfect their dispositions. These were fairly skilfully laid out, and reflect some other hand than Forster's.

Barricades were set up blocking the main entrances to the town, and proper use was made of the houses and narrow lanes as points of defence. The Jacobites possessed six cannon, and if these could have been properly manned the royalists, who were without artillery, would have been more severely mauled than was the case; but without trained gunners what little advantage they offered was chiefly psychological. Brigadier Mackintosh of Borlum commanded the barricade set up to the east of the church in the main street, and was supported by the Earl of Derwentwater's troops, who were in position in the churchyard. Another member of Clan Mackintosh commanded what was known as the windmill barrier, which was situated on the Lancaster road, while the one on the Liverpool road was under a Major Mills. Lord Charles Murray blocked a lane leading into fields across which General Carpenter's troops were expected. By midday on 12 November Preston was in a state of adequate defence.

General Wills, having discovered that the approach lanes to the town were clear and that the Jacobites had decided to make a stand, launched a two-point attack. Brigadier Honywood, commanding his own dragoons, and Preston's foot under Lord Forrester, attacked Borlum's post, while Brigadiers Dormer and Munden led a mixed force of infantry and dismounted cavalry against the Lancaster barricade. Little headway was made against this barrier and the attack does not seem to have been a very spirited affair. But on the Wigan side of the town the battle was fiercely contested and the Jacobites, firing from the protection of houses, inflicted considerable casualties on Wills's men.

The strength of Borlum's position was that between the double

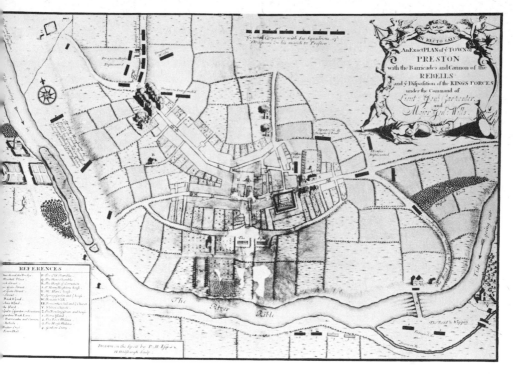

Above: Contemporary town plan of Preston
Below: Battle of Preston

barricade set up to the east of the church there stood two of the largest houses in the town. These belonged to Sir Henry Haughton and Mr Hare; both houses had been occupied by Highlanders. A frontal attack down the road had no chance of success so long as the attackers were subject to enfilade fire from these houses; but when Lord Forrester infiltrated his regiment through the gardens between the church and the two houses the position was dangerous, but by no means critical – that is, until the troops in the larger house (Haughton's) were withdrawn. It is not clear from contemporary accounts of the battle why Mackintosh did this, but it was a fatal error. Before nightfall Preston's regiment was in possession of both these houses, although in getting them they suffered the only heavy casualties of the whole battle.

A third attack had also been launched against Lord Charles Murray's barricade, but this had been held after heavy fighting in the course of which Murray had had to ask for reinforcements from Derwentwater. As night drew on and the whip-lash sound of close-range bullets became less persistent the Jacobites could be well content with the day's work, for all the barriers were still intact, although the one by the church had become dangerously vulnerable. However, all was not well among the rebel soldiery: royalist prisoners taken in the fighting soon dispelled all hopes that any of their colleagues would desert. Some Jacobites with cool heads, and cold feet, made their way out of the town while there was still time – for the next day General Carpenter arrived and immediately sealed off all exits.

Carpenter claimed the credit for the victory, but at the time he commended General Wills for the fighting on the 12th, and the only serious flaw that he could find in his dispositions was that the bridge and ford across the Ribble had been left unguarded. Once these exits had been closed the rebels were bottled up, but there was little doubt that they could have fought their way out. However, much to the disgust of the Highlanders, caitiff counsels in the end prevailed. On 14 November the English marched in and disarmed Forster's men. The number of prisoners taken was about 1,500, of which seventy-five were English noblemen or gentlemen and 143 Scottish. Most of the rank and file taken were Scotsmen and they were treated with considerable savagery. The important prisoners were taken to London and some were sentenced to death. Both Mackintosh of Borlum and Forster escaped from Newgate – but whereas Forster decided that exile in France was preferable to any further military forays, we shall meet Mackintosh again. The Jacobite casualties were only eighteen killed and twenty-five wounded, as opposed to about 200 royalists killed or wounded, most of whom were from Preston's regiment.

The Battle of Preston terminated the Jacobite insurrection in England; but at almost exactly the same time as Forster and his officers were negotiating the surrender in Lancashire an even more disastrous blow to James's cause was struck on a lonely moor near Stirling. Although Mar had scarcely stirred from Perth since his arrival there at the end of September, a constant stream of recruits had doubled his army to around 10,000 men,* and behind him almost the whole of Scotland was held for James. At last even Mar (whom James had made a duke in October) thought that his force was sufficiently formidable to permit him to venture forth, and on 10 November he left Perth with the intention of joining up with the Jacobites in Lancashire. He planned three diversionary crossings of the Forth, each with 1,000 men, in the neighbourhood of Stirling, while he himself crossed the river higher up with the main body. At Auchterarder General Gordon joined him from Doune, and he was put in command of the 3,000 men with orders to secure Dunblane as his first objective.

However, Argyll had quickly learned of Mar's plan, and he was not the man to let his small army be defeated in detail or to sit back in Stirling and await attack. He immediately called in his outlying garrisons and advanced to Dunblane before Gordon could reach the town. On the bitterly cold night of 12 November he had his army encamped on the high ground some two miles east of Dunblane, and on this commanding feature he awaited Mar. On becoming aware of Argyll's advance, General Gordon fell back on the main army, which in the meantime had marched down the drove leading from Greenloaning to Kinbuck. Here the army encamped, and at daybreak the next morning Mar marched for Sheriffmuir, where with a superiority in numbers of three to one he had reason to be confident of the outcome of any engagement.

Argyll was well acquainted with the site, for the name Sheriff-muir derives from the place's use as a training ground for the militia. When he found that the recent hard frosts had enabled his cavalry to ride over the usually wet Lynns he extended his line to reach from the high ground just above the present Dun-blane–Blackford road down the slope towards the Wharry burn. He formed his army into two lines. The first comprised six battalions of infantry, with each wing protected by three squadrons of

* This was probably the number after the Frasers had deserted Fraser of Fraserdale shortly before the battle when their chief (Simon Fraser, eleventh Lord Lovat) took the government's side.

dragoons and an additional squadron behind each of the wings; the second line had only two battalions of foot and one squadron of dragoons to each wing. Argyll commanded the right wing, General Wightman the centre and General Whetham the left.

Although Argyll from his vantage point near the Gathering Stone could see a part of the Jacobite army, neither commander was properly aware of the other's dispositions, for much of Mar's approach march from Kinbuck had been in dead ground. Mar also formed his army into two lines. The ten battalions of infantry in the first line were mostly Highlanders, and there were a further ten battalions in the second line with a reserve of 800 men. The Stirling squadron (who had charge of the standard) and two squadrons of Huntly's horse protected the right flank of the first line with the Perthshire and Fifeshire squadrons on the left; the Earl Marischal's squadron was on the right of the second line and the Angus squadrons on the left. The Earl Marischal was in overall command of the cavalry, while General Gordon commanded on the right of the line and General Hamilton on the left. Mar took position at the right centre of the front line.

Thus, shortly before midday on this cold November morning, these two armies formed up for battle within a very short distance of each other without either side being perfectly aware of what the other was about. The Jacobites, confident of victory, were in a mood of great exhilaration, tossing their bonnets in the air and emitting loud huzzas. After Mar had delivered to the heads of clans what even his sternest critics described as a stirring address, the order to advance was given. On the one side of the ridge colourful plaids and kilts, on the other brilliant uniforms with flaunted facings of scarlet and blue: a pageantry of splendour, so soon to become a sorry scene of disarray.

Contemporary accounts of the muddle into which the rebel army got itself as it advanced to the attack are confusing and, as each soldier-scribe is seeking to justify his action, often contradictory. But it appears that as soon as the Jacobites topped the crest of the ridge it was seen that the right wings of both armies overlapped the other's left. Both Mar's lines were advancing in column of battalions, and his hasty attempt to deploy and extend to his left resulted in the front and rear lines of that wing becoming entangled. What was more serious, the cavalry on the left – perhaps on account of the boggy ground – edged to their right, leaving the infantry unprotected.

Argyll was in a position to observe the confusion into which the Jacobite left had been thrown and he wasted no time in exploiting

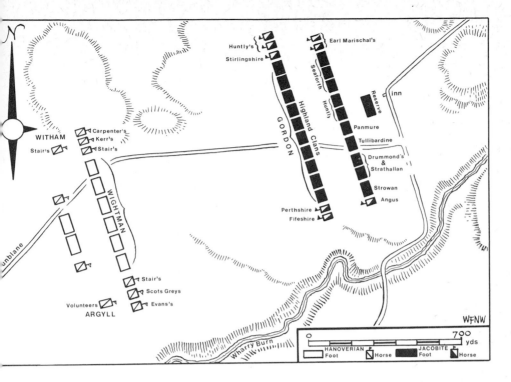

Above and below: Battle of Sheriffmuir

it. He went into the attack at the head of five squadrons of dragoons and five battalions of foot, as well as sixty mounted volunteers under the Earl of Rothes. Taken off balance, the Highlanders nevertheless put up an amazingly stout resistance, more especially when the Fife and Angus squadrons had dislocated themselves from the centre and come to their assistance. Wherever the ground was favourable this retreating left wing stood and fought with much stubbornness, but gradually they were pressed back in a two-mile half-circle to the river Allan, which they crossed – still under pressure – in the neighbourhood of Kinbuck.

Sheriffmuir was an inconclusive and untidy battle, for Argyll, although a greatly superior general to Mar, seems to have been guilty of going into the attack before he had assured himself that his left wing was adequately protected. In fact it too, although to a lesser degree than the Jacobite left, was still getting into position when Mar ordered the Highland clans on his right and two squadrons of horse into the attack. At the same time, unaware of what was happening on his left, he sent an aide-de-camp to General Hamilton with orders to advance that wing. Mar's attack opened with a sharp bout of musketry, both armies firing at almost point-blank range. The ranks shivered like corn in the wind, and among the Highlanders the popular Captain of Clanranald fell, but Glengarry rallied the clan and crying for revenge they discarded their muskets and were quickly among the militia with their broadswords. It was all over in a matter of minutes: Argyll's left was chased from the field and even to the outskirts of Stirling.

The field of battle was now almost deserted, for owing to lack of enthusiasm, if not actual disobedience of orders, the Master of Sinclair and his cavalry remained totally inactive throughout, and this allowed Argyll's centre to join in the pursuit of the Jacobite left. Both commanders learned of the disasters to their respective left wings while two miles from the scene of battle, both having assumed the victory to be theirs. Mar retraced his steps, with his right wing virtually intact, and occupied the high ground from Stonehill to the Gathering Stone. This wing alone was larger than the whole of Argyll's army, and he would have had little difficulty in annihilating the victorious royalist troops, whom he could clearly see from his commanding position above Kippendavie. But Mar in his weak, indecisive way lacked the manhood to dare, and he even allowed some enemy stragglers to pass underneath his hill unscathed. For the rest of the day the two protagonists, with what was left of their troops, remained passively watching each other. Then, as the early darkness closed in, Mar marched his men back

194

to Ardoch and Argyll camped in and around Dunblane.

If a victory was to be claimed by either side Argyll had that slender right, for on the next day he re-occupied the battlefield and gathered up the spoils – which were considerable. The royalists admitted to 290 killed, 187 men wounded and over 100 taken prisoner, most of whom were shortly released for want of means to accommodate them. Mar owned to the loss of only sixty men and eighty-two prisoners. Casualties were not too high, partly because artillery played no part in this battle, but certainly the Jacobites lost more than they admitted to – possibly 300–400 – and very probably the royalists did too. Apart from the Captain of Clanranald the Earl of Strathmore was the only Jacobite of importance to be killed, while the government troops lost the Earl of Forfar.

For the Jacobites anything less than a victory was a defeat. Loss of prestige was serious, resulting in many of the clansmen going home – Seaforth's people being hastened on their way by the news that the government had taken Inverness. There was now no chance of joining up with the army in England, and indeed the simultaneous defeat at Preston virtually brought the rebellion to a close, even though James was to arrive in Scotland in just over a month's time. The Hanoverian hand fell heavily on all who had come 'out' for the Chevalier. Nineteen Scottish and two English peerages were attainted; the Earl of Derwentwater* and Lord Kenmure were executed in 1716, and Lords Nithsdale and Winton saved their heads only through daring escapes.

The French did what they could to obstruct James's attempt to reach Scotland – even unloading the ship carrying a large quantity of arms that he had bought – and when he found their efforts unavailing Lord Stair (English ambassador in Paris) made his own arrangements to have the Chevalier murdered. The intended victim, however, having disappeared in the night from the court of Lorraine and run the gauntlet through France in a series of exciting adventures, eventually took ship from Dunkirk on 16 December and arrived in Peterhead harbour on the 22nd.

James's six-week stay in Scotland was one of almost continual disappointment. Tired and dispirited, ill and fevered, he made his way incognito through Aberdeen to Feteresso Castle, where he took to his bed for nine days. Then by way of Brechin and Glamis he reached Scone on 8 January 1716. Plans were made for his

* His brother Charles Radclyffe was imprisoned, but escaped and assumed the title—even though it had been attainted. He was captured at sea in 1746 and executed for his part at Preston.

coronation to take place there on 23 January, but by that time Argyll (and his difficult second-in-command General Cadogan) was stirring with an army three times the size of the one he commanded at Sheriffmuir, and the Jacobite court was preparing to move north.

James had not required the constant prompting of Bolingbroke and his nephew the Duke of Berwick to come to Scotland, but the latter's persistent refusal to accompany his uncle and the news – received just before he sailed – of Ormonde's second failure to invade England, were grievous blows, which he knew greatly diminished his prospects of success. Nothing occurred in Scotland to make him think otherwise. General Hamilton, whom he sent to France with an urgent appeal for help, had no luck there; Argyll, recently superseded and rightly considered to be discontented, nevertheless disregarded a letter from James, and Huntly was busy coming to terms with the Hanoverians. There were some still willing to join the pathetic remnants of the Jacobite army in Perth had James called them to arms, but many more would have done so had he arrived at the head of a well equipped French army. Mostly his Scotsmen were disappointed in him, and his weakness in agreeing to his advisers' foolish scorched earth policy before Perth did him personally, and the Cause generally, much harm.

By the end of January winter had the country in its firm grip, but Argyll commandeered the local people to clear the roads of snow and advanced on Perth. The Jacobite army retreated through Dundee to Montrose and here Mar persuaded James to embark for France in a ship that he had conveniently at hand. Mar said that the retreating army could make better terms without James – but he had no intention of staying himself to make these terms. James sailed for France on 4 February with Mar, the Earl of Melfort and Lord Drummond. A second boat sailed shortly afterwards with some other gentlemen.

The Jacobite army, now abandoned by both its sovereign and its commander-in-chief, continued its sorrowful way north in surprisingly good order. Argyll made what haste he could – although Cadogan thought otherwise – but he was never able to come to grips with the rebel army and probably took no more than 100 prisoners. Once into the Highlands this undaunted but sadly disillusioned band of men was safe from pursuit, and able to melt away to the comparative security of their remote fastnesses. The process of cleaning up, as it was euphemistically called, continued for over a year until with the Act of Pardon, passed in May 1717, Scotland was considered to be pacified.

The defeat at Preston, the fiasco of Sheriffmuir, the disheartening performance of James in Scotland, and the flight of many prominent Jacobite leaders to France had torn the entrails out of the movement for the time being. And when, just over three years later, an attempt was made to rekindle the flames of rebellion it quickly died of its own inanition.

The prime mover in the 1719 rising was the Spanish Cardinal Alberoni, whose policy had become increasingly hostile to England, France and Austria as a result of the Treaty of Utrecht in 1713, through which Spain lost both land and prestige. Matters went from bad to worse and on 17 December 1718 Britain declared war on Spain. Cardinal Alberoni decided to strike at England through the Jacobite movement; he was willing to supply money and what troops he could spare. The Duke of Ormonde was once more to attempt an invasion, landing on the south-west coast, and there was to be a smaller subsidiary landing on the west coast of Scotland. For this latter purpose the Earl Marischal and his brother James Keith were summoned to Spain and given instructions to return to France and recruit such prominent exiles as the Marquess of Tullibardine, his brother Lord George Murray, the Earl of Seaforth, John Cameron of Lochiel and Macdonald of Keppoch.

The main expedition under Ormonde, comprising 5,000 men and 15,000 arms in twenty-nine ships, sailed from Cadiz on 27 March (N.S.).* Two days later the fleet met with the usual Stuart weather at sea and was driven back to port with sufficient loss to incapacitate it. The smaller fleet, carrying the Jacobite leaders, 307 Spanish soldiers and a good quantity of arms and ammunition, sailed on varying dates and from different French ports. After an unpleasant and dangerous journey round the north coast, and a certain amount of island-hopping on the west coast, the fleet was finally united off Eilean Donan Castle at the head of Loch Alsh on 2 April (O.S.), but owing to the difficulty of finding boats it was not until 17 April that all the arms, powder and supplies had been safely landed.

Here the small force remained for several weeks while the leaders engaged in argument and recrimination. Tullibardine disputed the command with the Earl Marischal, basing his claim to leadership on an outdated commission from King James. Keith gave way so far as the land troops were concerned, but insisted

* The difference between dates prevailing on the continent to those in England was at this time eleven days, owing to our not adopting the Gregorian calendar (New Style (N.S.)) until 1752. The fleet would have left Cadiz on 6 April by Old Style (O.S.) dating.

197

on keeping command of the fleet. Two consequences of this disagreement were that Tullibardine and Keith set up camps separated by some two miles, which only increased existing difficulties, and that when Tullibardine showed signs of wishing to re-embark the troops and withdraw (which in the event would have been the wiser course) Keith sent the ships away. Lochiel and the Captain of Clanranald were sent to their own country to see how matters were, and letters were despatched to other clans urging them to rise. But most of the clansmen were loath to do so without some positive sign that numbers, so woefully misused at Sheriffmuir, were once more on their side.

The consensus among the leaders was that as theirs was only a diversionary operation no advance inland should be made before news of Ormonde's landing was received, but before the fate of the Duke's fleet was known matters at Eilean Donan had become critical. On 9 May three government warships appeared in Loch Alsh, and information (false as it turned out) was received that enemy troops were within twenty miles. It was clearly time for action to replace argument: an advance base for ammunition and stores was established at the Crow of Kintail,* and letters were urgently sent for Lochiel and Macdonald to rendezvous with as many men as they could. Soon some encouraging news was brought from Edinburgh: although the Duke of Ormonde had failed in his enterprise, he sent word from Spain that the Scottish rising should proceed and he promised to support it with arms and money. Now prodded from behind by the royalist navy and fed with vague promises from the front, the Jacobite force moved towards Glenshiel by two different routes. One party marched down the east bank of Loch Duich, while another went via Loch Long and then over the high ground north of Loch Duich.

About six miles south-east of Loch Duich the high hills on each side of the present road almost join; here the road, then nothing more than a cattle drove, winds through a pass not fifty yards wide. It was a place where a handful of resolute men might have held up an army for days. The Jacobites arrived at this pass towards the end of May. On 4 June Lochiel joined them with 150 men, Seaforth had raised 400 of his clan, and there were perhaps a further thousand Highlanders assembled. Three days later a party of Chisholm's men came in with information that a royalist army under General Wightman had passed through Fort Augustus

---

* A small garrison of forty soldiers and two officers left at Eilean Donan in charge of the main ammunition supply were forced to surrender to the men-of-war, and the castle was destroyed.

and was now marching down Glen Moriston. The Jacobites had had plenty of time in which to prepare their dispositions (some sangars had been constructed in the pass), and when on the 9th they learned that the enemy was encamped for the night at the head of Loch Cluanie they were ready to give battle the next day.

The narrow pass is just to the west of where there is now a conifer plantation. The Jacobite right, under Lord George Murray, took up a position on the foothills immediately to the south of the drove, with advance patrols some way forward. The 250 Spaniards held the rocky hillside immediately north of the drove, and above them came Lochiel and his 150 clansmen, then forty of Rob Roy's rascals, and further up were men under commanders such as Sir John Mackenzie, Brigadiers Campbell of Ormidale and Glendaruel, and Brigadier Mackintosh of Borlum. Lord Seaforth, with 200 of his best men, was in a commanding position about half a mile up the steep hill.

Against this Jacobite force of 1,600 Highlanders and 250 Spaniards, General Wightman had 850 foot, 120 dragoons and 136 Highlanders. This was no country for cavalry, so the dragoons had been dismounted on entering the glen. They, together with the six coehorn mortars advanced along the line of the drove. On the extreme right Wightman placed his Mackays from Sutherland, then came some 200 Grenadiers under Major Richard Milburn, the 11th

Battle of Glenshiel

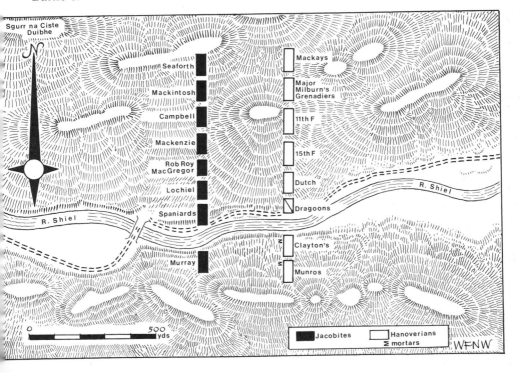

and 15th Foot, and a Dutch contingent. This right wing was com-manded by Colonel Clayton, whose own regiment, under Lieutenant-Colonel Reading, formed part of the left wing which advanced south of the drove with the Monros on the extreme left.

The engagement began on the Jacobite right soon after midday, when Lord George Murray's advance picquets contested ground as they gradually fell back onto the main position, but it was not until after 5 p.m. that the battle proper began. Undoubtedly the mortars played an important part in this short fight. They were used in the first instance against Lord George's men, who promptly withdrew from the very exposed hillock to the south of the drove, thus leaving the pass virtually unguarded. They were then turned upon the Spaniards, and firing at extreme range they probably did little harm, but they set the heather on fire, which must have caused confusion in the ever-narrowing funnel of attack. Mean-while the Mackays, having made light of the steep and rocky ascent, had got round Seaforth's flank, and in the short bout of musketry that followed the Earl got a ball in the arm. Soon the Jacobite left was in retreat, and although the Earl Marischal and Brigadier Campbell of Ormidale held the centre steady for a while it was not long before these men, and then Lord Tullibardine with the Spaniards, were seen to be scampering up the hillside and away through the pass that leads round the north side of the Sgurr na Ciste Duibhe. Before darkness fell on 10 June 1719 the Jacobite army had disintegrated and the Pretender's troops in Scotland had suffered the last of the repeated blows of fortune.

The surprising ease with which the King's army rolled up the rebels is no indication of the Highlanders' inability to hold an almost impregnable position. The fact is that this was just a face-saving affair. The will to win was lacking, for no one would have known what to do with the victory had it been gained. The battle was chiefly notable in that it was probably the only one in which Highlanders fought without charging or engaging in hand-to-hand grapple. The Spaniards, being unable to melt into the countryside, had to surrender, but the battle casualties were quite insignificant. Wightman lost twenty-one killed and perhaps double that number wounded, while there is no reliable record of any Jacobites being killed. However, some there must have been; and no doubt the figure of less than ten mentioned in Field-Marshal Keith's memoir is about right. Lord George Murray was among those wounded, but he soon recovered and almost thirty years later, when another and more romantic Jacobite prince resolved to venture upon the hazards of invasion, he was to play a most important part.

200

CHAPTER 11

The Second Jacobite Rebellion

Prestonpans, Falkirk and Culloden

21 September 1745, 23 January 1746 and 16 April 1746

Prestonpans and Falkirk were fought not far from Pinkie Cleuch and Falkirk (1298) respectively. The Prestonpans site is not very rewarding, as too much of it is now built over. About half a mile south of the crossed swords on the one-inch Ordnance Survey map (sheet 62) the local authority has marked the site of the battle with a notice and a useful description and plan, but sadly this has been greatly defaced. This noticeboard stands beside the A198 road between the road and the railway line, and is backed by some hideous slag heaps. The ruin of Colonel Gardiner's house still stands about half a mile north-west of Tranent church, where the Colonel was buried.

At Falkirk a stone stands on the side road just off the B803 road leading out of Falkirk to the south-west. This monument is close to where the fight took place; from it a footpath leads north along the side of the ravine which was such an important feature on the Hanoverian right and Jacobite left. The ground on either side of the ravine is still open country, as it is to the south of the stone where the battle was chiefly fought – although what was wet moorland is now good agricultural land. One can get a fair idea of the lie of the land either from an open field about a quarter of a mile down the footpath, or from vantage points just off the B803 road south of the stone.

The field of Culloden is very accessible, being only a little east of Inverness, off the Inverness–Perth road (A9). The B9006, which runs east from the A9 to Nairn, takes the visitor to the National Trust for Scotland's Information Centre on the site of the battle. It is possible to walk over much of the battlefield, but the Forestry Commission plantations prevent one from seeing the ground as a whole – no trees obscured the superb views of the Moray and Beauly Firths at the time of the battle. However, what disadvantages there may be from the restricted view of the site are compensated for by the National Trust for Scotland, who have at their centre a very useful audio-visual exhibit running during the summer season which supplements an excellent guidebook and most interesting museum.

201

On 23 July 1745 the little frigate *La Doutelle* dropped anchor off the island of Eriskay. After an eventful and exciting sea journey of eighteen days Prince Charles Edward Louis Philip Casimir Stuart had come home.

For the past two years messengers had been travelling between Edinburgh and Paris, and the hopes of Jacobites were high. The political climate was far less favourable for their cause than it had been thirty years before (see chapter 10); nevertheless there was reason for cautious optimism. The French defeat at Dettingen in June 1743 had so infuriated Louis XV that he at last agreed to mount a full-scale invasion of England and Scotland with a force of 13,000 troops under Marshal Saxe, and the Chevalier de St George, himself no longer fit for active service, sent his eldest son from Rome to accompany the Marshal on his important enterprise. But the weather, which never ceased to play scurvy tricks on the Stuarts, battered and scattered the warships and transports before they had even left Dunkirk and other embarkation ports: the invasion was off.

Prince Charles Edward returned to Paris, and after a year of frustration as a seemingly unwanted pawn on Louis's political chessboard he decided that he could wait no longer on the whims of the French king. Without French aid his prospects were doubtful, but he was well aware that time was running out: the Stuart flame

Entry of Prince Charles Edward Stuart into Edinburgh

was flickering and might soon be extinguished. Therefore with a handful of companions, who became known as the Seven Men of Moidart, for it was on the borders of Arisaig and Moidart that the party first stepped ashore on the Scottish mainland, he set forth on a venture that was hazardous in the extreme.

At the time that he landed in Scotland the Prince was not quite twenty-five years old; he was a tall, good-looking young man much more given to the field than the drawing room. He possessed many outdoor accomplishments and great physical stamina; his courage was undoubted and his capacity to endure hardships unrivalled, but although his charm and debonair manner have in retrospect irradiated the last years of a doomed dynasty, these and other popular qualities tend to be exaggerated. History has clothed his name with a romantic aura, but in truth this prince was seldom 'bonnie', and although he contrived to behave with fortitude and dignity in times of misfortune his mercurial temperament quickly plunged him from the pinnacle of optimism to the depths of despair, and he found it more difficult than his father had to bear the disappointments and disillusionments that crowded upon him.

The immediate response of the Highlanders to their prince's landing was not encouraging – indeed even at the height of his success he never commanded more than 9,000 men out of an estimated warrior strength, if the clans could ever be united in a common cause, of some 32,000. The romantic conception of the Forty-five as a popular and glorious crusade is misplaced. Charles, arriving unaided, was in the main unwanted, and only his determination and an early display of loyalty by Lochiel and one or two other chiefs saved the day. When Alexander Macdonald of Boisdale, almost the first chief to meet him, advised the Prince to go home, Charles replied, 'I am come home, sir, and I will entertain no notion at all of returning to that place from whence I come; for that I am persuaded my faithful Highlanders will stand by me.' And in the event a great many of them did. By 19 August, when the huge white, red and blue silk standard was broken at Glenfinnan, there had gathered some 200 Clanranald Macdonalds, and Alexander Macdonald of Keppoch was on his way with 300 more men. And we can readily imagine what joy there must have been in that little valley flanked by mountains of timeless antiquity when the sound of the Cameron pipers could be heard in the distance leading 700 of their clansmen towards the royal standard. Donald Cameron of Lochiel had been one of those who advised the Prince to return, but when he saw the spirit of the man he declared, 'I'll share the fate of my prince; and so shall every man over whom nature or fortune hath given me any power.' And, like many others, he never wavered in his loyalty to the very end.

The march to Edinburgh and the south had begun. The road was not to be broad and easy, and in the many hazards that lay ahead only success would keep the clans together and hold the wolves at bay – and at first success attended them everywhere. General Cope, with an English army of not more than 3,000 men, most of them raw recruits in whom he could place little trust, failed to intercept the Highlanders or prevent them from taking Edinburgh. But shipping his army from Aberdeen to Dunbar, he set off immediately on disembarkation to oppose them. At a council of war held in the Highlanders' camp near Duddingston it was agreed that their army should not wait for the English to attack, but should march against them. By now the Prince had a fighting force of about 2,500 men, although he was completely without artillery and his cavalry arm consisted of only some forty horsemen under Lord Strathallan. Against this force General Cope mustered 2,300 men, which included the 13th and 14th Dragoons, and six cannon – the latter manned by a team of very inadequate nautical gunners.

On the morning of 20 September, when the clans had been assembled and were ready to leave camp, the Prince addressed the chiefs. Having reminded them of the good cause for which they were about to fight he ended by dramatically drawing his sword from its scabbard and declaring, 'Gentlemen, I have flung away the scabbard; with God's help I will make you a free and happy people.' Shortly afterwards Lord George Murray,* the Prince's most able commander, led the army out of camp, across the river Esk and on towards the enemy. Soon they reached Fawside Hill, and moving along its crest they were within half a mile of the village of Tranent when the English army came into view. Sir John Cope was in the vicinity of Seton when Lord Loudoun brought him the news that the Jacobites were on the march. But he was in no way alarmed, for he reckoned he had reached the ideal battleground for his horse and foot. Certainly his first position facing west was a very strong one, being protected on three sides – to the north the sea and villages, to the west a ten-foot boundary wall

---

* Lord George Murray, who as a young man had fought at Glenshiel (see pp. 198–200), joined the Prince at Perth; he was the younger brother of William Murray, the Jacobite Duke of Atholl. Made a lieutenant-general in the army, he usually held the most important command in the field, although the Prince was titular commander-in-chief. He had many enemies among the Prince's cronies, and there was often friction between him and the Prince with most unfortunate consequences to the Cause.

surrounding Preston House park, and south of that Colonel Gardiner's house, which was almost surrounded by what Cope believed to be an impenetrable marsh. When he discovered that the rebel army was facing him from the south and not the west he swung his army round to what was an even stronger position, for the marsh was then on his immediate front.

The Forty-five campaign was throughout bedevilled by the fractious conduct of the senior officers, and the fact that command was based on the principle of limited liability. Only at Culloden did the Prince take actual command of the army, and nearly every decision – even after he had stopped holding councils – was imposed upon him, often against his better judgement, by a cabal of ill assorted advisers. One of the Seven Men of Moidart was an Irishman called Colonel John William O'Sullivan, who on account of his supposed military knowledge had been made adjutant-general and quartermaster-general of the army; this man disliked Lord George Murray intensely, and the dislike was reciprocated. Their incapacity to cooperate manifested itself for the first time just before the battle began, when Lord George, who on this occasion shared the command with the Duke of Perth, proceeded to make and execute a plan without informing either the Prince or the Adjutant-General.

Earlier Lord George had sent Colonel Ker of Graden to reconnoitre the enemy position, and on learning from him that it was almost impregnable he decided that the enemy could only be attacked from the east. Accordingly he led off with the Camerons, sending a message back to the Prince asking him to follow with the remaining front line troops, less the Atholl brigade and a reserve to be temporarily left on Fawside to confuse the enemy. This exposure of his flank to the enemy in broad daylight violated all the principles of O'Sullivan's military training – but his protests were in vain. Cope was certainly somewhat confused, but until he knew what Murray was about he was determined not to be taken by surprise, and he had outposts guarding the narrow defile between Preston and Bankton Houses and all other approaches. But although the Athollmen and the reserves did not rejoin the main army until after dark the barking of the dogs as they passed through Tranent clearly indicated the design. Cope then swung his line round once more, this time to face almost due east. He now prepared for battle with the 44th regiment on the right, the 46th on the left, and eight companies of the 47th and two of the 6th in the centre (for table of regiments in the English army see page 224). His guns were all on the right of the line. On the right of the foot were two squadrons of the 13th Dragoons, and on the left two squadrons of the 14th. In reserve there was a single squadron from each cavalry regiment.

The Jacobite army, having passed through Tranent and round the front of the enemy, still had to cross the marsh before reaching suitable ground over which to attack. One of their number, a local man called Robert Anderson, volunteered to show them a track that he knew well from snipe-shooting, and in the early hours of the morning he led the way. The mist swirled up from the bog as the wraith-like army wound its silent way through a defile near Riggonhead Farm and on through the morass. Suddenly there was a challenge from an enemy patrol, who scurried back to give the alarm, but as day was breaking Anderson had the army safely across the bank that divided the marsh from an open stubble field. The Duke of Perth led the van, and in the half-light he mistook the distance he had to go to ensure that the rear was clear of the bog before facing left. In consequence there was a large gap between the two halves of the army which might have proved serious had the English cavalry been able to exploit it – but the dragoons, who had already made an undignified exit from Edinburgh, were again to be found unworthy of their calling. This need to clear the end of the marsh also meant that the Jacobite left was not exactly opposite the English right, and the greatly extended line not only gave Cope a mistaken idea of the enemy numbers but posed a threat to his left flank. He therefore sent his aide-de-camp to fetch two guns from the right of the line. But he was too late: the civilian drivers and nautical gun crews had already left the field.

Murray, in personal command of the left wing, went into the attack somewhat before the right half of the Jacobite army. The sun was just rising, drawing more vapours from the marshes, as with a great yell 500 Camerons, 250 Appin Stewarts and 200 men of the Duke of Perth's charged obliquely to their left across the 200 yards that separated them from the English line. At once Colonel Whitefoord and another officer manipulated the guns so shamefully abandoned by their recreant crews; they managed to discharge five of the 1½-pounders and all the mortars, although the latter were of little effect. For a moment the Highland line reeled and there were a few casualties, but without trained gun crews the artillery was powerless against the irresistible charge of the clansmen. When the outposts had been called in there had been insufficient time to send the men to their regiments, so they had been told to fall in on the right of the line. This cramped the 13th Dragoons for space and necessitated one squadron being formed

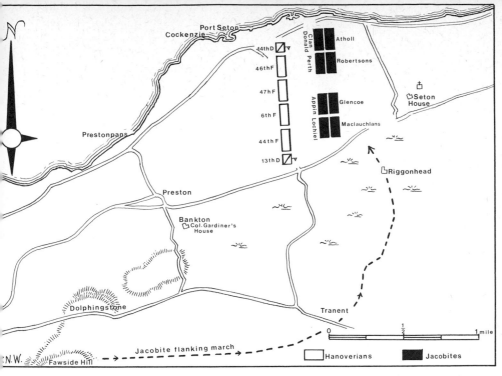

Battle of Prestonpans

up in the rear. The crowded position in which they found themselves may also have had some bearing on their refusal to charge.
Both Colonel Whitney's squadron, and Colonel Gardiner's which
was in the rear, failed to obey their commanders, one volley from
the Highlanders being sufficient to put the troopers to flight.

The position for the English was as grim at the other end of the
line. Here the Macdonalds were coming on in steadier formation
than the Camerons and Stewarts, who had charged with equal
élan but in small groups, and as they swung in towards the English
left the 14th Dragoons, in spite of the courageous example of their
commander, soon panicked and left the field without inflicting any
damage on the enemy. The royalist infantry now had the unenviable task of facing the full fury of a Highland charge. Both wings
came on remorselessly, and, as was their wont, having discharged
a volley the Highlanders threw away their muskets and relied
upon their broadswords, which, wielded with accuracy and vigour,
bit deeply into the heads and limbs of the badly shaken redcoats.
General Cope and Lords Loudoun, Drummore and Home did their
best to rally the terrified royalists: parties of dragoons were
rounded up, and infantrymen urged at pistol point to stand again
and dirty their muskets and blood their bayonets. But all was

chaos and confusion, and in a white heat of undisciplined passion the Highlanders laid about them, scattering the English army, until eventually the few officers and men who had tried to stem the flood joined the broad stream of fleeing men.

In the rout that followed considerable execution was done by the wildly excited and triumphant Highlanders and the fields around were strewn with wounded soldiers and severed limbs. The Battle of Prestonpans, or Gladsmuir as it at first came to be called, was a disaster for King George's army and a tremendous morale-raiser for the Jacobites: the former probably lost no more than 300 dead, most of whom were killed in flight, but eighty officers and more than a thousand men, together with all the baggage, were captured. The Jacobites lost six officers and somewhere around forty men. The English death roll might well have been heavier had not the Duke of Perth and Lord George Murray, acting under the Prince's orders, made sure that all the wounded got the best medical attention available.

After the battle Charles returned to Edinburgh and Cope hastened to Berwick, where Lord Mark Kerr remarked somewhat unkindly that he must be the only general in Europe to be the first to bring the news of his own defeat. Both sides now gathered strength for the next round. The Jacobites more than doubled their numbers and Lords Elcho and Pitsligo had around 500 horse under command. Moreover, there was better news from France: arms and ammunition (including six four-pounders) had recently been landed and the Marquis d'Aiguilles, Louis's unofficial ambassador, held out promise of further aid. To meet this formidable threat the Whig government hurried troops across from Flanders, including 6,000 Dutch, and sent General Handasyde to replace Cope.

Charles favoured a march on Newcastle to meet General Wade's force before it could be strengthened. Had this been done soon after Prestonpans who could say that he was not right? English morale was low – in fact it had almost reached panic proportions in certain circles – and once the fortified area of Newcastle was overcome the road to London would be virtually open. But by the end of October, when the need for a decision had become imperative if the daily desertions were to be halted, it may have been too late, and Lord George's advice, backed by many of the Highland chiefs, was probably the best. He argued that to march by Carlisle was a sounder plan: the route was better and the capture of Carlisle would rally English Jacobite support, making it easier to defeat Wade's newly reinforced army. The Prince reluctantly agreed.

208

Carlisle and its castle surrendered on 14 November after a siege lasting no more than six days. Wade had moved slowly towards its relief, but got no further than Hexham, and after Carlisle Penrith, Lancaster, Preston and Manchester were quickly occupied. Except in Manchester, where some 300 volunteers had been formed into a special regiment (later to be sacrificed in garrisoning Carlisle), the English response to the Jacobite cause had been disappointingly small, and when the army entered Derby on 4 December it numbered only about 4,500 men. The decision taken at Derby to return to Scotland was perhaps the most momentous of the whole campaign, and the rights and wrongs of it have long been argued. It could be said that the Stuart dynasty died at Derby. Certainly the Prince, whose earnest entreaties were overruled by Murray and most (but not quite all) of the chiefs, was convinced that the decision to retreat had irreparably marred his fortunes, and from that time of torment there emerged a deeply disappointed and slightly embittered man.

The return to Scotland was not entirely uneventful. The Duke of Cumberland, whose attempt to intercept the army on its way south had been cleverly foiled by Murray's tactical competence, was now in close pursuit with a force of 4,000 men. At Clifton, near Penrith, his cavalry caught up with the Jacobite rearguard under Lord George. By the light of a partially obscured moon three dragoon regiments were put to rout in a short, sharp engagement by the Glengarry Macdonalds, the Stewarts of Appin and Cluny Macpherson's men. There were no more than fifty casualties altogether, but this fierce little skirmish effectively checked Cumberland's pursuit. Carlisle was reached on 19 December. Here it was decided to abandon all the artillery, less three field guns, and on the Prince's insistence a garrison of 400 men was left there – soon to fall victims of Cumberland's avenging army.

The Highlanders crossed the Esk into Scotland on 20 December 1745. It was, by the English Old Style of reckoning, the Prince's twenty-fifth birthday. Charles spent a week in Glasgow trying to maintain some state amongst a population that for the most part had never been sympathetic to the Jacobite cause, and on 3 January he left for Stirling. Welcome reinforcements joined him here, including a contingent from France. While the army had been trekking through England 800 men under Lord John Drummond had landed on the east coast of Scotland (mostly Irish troops in the French service), and with them came two sixteen-pounders, two twelve- and two eight-pounders. However the majority of the new recruits came from all over Scotland: Frasers, Farquharsons,

Macdonells, Grants, Mackenzies and Ogilvys – more than 3,000 in all. The Jacobite army had now reached the moment of its fullest efflorescence: 9,000 warriors, of whom 1,300 were cavalry, and a good train of artillery. Stirling town surrendered on 6 January, but General Blakeney retired to the castle and prepared to withstand a siege. It is doubtful if the futile attempts of Charles's French engineer, M. Mirabel de Gordon, would ever have made any impression on the redoubtable castle perched on its precipitous rock, but events to the south caused the Prince to march to meet the enemy, leaving only a containing force at Stirling.

After capturing Carlisle the Duke of Cumberland returned to London, and his troops were kept in the south against the possibility of a French invasion. Wade was rightly considered too old for his post and was superseded by General Henry Hawley as commander-in-chief in the north, a fierce disciplinarian, but not a general of any particular merit. On arrival at Edinburgh Hawley found that he had under his command twelve battalions of infantry and three regiments of dragoons, but although their paper strength was formidable he complained that many of the men were 'no better than militia', and his artillery was a very scratch lot. Hawley might maunder over an inadequate army, but he was no poltroon refusing to come to grips with the foe. On 13 January his second-in-command, Major-General John Huske, marched from Edinburgh with the vanguard and two days later the whole English army was encamped near Falkirk. Here it was joined by Colonel John Campbell with three companies of Lord Loudoun's regiment, one of Lord John Murray's and twelve of the Argyll militia. The royalist force now numbered 8,000, and as Charles had left 1,000 to contain Stirling Castle the two armies were about equal.

The battle was fought to the west of Falkirk where the ground rises steeply from the Forth and Clyde Canal to a rough plateau called Falkirk Moor. The ascent was over a broken and rugged hillside, and there was a deep ravine that ran up its face for several hundred yards. Lord George Murray pressed upon the Prince the need to seize this high ground before the English, who were encamped only a mile away, got to it first. This was agreed, and after elaborate plans for deception had been worked out Murray, at the head of three Clan Donald regiments, marched out of the camp at Plean about midday on 17 January. He had a fair knowledge of the ground, and took a circuitous route southwards under cover of Torwood, crossing the river Carron (after ignoring O'Sullivan's and the Prince's request that he wait until night) at Dunipace. As the Highlanders advanced towards their objective a heavy

Above: Dragoon, infantry sergeant and private, 1745. The sergeant is armed with a halberd. Below: Highland clansmen, 1745. Left: The belted plaid (large plaid kilted and belted about waist, upper portion pinned on left shoulder) was worn from about 1599. The clansman carries a Lochaber axe. Right: The short kilt (philabeg) was introduced about 1730. The clansman carries broadsword, targe, dirk, Highland dag (slung pistol) and musket (fired and thrown down before the charge)

storm broke across this wild, primeval place of bog and bramble, but the driving rain was on their backs and in the faces of the enemy, who were scrambling unseen up the other side of the hill.

General Hawley, having examined the ground early that morning with Colonel Wolfe (later to gain immortal fame on the Heights of Abraham), retired to his billet apparently confident that the Jacobite army would never dare to attack him. His conduct at this stage was negligent in the extreme, for not only did he prefer the generous hospitality so purposefully plied by his hostess Lady Kilmarnock* to the rigours of the camp, but he failed to see that his army took elementary precautions against surprise even when an officer warned him that the Highlanders would be upon him before dark. When at last he grasped the seriousness of the situation the camp was startled by the sight of their dyspeptic-looking general arriving at the gallop hatless and breathless. However, he wasted no time in sending the three cavalry regiments up the face of the hill, led by Colonel Francis Ligonier in command of the 13th Dragoons. The cavalry was followed by the front line infantry with six regiments forward and six in the second line, with the Glasgow militia in rear of the cavalry and the Argyll militia on the right at the bottom of the hill.

As Lord George Murray breasted the hill at the head of the army, with the three Macdonald regiments in the van, the rain was lashing down, and on such an afternoon darkness would come early. It was already after half past three. The Highlanders formed line with the Macdonalds on the right with their flank protected by an impenetrable bog; the long front line extended to the edge of the ravine where the Appin Stewarts held the left. In between them and the Macdonalds were the Camerons, Frasers, Macphersons, Mackintoshes, Mackenzies and Farquharsons. The second line was made up of two battalions each of Lord Lewis Gordon's and Lord Ogilvy's together with three battalions of the Atholl brigade. Lord John Drummond, whose troops had taken part in the deception march, was in command of the reserve. It is sometimes said that he commanded the left of the Jacobite line, but in fact no one was appointed to this post, an oversight that could have proved disastrous. The artillery of both armies found immense difficulties in the terrain they were attempting to cross and played little part in the battle. No sooner had the line been formed than the acidulous adjutant-general was, as usual, criticizing Murray's

* She was the wife of the fourth Earl of Kilmarnock, who was captured at Culloden and later executed. A staunch Jacobite herself, she did what she could to keep the not unwilling Hawley from his command.

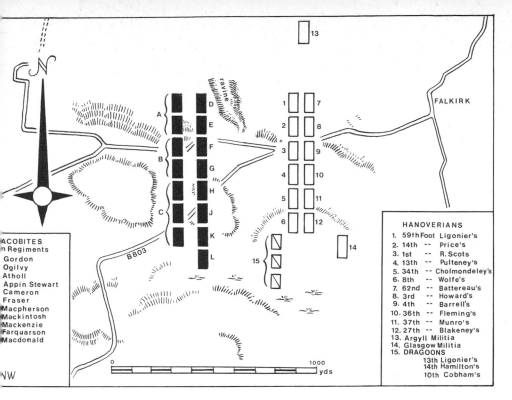

Battle of Falkirk

dispositions and – also as usual – getting a markedly cold response.

Displaying a confidence in the ability of his cavalry to defeat Highlanders which was not shared by their commander nor borne out by events at Prestonpans, General Hawley ordered them into the attack unsupported by the infantry, who were still forming up. Colonel Ligonier's three regiments of dragoons were on the left of the English line, and as they advanced Murray ordered the Highland right to hold their fire until the horsemen were within about fifteen paces. At least eighty horses went down under that first murderous volley which thundered down the line from the Macdonalds to the Frasers. The terrified cavalrymen, with their unenviable record of past failures, were again thrown into confusion; a few reached the Jacobite line only to be hacked and stabbed by Scottish dirks, but most of them wheeled about and only Cobham's regiment took any further part in the fighting.

The shattering volley that repulsed the dragoons was fired at about 4 p.m.; the rest of the battle, which lasted for less than half an hour, was an untidy, muddled affair. Murray tried in vain to hold the Highland right steady, but two of the Macdonald regiments could not be restrained and were soon lost to the battle in pursuit of the dragoons, who had themselves ridden down and scattered men of their own left. The centre Jacobite regiments then swung in on these hard-pressed men. Attacked from the front and the flank, their cartridges damp and their muskets misfiring, it was not long before both the first and second lines gave way. But on the Highlanders' left, where there was no one in overall command, the position was very different. Here three royalist regiments, whose front was protected by the ravine, stood firm, and poured a withering fire into the flank of the advancing Jacobites. The left of the rebel army, unable to close with the English across the ravine, suddenly found Cobham's dragoons taking them in the rear. The situation looked dangerous, and in the confusion of order and counter-order some of the clansmen were leaving the field thinking the battle lost. But the Prince, realizing the position, ordered up the Irish picquets, and on the appearance of these fresh troops the English right fell back towards Falkirk, the dragoons covering this comparatively orderly retreat.

The royalist army, abandoning most of their camp, seven cannon and a quantity of ammunition, made for Linlithgow. The Prince, in spite of English denials, had won another victory. It was to be his last. Jacobite losses amounted to only about fifty killed and seventy or eighty wounded, while General Hawley left some 300 men dead on the field, including at least twelve officers of which five were of field rank, and upwards of 200 prisoners were taken by the Scots. That night the Prince entered Falkirk in triumph.

But the Jacobite leaders had never displayed that spirit of concord so essential for ultimate success, and now recriminations for the conduct of the battle soured victory and laid the foundation for future disaster. Opinions were divided as to how to proceed. There were those in favour of pursuing Hawley's demoralized army and striking it a decisive blow while it was off balance; success would have been almost certain, but the road to London was no longer open. Others advocated the need to reduce Stirling Castle. The Prince was hesitant, but finally agreed upon a continuance of the siege. It was a forlorn enterprise in spite of all Monsieur Mirabel's gasconades, for the castle was well provisioned and from its commanding position the royalist armament was quickly able to silence the Jacobite batteries. Highlanders could never be inactive for long, and while preparations for the siege were going on many drifted away. They did not all intend to desert – but a sufficient number disappeared to seriously alarm the chiefs. Once again Lord George Murray and his colleagues presented their prince with a memorial (written representation), this time urging upon him the necessity to retire northwards for the winter and to recoup their strength. Charles was bitterly disappointed, although

214

as before he had to comply: he offered no reproaches, but he made it clear that it was a decision taken against his wishes. On 1 February the Jacobite army crossed the Forth and marched north.

The march to Inverness, in appalling weather conditions through a poverty-stricken countryside, whose primitive agriculture was far less capable of supporting an army than the Lowlands now abandoned to the enemy, was carried out under the Prince and Lord George Murray along separate routes. On 21 February the two divisions were reunited at Inverness, which had been evacuated by Lord Loudoun's troops a few days earlier, and Colonel Grant of Rothiemurchus was not long in surrendering the castle. During the next six weeks, while their prince amused himself shooting and enjoying the social life of Inverness, his troops were busy on a variety of military ventures. Fort Augustus was taken and Lord George, aided by Macpherson of Cluny, conducted a most successfull raid on the English outposts in Atholl territory, although he failed to take Blair Castle. At the insistence of the Camerons Fort William was besieged, but this was found to be too hard a nut to crack. Neither did the cause gain much from the exertions of Lord Cromarty. This nobleman was no soldier, and having failed (until supported by the Duke of Perth) to make headway against Lord Loudoun's force in the north, he later allowed himself to be ambushed and captured while endeavouring to rescue the valuable contents of the *Prince Charles,* which had been seized by Lord Reay's troops when that vessel was disabled in the Pentland Firth.

At the beginning of April, when the net was inexorably tightening around them, the Jacobite army was still scattered and in poor shape. The Duke of Perth and Lord John Drummond, with a totally inadequate force, were watching the Spey in the neighbourhood of Fochabers, Murray was still besieging Blair Castle, Cluny was in Badenoch with at least 300 clansmen, the Camerons were before Fort William, the Master of Lovat was said to be marching towards Inverness with a second Fraser regiment, and Lord Cromarty was still in the north with the Mackenzies and MacGregors. Urgent messages to these distant clansmen succeeded in rallying them just in time, save for those men with Cluny, Lord Cromarty and the Master of Lovat, all of whom took no part in the coming battle. When the Prince at the head of his shrunken army moved to Culloden House he had under command somewhere around 5,000 men. His artillery was not worthy of the name, and his cavalry was scarcely any better – Lord Elcho's Life Guards, originally formed as a *corps d' élite* of landed gentry but now sadly diminished, and all that was left of a squadron of FitzJames's horse that had landed from France in February: in all two troops numbering perhaps 150 horse. The morale of the whole army was at a low ebb: the treasure chest was empty and the men were lamentably short of pay and food. Yet there is a touch of grandeur in the death throes of this Jacobite army, desperate, demoralized but in a strange way still undaunted.

Meanwhile, how did the Whig government set about repairing the disaster of Falkirk? The answer was provided in the person of the King's second son, William Augustus Duke of Cumberland, 'Billy the Martial Boy' or 'the Butcher', depending which side you were on. Only a few months younger than Prince Charles, this unattractive Hanoverian had gained rapid military promotion, even allowing for his position and the times. Although by no means a brilliant commander he was not without ability: his courage and powers of leadership had been tested and proved at Dettingen and Fontenoy, and he was certainly a considerable improvement on his three predecessors. Now that the French threat to the south had been removed Cumberland was sent north at the end of January. He immediately set out to relieve Stirling, and pursued the Jacobite army as far as Perth. From here he marched to Aberdeen, where he arrived on 27 February and where he was to remain until 8 April. Before he left Perth his command had been reinforced by some 5,000 Hessian troops, who had landed at Leith under Prince Frederick of Hesse-Cassel. These troops were of great assistance in guarding Cumberland's lines of communication.

In March Cumberland had sent one division under Major-General Bland into Strathbogie, and on 11 April he joined him at Cullen with the rest of the army. The Spey was crossed unopposed* on 12 April, and the English army reached its camp at Balblair (a mile south-west of Nairn) on 14 April. Cumberland had under command fifteen infantry battalions, three regiments of horse and a formidable train of artillery; there were also several companies of Argyll militia (Campbells), bringing his total force up to not far short of 9,000, of whom 2,400 were cavalrymen. Since the introduction, in about 1720, of the iron ramrod the infantryman's rate of fire had been greatly increased – and these men, who had spent the last two months perfecting their musketry, could probably fire

---

* It is sometimes argued that the Jacobite army would have had more chance of success had they opposed the crossing of the Spey in strength. But apart from the fact that Cumberland had moved too quickly for them, their armament and method of fighting were quite unsuitable for this sort of action.

216

three effective volleys in a minute. It is also noteworthy that the battle about to be fought was the first major action on British soil in which the cannon were manned by men of the Royal Regiment of Artillery, which had been formed in 1716.

The fifteenth of April was Cumberland's twenty-fifth birthday and the English troops, well provisioned by the fleet, were permitted a day's rest to celebrate the event. Twelve miles away, however, all was bustle in the Jacobite camp. Lochiel's men had only come in from Fort William the previous day, and many of the clansmen were still being rounded up from fighting and foraging expeditions near and far. But the Prince was determined to give battle, and ordered his men to move into position on the high ground to the south of Culloden House known as Drummossie Moor. This almost flat, gently rolling piece of land is some 470 feet above sea level; it is about a mile in width at the place where the Prince elected to deploy, falling quite steeply to the river Nairn on its south edge. There were few trees on the ground, but some of the small cultivated areas that existed were enclosed by turf or loose stone walls, particularly on either side of the Jacobite battle position where parts of Culloden park were enclosed.

Murray, who was well aware of the limitations of the Highland army, was violently opposed to offering battle on this open expanse, so suitable for properly equipped, well trained troops to operate on. He had been sent, a few days earlier, to reconnoitre the ground between Culloden and Nairn and had found near Dalcross some much rougher and more suitable terrain, but had been overruled by O'Sullivan. Now, on his own initiative, he had sent Brigadier Stapleton and Colonel Ker to examine the ground to the south of the Nairn. Their report was most encouraging for the land being steep and rugged was useless for cavalry and ideal for Highlanders. However, Lord George's advice went unheeded.

He did, however, gain approval for a night march against the enemy camp. His argument, that the army could cover the distance in time to deliver a two-pronged surprise attack in the early hours of the morning, when the English could be expected to be suffering from the aftermath of their commander's birthday celebrations, had some merit. If the march had been undertaken with a full force of fit men it might well have succeeded and – as at Sedgemoor – a surprise attack certainly offered more chance of success than taking on the powerful English army on open ground. But in the circumstances it was asking too much of the troops.

When the time came to set off (about 8 p.m.) many of the Highlanders were absent in search of food, and no man in the two columns had eaten more than a biscuit or small loaf all that day. The commissariat under John Hay of Restalrig had completely broken down. Murray led the first and largest column, and the Duke of Perth was with the Prince at the head of the second one. The night was dark, the route extremely rough, and few save the Mackintosh guides had any sense of direction. As the hungry men trudged through the heather in black silence many fell out 'by faintness from want of food', and Murray's column had constantly to halt to allow those in the rear to catch up. By 2 a.m. the leading men had only reached Knockanbuie, some three miles from their objective, and it was obvious that the attack could not go in under cover of darkness; moreover, drums could be heard in the English camp, clearly indicating loss of surprise. There was nothing for it but to return, and although the Prince was at first eager to proceed he came to see that the decision was inevitable. It was 5 a.m. on 16 April when the dismayed and utterly exhausted troops got back to Drummossie Moor. Here many weary and faithful feet that had tramped through half England and most of Scotland were soon to find their final rest.

No one thought of anything but sleep. For some reason the Jacobite leaders considered it most unlikely that the English would advance to the attack that day. But no sooner had Cumberland learned of the disastrous night march than he ordered his troops forward. The first news reached the Jacobite camp at about 10 a.m., when a patrol announced that the enemy were within four miles. Even before Charles had laid down to rest the Marquess d'Aiguilles had sought an interview and besought him not to offer battle, but to retire – even if it meant abandoning Inverness – and recoup his strength, later to offer battle on better ground. This sensible plea was joined by those of Murray, Macdonald of Keppoch and Lochiel. Alas, that stubborn streak of Stuart obstinacy asserted itself and no further mention of retreat was permitted.

When the Highland army deployed for battle Lord George begged the right for his Atholl brigade and the Prince, perhaps as an emollient for his earlier rebuttal over choice of ground, granted it to him. The Macdonalds are said to have been greatly offended at being denied their time-honoured position in the line, and it is often suggested that their performance in the battle suffered in consequence. However, there is reason to believe that this thorny question was first raised before Prestonpans, and that the Macdonalds – albeit reluctantly – agreed that the right should be taken in rotation. In any case many other factors weighed heavily against the Macdonalds in the confusion of the battle, and

218

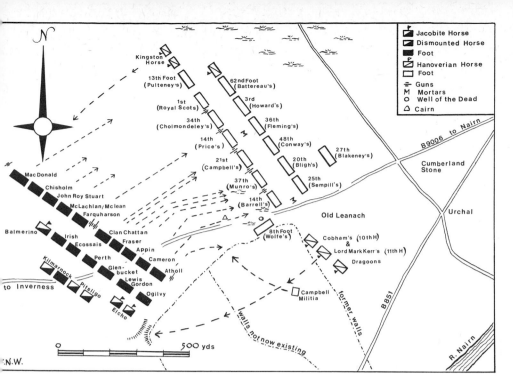

Map legend:
- Jacobite Horse
- Dismounted Horse
- Foot
- Hanoverian Horse
- Foot
- ⇌ Guns
- M Mortars
- O Well of the Dead
- △ Cairn

N

Kingston Horse

13th Foot (Pulteney's)

62nd Foot (Battereau's)

1st (Royal Scots)

3rd (Howard's)

34th (Cholmondeley's)

36th (Fleming's)

14th (Price's)

48th (Conway's)

21st (Campbell's)

20th (Bligh's)

27th (Blakeney's)

37th (Munro's)

25th (Sempill's)

14th (Barrell's)

Old Leanach

8th Foot (Wolfe's)

Cobham's (10th H) & Lord Mark Kerr's (11th H) Dragoons

Campbell Militia

MacDonald
Chisholm
John Roy Stuart
McLachlan/Mclean
Farquharson
Balmerino
Irish Ecossais
Clan Chattan
Fraser
Appin
Perth
Cameron
Kilmarnock
Pitsligo
Glen-bucket
Lewis Gordon
Atholl
to Inverness
Ogilvy
Elcho

B9006 to Nairn

Cumberland Stone

Urchal

walls not now existing

former walls

B851

R. Nairn

500 yds

N.W.

Above and below: Battle of Culloden

HANOVERIAN ARMY

Cumberland Stone

Urchal

Information Centre
Old Leanach

Well of the Dead

Cairn

N

JACOBITE ARMY

King's Stables

Irish Memorial

it cannot be definitely said that their courage and loyalty suffered from wounded pride.

The Camerons formed up on the left of the Athollmen and then came the Stewarts of Appin and the Frasers; this wing was commanded by Murray. In the centre of the front line were the Mackintoshes and Farquharsons (Clan Chattan), the combined MacLachlan–Maclean regiment, John Roy Stuart's regiment and the Chisholms, all under the command of Lord John Drummond. And the left, commanded by the Duke of Perth, comprised the Clanranald, Keppoch, Glencoe and Glengarry Macdonalds. The exact composition of the second line remains uncertain, but it seems to have been widely spaced with Lord Elcho's and Fitz-James's horse and Lord Ogilvy's troops on the right, the Irish picquets and the French regiment known as the Royal Scots (under Lord Lewis Drummond) together with Lord Lewis Gordon's regiment in the centre, and on the left another Gordon regiment under the septuagenarian John Gordon of Glenbucket. Brigadier Stapleton commanded the second line. The Prince assumed overall command, and having inspected both lines took up his position initially just to the rear of the second line. His ineffectual cannon, manned mostly by inexperienced Highlanders, was placed in batteries of four on the right, centre and left of the front line.

The Duke of Cumberland's army reached their final position, with their left on the Leanach Farm enclosure, a little after midday. There was then about 500 yards separating the two armies. Cumberland had already halted some way back and deployed his columns into line, originally with six regiments in each of the first two lines and three in reserve; but on finding that he had advanced beyond the protective bog to his right he ordered up two battalions from the reserve to take position on the right of the first and second lines respectively. He also ordered Wolfe's regiment, who were on the left of the second line and standing ankle-deep in water, to take position immediately on the left of the front line and at right angles to that line (*en potence*), so that they could pour flanking fire into any attack. The English artillery, which was in the capable hands of Colonel Belford and had with difficulty been manhandled over the boggy ground, was now placed at intervals between the front line regiments. The Duke also had six coehorn mortars which were formed into batteries of three and posted in advance of the regiments forming the right and left wings of the second line. The cavalry, under General Hawley, was divided and placed on the right and left of the front lines.

The cold north-east wind now began to blow rain and sleet into the Highlanders' faces, and there could have been few among those weary, wasted men who were not to some degree awed by the long lines of red- and blue-coated soldiers that confronted them, bristling with bayonets fixed and sabres drawn. Soon to the drums and fifes that they heard – yes, and even their own music from the Campbell pipes – would be added the terrifying accompaniment of Belford's blazing batteries.

It was just after 1 p.m. that the cannonade started. The Prince's feeble guns fired first, but without any noticeable effect. Then the royalist pieces took up the challenge, and firing in one great roll the noise was deafening and the damage devastating. As the Highlanders stood straining at the leash waiting for the order to charge – the order that seemed never to come – the English guns kept up their remorseless pounding. Through the dust and smoke drifting across on the wet wind the gunners could be dimly seen sponging out their reeking barrels and ramming home more powder and shot. Opinions differ as to how long this fearful bombardment lasted. John Home* puts it at almost an hour, but this must be wrong, for the whole battle was over in forty minutes. Almost certainly it was no more than fifteen minutes before the Highlanders charged; but then Belford switched from ball to grape and the air was thick with pieces of iron, nails and small shot that burst from the flimsy canisters.

It is difficult to know why the Prince was so dilatory in giving the order to charge: it was the one very slender chance that his men had of victory. By the time the order eventually reached the front line troops Cumberland's guns had made defeat inevitable. Maybe he was convinced that the English would come at him and thereby close the gap over which his men had to charge, but more probably he was too far back to have proper control of the battle and did not see to what extent the Highland lines were being torn apart. When at last he did give the order his aide, young Lachlan MacLachlan, was struck down as he rode across to the left, for these troops being somewhat retarded should have got the order to advance first. But the right and centre could be restrained no longer, and whether the Prince's order ever reached them is of small consequence: they had waited too long and now they were off.

Once the Highlanders were committed to the charge the story is soon told. The short fight was contested with fearful savagery, but the odds against the rebel army were too great. Indeed, we cannot but be amazed at the courage and determination which

* John Home, *The History of the Rebellion in the Year 1745*, p. 230.

carried their right and centre into the second line of English infantrymen. The actual fighting casualties were heaviest on this front, and in the mêlée that ensued once the two sides had closed in hand-to-hand combat it is probable that Wolfe's men did as much damage to their own ranks as to those of the enemy. The impact upon the English left, which almost overwhelmed them at this point, was caused by the Clan Chattan swerving to their right as they charged up the drier ground of the old road. The unwieldy mass thus formed momentarily pushed back the English by sheer weight of numbers, but made it impossible for the clansmen to use their firearms and exposed them to the pitiless fire of Cholmondeley's and Price's regiments in the English centre.

The Highland casualties were grievous in the extreme: eighteen officers of Clan Chattan fell before they even reached the English line, and the Atholl brigade lost more than twenty, most of them shot down by Wolfe's men as the swerving centre pressed them against the park wall. Nevertheless, the Highlanders with their broadswords did great damage to Barrel's and Munro's regiments, and it was not until Cumberland ordered Major-General Huske to bring forward Sempill's and Bligh's regiments that the Highlanders were finally repulsed. Lord George Murray, who was soon unhorsed, continued fighting ferociously on foot until borne away in the stream of retreating men. The heroic and legendary Alexander MacGillivray of Dunmaglas, commanding the centre in Lord John Drummond's absence, stormed his way through the first line only to be shot down by men of Sempill's or Bligh's.

The Macdonalds, on the left of the Jacobite line, never reached the English right. There is no doubt that at first they paid little heed to the exhortations of the Duke of Perth and his brother, and even when Alexander Macdonald of Keppoch, so soon to meet his death, appealed to their honour they advanced only in short rushes firing their muskets at random. The usual explanation for this is, as we have noted, that they were aggrieved at their position in the line; but other possibilities must be considered. They had by far the furthest distance to charge, and they had already been devastated by the enemy artillery. As soon as they advanced, their left, now protected by the Culloden enclosures, would be exposed, just as their right already was because of the swerving of the centre. Moreover, before the reserve could plug this gap Kingston's Dragoons were through it and in the rear of the Macdonalds. When these clans did eventually get near enough to Pulteney's and the Royals they were shot down like rabbits, and seeing the right and centre give way they too fell back. The Irish picquets and the

Royal Scots under Brigadier Stapleton ably covered their withdrawal and fought bravely in this closing stage of the battle.

Even before the cannonade had begun Lochiel and Murray had espied a party of Campbells and dragoons making their way round the Jacobite right flank. This flank was protected by the park walls, but dry-stone walls are not difficult to pull down and this the Campbells set about doing. As soon as he realized the danger Murray ordered some of Lord Lewis Gordon's men to face that front, but they were not able to prevent the Campbells from making a passageway for Hawley's cavalry. In the rout that followed the breaking of the Highland line the Campbells were able to pour volley after volley into their Cameron enemies from the protection of the walls, and the dragoons, charging through the gaps, added to the general destruction.

There are many conflicting accounts of the Prince's action at the end of the battle. Lord Elcho put it on record that as soon as the left broke Charles, escorted by a party of FitzJames's horse, rode quickly to safety; but this was probably only a half-truth. By nature an optimist, he must at last have seen defeat outstaring him. He seems to have made some effort to rally the regiments on the left wing, but realizing the impossibility of the task he allowed himself to be taken from the field by Sir Thomas Sheridan, Hay of Restalrig and a few others. No doubt he never envisaged retreat, but the event should have been catered for and a rallying point made. As it was most of those on the right who survived made across the Nairn and into Badenoch, while those on the left took the road to Inverness. The Prince first drew rein some four miles from the battlefield at Faillie, and again Lord Elcho tells us that he had no word for the Scots, but seemed only concerned for the welfare of his Irish and exile French troops.

The carnage of the field was appalling, and Cumberland's men had orders not to spare the wounded. The exact number of casualties on both sides has long been in dispute, but the Highlanders certainly lost 1,000 men killed in battle or murdered on the field – and probably more. Most of the English casualties occurred in Barrel's, Munro's, Bligh's and Sempill's regiments, for they were virtually the only infantry seriously engaged, and were said to number 364 killed and wounded. Vast quantities of muskets, broadswords and ammunition fell to the victors, as well as fourteen standards.

The destiny of a dynasty flowed with the blood of these proud Jacobite warriors. The victories that had been gained in the past, the final disaster at Culloden and the hardships that they and their prince were still to endure, ensure for them a lasting renown.

Table Showing the Regiments of the English Army (1746: Culloden)

Name of the commander	Number of regiment	What the regiment later became
CAVALRY		
Gardiner's } Ligonier's }	13th Dragoons	13th Hussars
Hamilton's	14th Dragoons	14th Hussars
Cobham's	10th Dragoons	10th Hussars
Lord Mark Kerr's	11th Dragoons	11th Hussars
Kingston's horse	—	Disbanded
REGIMENTS OF THE LINE		
The Royals (or the Royal Regiment of Foot)	1st	The Royal Scots
Howard's	3rd	The Buffs (Royal East Kent Regiment)
Barrell's	4th	The King's Own Royal Regiment (Lancaster)
Wolfe's	8th	The King's Regiment (Liverpool)
Pulteney's	13th	Somerset Light Infantry
Price's	14th	West Yorkshire Regiment
Bligh's	20th	Lancashire Fusiliers
Campbell's	21st	Royal Scots Fusiliers
Sempill's	25th	King's Own Scottish Borderers
Blakeney's	27th	1st Battalion Royal Inniskilling Fusiliers
Cholmondeley's	34th	1st Battalion The Border Regiment
Fleming's	36th	2nd Battalion Worcestershire Regiment
Munro's	37th	1st Battalion Hampshire Regiment
Conway's	48th	1st Battalion Northamptonshire Regiment
Battereau's	62nd	Disbanded 1748
Argyll militia	—	Disembodied after suppression of rising
Guise's	6th	Royal Warwickshire Regiment
	44th } 46th } 47th }	These regiments were marine regiments and were disbanded in 1748

At the time of Culloden all regiments would usually have been known by the colonel's name—and this was constantly changing. The Clothing Regulations of 1747 required regiments to bear their precedence numbers on their colours, and from this date onwards regiments began to refer to themselves by numbers rather than by names of colonels.

Bibliography

Chapter 1: The First Civil War
Barrett, C. R. B., *Battles and Battlefields in England*, A. D. Innes, 1896.
Burne, A. H., and Peter Young, *The Great Civil War*, Eyre and Spottiswoode, 1959.
Clarendon, Edward, Earl of, *The History of the Rebellion*, Clarendon Press, 1704.
Firth, Charles, *Cromwell's Army*, Methuen, 1912.
Fortescue, J. W., *History of the British Army*, Vol. I, Macmillan, 1899.
Fraser, Antonia, *Cromwell—Our Chief of Men*, Weidenfeld and Nicolson, 1973.
Gardiner, S. R., *History of the Great Civil War, 1642-1649*, 4 vols, Longmans, 1911.
Rogers, H. C. B., *Battles and Generals of the Civil Wars, 1642-1651*, Seeley Service, 1968.
Roper, H. R. Trevor-, *Archbishop Laud 1573-1645*, Macmillan, 1962.
Trench, Charles Chevenix, *A History of Horsemanship*, Longmans, 1970.
Wedgwood, C. V., *The Great Rebellion, Vol. I: The King's Peace*, Collins, 1955.
Wedgwood, C. V., *The Great Rebellion, Vol. II: The King's War*, Collins, 1958.
Woolrych, Austin, *Battles of the English Civil War*, Batsford, 1961.
Young, Peter, *Edgehill 1642*, Roundwood Press, 1967.
Young, Peter, *The British Army 1642–1970*, William Kimber, 1967.
Young, Peter, and John Adair, *Hastings to Culloden*, G. Bell, 1964.

Chapter 2: Edgehill
Burne, A. H., *Battlefields of England*, Methuen, 1950.
Burne, A. H., and Peter Young, *The Great Civil War*, Eyre and Spottiswoode, 1959.
Davies, Godfrey, 'The Battle of Edgehill', *English Historical Review*, XXXVI, 1921.
Firth, Charles, *Cromwell's Army*, Methuen, 1912.
Gardiner, S. R., *History of the Great Civil War, 1642 1649*, Vol. I, Longmans, 1911.
Rogers, H. C. B., *Battles and Generals of the Civil Wars, 1642–1651*, Seeley Service, 1968.
Wedgwood, C. V., *The Great Rebellion, Vol. II: The King's War*, Collins, 1958.
Young, Peter, *Edgehill 1642*, Roundwood Press, 1967.
Young, Peter, and John Adair, *Hastings to Culloden*, G. Bell, 1964.

Chapter 3: The First Battle of Newbury
Barrett, C. R. B., *Battles and Battlefields in England*, A. D. Innes, 1896.
Burne, A. H., *Battlefields of England*, Methuen, 1950.
Burne, A. H., and Peter Young, *The Great Civil War*, Eyre and Spottiswoode, 1959.
Clarendon, Edward, Earl of, *The History of the Rebellion*, Book VII, pp. 205–14, Clarendon Press, 1704.
Firth, Charles, *Cromwell's Army*, Methuen, 1912.
Gardiner, S. R., *History of the Great Civil War, 1642–1649*, Vol. I, Longmans, 1911.
Money, Walter, *The First and Second Battles of Newbury*, Simpkin, Marshall, 2nd edition, 1884.
Rogers, H. C. B., *Battles and Generals of the Civil Wars, 1642–1651*, Seeley Service, 1968.
Wedgwood, C. V., *The Great Rebellion, Vol. II: The King's War*, Collins, 1958.
Young, Peter, and John Adair, *Hastings to Culloden*, G. Bell, 1964.

Primary Sources
Codrington, Robert, *The Life and Death of the Illustrious Robert, Earle of Essex*, London, 1646.
Thomason Tracts, E.69 and E.70 (which include Sir John Byron's account of the battle).

Chapter 4: Cheriton
Adair, John, *Cheriton 1644*, Roundwood Press, 1973.
Burne, A. H., *More Battlefields of England*, Methuen, 1952.
Burne, A. H., and Peter Young, *The Great Civil War*, Eyre and Spottiswoode, 1959.
Clarendon, Edward, Earl of, *The History of the Rebellion*, Book VIII, Clarendon Press, 1704.
Gardiner, S. R., *History of the Great Civil War*, Vol. I, Longmans, 1911.
Godwin, G. N., *The Civil War in Hampshire*, revised edition, Southampton, 1904.
Rogers, H. C. B., *Battles and Generals of the Civil Wars, 1642–1651*, Seeley Service, 1968.
Walker, Sir Edward, K. G., *Historical Discourses upon Several Occasions*, London, 1705.
Wedgwood, C. V., *The Great Rebellion, Vol. II: The King's War*, Collins, 1958.
Woodward, B. B., T. C. Wilks and C. Lockhart, *A General History of Hampshire*, Vol. II, London, 1861-9.

Primary Sources
Healey, Charles, ed., *Bellum Civile* (Hopton's account of the battle), Somerset Record 18, 1902.
Military Memoir of Colonel John Birch, written by Roe, his secretary, ed. Rev. T. W. Webb, Camden Society, 1873.
Thomason Tracts, E.40 (including Elias Archer's and Harley's accounts of the battle).

Chapter 5: Marston Moor

Barrett, C. R. B., *Battles and Battlefields in England*, A. D. Innes, 1896.

Burne, A. H., *Battlefields of England*, Methuen, 1950.

Burne, A. H., and Peter Young, *The Great Civil War*, Eyre and Spottiswoode, 1959.

Firth, Charles, *Cromwell's Army*, Methuen, 1912.

Fraser, Antonia, *Cromwell—Our Chief of Men*, Weidenfeld and Nicolson, 1973.

Gardiner, S. R., *History of the Great Civil War, 1642–1649*, Vol. I, Longmans, 1911.

Leadman, A. D. H., *Battles Fought in Yorkshire*, London, 1891.

Rogers, H. C. B., *Battles and Generals of the Civil Wars, 1642–1651*, Seeley Service, 1968.

Wedgwood, C. V., *The Great Rebellion, Vol. II: The King's War*, Collins, 1958.

Young, Peter, *Marston Moor 1644*, Roundwood Press, 1970.

Young, Peter, and John Adair, *Hastings to Culloden*, G. Bell, 1964.

Primary Sources
Thomason Tracts, E.54 (7, 8, 19: Watson, *A Full Relation of the Late Victory*), E.2 (14: Stewart, *A More Exact Relation of the Late Battell*).

Chapter 6: Naseby

Buchan, John, *Oliver Cromwell*, Hodder, 1934.

Burne, A. H., *Battlefields of England*, Methuen, 1950.

Burne, A. H., and Peter Young, *The Great Civil War*, Eyre and Spottiswoode, 1959.

Clarendon, Edward, Earl of, *The History of the Rebellion*, Book IX, Clarendon Press, 1704.

Dore, R. N., 'Sir William Brereton's Siege of Chester and the Campaign of Naseby', *Transactions of the Lancashire and Cheshire Antiquarian Society*, Vol. 67, 1957.

Firth, Charles, *Cromwell's Army*, Methuen, 1912.

Fortescue, J. W., *History of the British Army*, Vol. I, Macmillan, 1899.

Fraser, Antonia, *Cromwell—Our Chief of Men*, Weidenfeld and Nicolson, 1973.

Gardiner, S. R., *History of the Great Civil War, 1642–1649*, Vol. II, Longmans, 1911.

Markham, C. R., *The Life of the Great Lord Fairfax*, Macmillan, 1870.

Rogers, H. C. B., *Battles and Generals of the Civil Wars, 1642–1651*, Seeley Service, 1968.

Walker, Sir Edward, K. G., *Historical Discourses upon Several Occasions*, London, 1705.

Wedgwood, C. V., *The Great Rebellion, Vol. II: The King's War*, Collins, 1958.

Woolrych, Austin, *Battles of the English Civil War*, Batsford, 1961.

Young, Peter, 'The Northern Horse at Naseby', *Journal of the Society for Army Historical Research*, 1954.

Young, Peter, and John Adair, *Hastings to Culloden*, G. Bell, 1964.

Primary Sources
Sprigge, Joshua, *Anglia Rediviva*, London, 1647.
Thomason Tracts, E.288.

Chapter 7: Montrose's Battles

Buchan, John, *The Marquis of Montrose*, Nelson, 1913.

Clarendon, Edward, Earl of, *The History of the Rebellion*, Book 9, Clarendon Press, 1704.

Gardiner, S. R., *History of the Great Civil War, 1642–1649*, Vols II and III, Longmans, 1911.

Morris, Mowbray, *Montrose*, Macmillan, 1901.

Wedgwood, C. V., *Montrose*, Collins, 1952.

Chapter 8: Charles II's Civil War

Abbott, W. C., *The Writings and Speeches of Oliver Cromwell*, Vol. II, Harvard University Press, 1939.

Barrett, C. R. B., *Battles and Battlefields in England*, A. D. Innes, 1896.

Blount, Thomas, *Boscobel*, London, 1660: revised edition Tylston and Edwards, 1894.

Buchan, John, *Oliver Cromwell*, Hodder, 1934.

Bund, J. W. Willis, *The Civil War in Worcestershire*, Birmingham, 1905.

Burne, A. H., *Battlefields of England*, Methuen, 1950.

Clarendon, Edward, Earl of, *The History of the Rebellion*, Book XIII, Clarendon Press, 1704.

Firth, Charles, *Cromwell's Army*, Methuen, 1912.

Fortescue, J. W., *History of the British Army*, Vol. I, Macmillan, 1899.

Fraser, Antonia, *Cromwell—Our Chief of Men*, Weidenfeld and Nicolson, 1973.

Rogers, H. C. B., *Battles and Generals of the Civil Wars, 1642–1651*, Seeley Service, 1968.

Young, Peter, 'The Northern Horse at Naseby', *Journal of the Society for Army Historical Research*, 1954.

Young, Peter, and John Adair, *Hastings to Culloden*, G. Bell, 1964.

Primary Sources
C.S.P. Domestic Series, 1651.
Hobman, D. L., *Memoirs of Captain Hodgson*.
Thomason Tracts, E.641.

Chapter 9: 'Let Monmouth Reign'

Burne, A. H., *Battlefields of England*, Methuen, 1950.

Churchill, Winston S., *Marlborough: His Life and Times*, Vol. I, Harrap, 1947.

'Oyley, Elizabeth, *James, Duke of Monmouth*, Bles, 1938.

ea, Allan, *King Monmouth*, John Lane, 1902.

ortescue, J. W., *History of the British Army*, Vols I and II, Macmillan, 1899.

acaulay, Lord, *The History of England*, Vol. I, Macmillan, 1914.

age, Maurice, *The Battle of Sedgemoor*, Page, 1930.

oberts, George, *The Life, Progress, and Rebellion of James, Duke of Monmouth*, Vols I and II, Longmans, 1844.

rench, Charles Chevenix, *The Western Rising*, Methuen, 1950.

olseley, Viscount, *The Life of John Churchill, Duke of Marlborough*, Richard Bentley, 1894.

oung, Peter, and John Adair, *Hastings to Culloden*, G. Bell, 1964.

rimary Sources

alrymple, Sir John, *Memoirs of Great Britain and Ireland*, Vol. I, revised edition, 1790.

anuscripts of Mrs Stopford Sackville, Historical Manuscripts Commission, 9th Report, Parts I to III, London, 1883.

Ir Nathaniel Wade's Confession, Harleian MSS. 6845, Folio 264.

aschall, Andrew: facsimiles of his account of the battle are in Weston Zoyland church and the Blake Museum, Bridgwater.

hapter 10: The First Jacobite Rising

non, *The Battle of Sheriffmuir*, Eneas Mackay, 1898.

unningham, Audrey, *The Loyal Clans*, Cambridge University Press, 1932.

uke, Winifred, *Lord George Murray and the 'Forty-five*, Milne and Hutchinson, 1927.

ortescue, J. W., *History of the British Army*, Vol. II, Macmillan, 1899.

etrie, Charles, *The Jacobite Movement*, Eyre and Spottiswoode, 1959.

hield, A., and Andrew Lang, *The King Over the Water*, Longmans, 1907.

ayler, Alistair and Henrietta, *1715: Story of the Rising*, Nelson, 1936.

ayler, Alistair and Henrietta, *The Old Chevalier*, Cassell, 1934.

erry, Charles Sanford, ed., *The Jacobites and the Union*, Cambridge University Press, 1922.

hapter 11: The Second Jacobite Rebellion

nderson, Peter, *Culloden Moor*, William Mackey, 1920.

uke, Winifred, *Lord George Murray and the 'Forty-five*, Milne and Hutchinson, 1927.

Duke, Winifred, *Prince Charles Edward and the 'Forty-five*, Robert Hale, 1938.

Fortescue, J. W., *History of the British Army*, Vol. II, Macmillan, 1899.

Home, John, *The History of the Rebellion in the Year 1745*, p. 230, London, 1802.

Paton, Henry, ed., *The Lyon in Mourning*, 3 vols, Edinburgh, 1895.

Petrie, Charles, *The Jacobite Movement*, Eyre and Spottiswoode, 1959.

Porcelli, Baron E. G. M., *The White Cockade*, Hutchinson, 1949.

Prebble, John, *Culloden*, Secker and Warburg, 1961.

Taylor, Iain Cameron, *Culloden*, National Trust for Scotland, 1970.

Terry, Charles Sanford, ec., *The 'Forty-five*, Cambridge University Press, 1922.

Tomasson, Katherine, and Francis Buist, *Battles of the '45*, Batsford, 1962.

Wilkinson, Clennell, *Bonnie Prince Charlie*, Harrap, 1932.

Young, Peter, and John Adair, *Hastings to Culloden*, G. Bell, 1964.

List of books studied in connection with armour, weapons and uniforms

Ashdown, C. H., *British and Foreign Arms and Armour*, T. C. and E. C. Jack, 1909.

Barnes, R. M., *History of Regiments and Uniforms of the British Army*, Seeley Service, 1957.

British Military Uniforms, Stamp Publicity, 1971.

ffoulkes, Charles, *Armour and Weapons*, Clarendon Press, 1909.

Hunter, Edmund, *Arms and Armour*, Wills and Hepworth, 1971.

Laver, J., *British Military Uniforms*, King Penguin, 1948.

Lawson, C. C. P., *History of the Uniforms of the British Army*, Kaye and Ward, 1967.

Luard, J. L., *History of the Dress of the British Soldier*, Clowes, 1852.

Martin, Paul, *Armour and Weapons*, H. Jenkins, 1968.

Maxwell, S., and Hutchinson, R., *Scottish Costumes 1550–1850*, A. and C. Black, 1958.

Norman Vesey, *Arms and Armour*, Weidenfeld and Nicolson, 1964.

North, Rene, *Military Uniforms*, Hamlyn, 1970.

Potter, R., and Embleton, G. A., *The English Civil War*, Almark Publications, 1973.

Talbot-Booth, E. C., *British Army Customs, Traditions and Uniforms*, Sampson Low, Marston, 3rd edition, 1941.

Tylden, Major G., *Horses and Saddlery*, J. A. Allan, 1965.

Wilkinson, F., *Arms and Armour*, Hamlyn, 1972.

Wilkinson, F., *Small Arms*, Ward Lock, 1965.

Wilkinson Lathan, R. and C., *Cavalry Uniforms of Britain and the Commonwealth Including Other Mounted Troops*, Blanford Press, 1969.

Index

The B.AT

This View of the Glorious Victory obtained over the Rebels Shews His MAJESTIES Army commanded by

Body of Reserve composed of Four — Part of the Highland Army is here represented as furiously attemp

Bayonets of Barrels by Munro's intrepid Regiments. The right wing of the Rebels being cover'd by a sto

Rebels w.ch put them into immediate confusion Kingstons Horse wheel'd off at the same time by the righ

Publish'd 1.st November 17